PARTY GOVERNMENT AND POLITICAL CULTURE IN WESTERN GERMANY

This book is a collection of papers by a selection of German and British political scientists, sociologists and historians. The standpoints and theoretical orientations of these essays are naturally diverse, but the common concern with the problems and preconditions of party government imparts a unifying focus to the whole book. Several of the essays complement one another in a quite unforced way.

This study represents a sustained attempt to unravel some of the key relationships in the German political system – in the connections between political culture, the party system and parliamentary government – and account has been taken of the fact that a wider audience may be unacquainted with the debates on the various topics. It gives a flavour of current academic concerns both in Britain and Germany.

Herbert Döring is Lecturer in German History at the School of Slavonic and East European Studies, University of London and Member of the Institut für Sozialwissenschaften, University of Mannheim.

Gordon Smith is Reader in Government at the London School of Economics.

Party Government and Political Culture in Western Germany

Edited by

Herbert Döring and Gordon Smith

First published 1982 by
THE MACMILLAN PRESS LTD
London and Basingstoke
Companies and representatives
throughout the world

ISBN 0 333 29082 8

Printed in Hong Kong

Contents

Contents

Preface

The idea for this book emerged as a result of a series of lectures given in London during 1979 to mark the thirtieth anniversary of the founding of the Federal Republic. Those original lectures have been incorporated in the present volume in an extended form, and the scope of the book was widened considerably by inviting a number of additional contributions.

The title of *Party Government and Political Culture in Western Germany* should provide a good indication of the extensive interests of the contributors – a 'healthy mix' of German and British political scientists, sociologists and historians. Their standpoints and theoretical orientations are naturally diverse, but the common concern with the problems and preconditions of party government imparts a unifying focus to the whole book. It was particularly gratifying to find how much the individual essays complemented one another in a quite unforced way.

This study represents a sustained attempt to unravel some of the key relationships in the German political system – in the connections between political culture, the party system and parliamentary government – and account has been taken of the fact that a wider audience may be unacquainted with the debates on the various topics. Nonetheless, the presentation of the book seeks to avoid a treatment that would be mainly introductory or descriptive. We hope it will succeed in giving the flavour of current academic concerns both in Britain and Germany.

Our thanks in particular go to Dr Klaus Schulz, Director of the Goethe Institut in London, for his interest and his help in mounting the original series of lectures.

H.D.

G.S.

Notes on the Contributors

Herbert Döring is Lecturer in German History at the University of London (SSEES) and Member of the Institut für Sozialwissenschaften, University of Mannheim. He is the author of *Der Weimarer Kreis: Studien zum politischen Bewusstsein verfassungstreuer Hochschullehrer* (1975), and he is at present completing a research study on 'Modern Political Parties and Democratic Theory'.

Kenneth Dyson is Senior Lecturer in Politics at the University of Liverpool. He has written widely on West European politics and public administration. His recent publications include: *Party, State and Bureaucracy in Western Germany* (1977) and *The State Tradition in Western Europe* (1980).

Nevil Johnson is Nuffield Reader in the Comparative Study of Institutions at Oxford and Professorial Fellow of Nuffield College. He has written widely on British and German politics. He is the author of *In Search of the Constitution: Reflections on State and Society in Britain* (1977) and *Government in the Federal Republic of Germany* (1973).

M. Rainer Lepsius is Professor of Sociology at the University of Heidelberg. His recent publications have dealt with aspects of political, historical and comparative sociology. At present he is co-editing the collected works and letters of Max Weber.

Martin McCauley is Lecturer in Russian and Soviet Institutions at the School of Slavonic and East European Studies, University of London. His recent books include *Marxism–Leninism in the German Democratic Republic: The Socialist Unity Party* (1979) and *Communist Power in Europe, 1944–1949* (revised edition, 1979).

Franz Urban Pappi is Professor of Sociology at the University of Kiel. He was editor of *Sozialstrukturanalysen mit Umfragedaten* (1979), and was co-author, with E. O. Laumann, of *Networks of Collective Action* (1976). His current research includes work on community power structures and the concept of the rational voter.

William E. Paterson is Senior Lecturer in Politics at the University of Warwick. He has written extensively on West German politics, foreign policy and European integration, and he was co-editor of *Social Democratic Parties in Western Europe* (1977). Currently he is working on the European policy of the Federal Republic and factionalism in West German parties.

Geoffrey Pridham is Lecturer in European Politics at the University of Bristol. He is the author of *Christian Democracy in Western Germany* (1977). His most recent books are: *Transnational Party Cooperation and European Integration* (with Pippa Pridham), and *The Nature of the Italian Party System*, both to appear in 1981.

Peter Pulzer is Official Student (Fellow) of Christ Church and University Lecturer in Politics, Oxford. His books include: *The Rise of Political Anti-Semitism in Germany and Austria* (1964) and *Political Representation and Elections in Britain* (third edition, 1975).

Gordon Smith is Reader in Government at the London School of Economics. His recent publications include *Democracy in Western Germany* (1979) and *Politics in Western Europe* (third edition, 1980). He is co-editor of the journal *West European Politics*.

Michael Terwey is a Research Associate at the Institut für Soziologie, University of Kiel. He has just completed a study of the relationship between social thought and empirical research in the work of Ferdinand Tönnies, and he has recently been concerned with research on income distribution and class structure in Western Germany.

1 Introduction

HERBERT DÖRING and GORDON SMITH

As this book came about through collaboration between a number of German and British academics, it is appropriate to introduce the theme of 'party government and political culture' by making some comparisons between the political systems of the two countries. Since both Britain and West Germany are based on the tenets of liberal democracy and parliamentary government, we should expect the similarities to be numerous. But Germany had only inherited a precarious parliamentary tradition that first developed within the shell of an authoritarian state. It was a legacy which did not promise well for the future of liberal democracy. Yet the ground rules of party government were not just imposed by the occupying powers – they were also accepted by the German political elites. The Federal Republic has now moved towards the practice of alternating government based on two competing party blocs, and any doubts about the working of parliamentary democracy were dispelled in 1969 when the constitution was tested by the first post-war change of government.

Precisely the extent of apparent likeness between the two systems at the present time may be misleading, and the same institutional labels can deceive the casual observer. It is tempting to assume that Western Germany has followed the British model, especially so since several German political scientists have expressed a preference for a two-party system and for a British-type electoral system. However, one of the results of the examination made in this book is to expose the limitations of any tendency to measure the Federal Republic against a Westminster style of parliamentary politics.

It is difficult, anyway, to judge the two democracies on the same scale, even though they both have a reputation for political stability. In the case of Britain, her parliamentary democracy evolved gradually and with a certain grandeur, the envy to some extent and the desired model of many constitutional liberals in Germany. In contrast, German progress was chequered, marred by a whole series of fundamental ruptures until the arrival of the

Federal Republic, nothing grand, no 'Glorious Revolution', and yet all uncomfortably convulsive.

Their contrasting historical experience may lead to different evaluations of the same evidence of current stability, a feeling that whatever the objective indicators of political stability show, qualitatively there is no real comparison. The view may even be expressed that political stability will persist in Britain whatever happens, while in Germany it will only last until something does happen. When such an observation is made from the British side it reveals a rather complacent hubris, and a similar German comment naturally displays the anxieties bound to be felt in a country where political cataclysms have burned into the public mind. Yet, neat as the formulation is, it takes into account neither the evidence of an increasing political and constitutional malaise in Britain, nor the signs in the Federal Republic of a stable symmetry emerging between party and parliamentary institutions and political culture. Perhaps there is a case not only for putting the two democracies on the same scale of performance but also for showing that their paths on it may have crossed, the one upwards, the other down.

It has to be admitted that the British practice of parliamentary and party government continues to conform to all the accepted criteria: governments are stable, they are normally majoritarian, and they alternate smoothly and regularly between the two parties. In spite of a few hiccups – Liberal 'revivals' and sporadic nationalist upsurges – the 'pristine beauty' of the British two-party system remains largely intact. A blind eye is turned to the fact that during the hundred years, from 1871, almost one year in four saw a coalition government – apart from such tacit alliances as the one between Callaghan and the Liberals. The cherished view that Britons do not like coalitions continues to hold sway, and with the defeat of devolution plans for Scotland and Wales, the classic doctrine of the supremacy of Parliament still reigns supreme.

Yet there is dissatisfaction. A certain weariness and frustration is evident: the 'accepted criteria' are all met, but without the beneficial results. Alternating party government tends to lead to quick reversals of policy rather than to purposeful direction. The two-party system itself hardly reflects electoral realities, and the significant decline in the aggregate share of the vote taken by the Conservative and Labour parties in recent years has not been accompanied by a commensurate increase in seats for other parties. The unease is compounded by the almost obsessively adversary style of confrontation that the entrenched two-party system encourages, even enforces, on the participants.

If it were only a question of style, suited to the dramatisation of the dichotomy of Government and Opposition, not too much would be at stake;

but the rhetoric has also become a reality, and the basic consensus needed to make the concept of 'alternating government' work is weakened with each ratchet of party polarisation. The outcome could conceivably be an increase of social cleavage, the appearance of two 'armed camps' in place of a rather comfortable coexistence. But that development is improbable; instead the strains are shown in other ways: the continual switches of policy from one government to another, or even within the life of a single government, lead to a sense of drift, of vacillation and impotence.

The political malaise may well reflect economic ills as well as a social disorientation. A loss in the authority of government follows a weakness in its performance. Such repercussions are felt in other countries as well as Britain: the concept of 'government overload' and the forecasts of crises of 'governability' have become commonplace throughout the Western world and in the literature of the social sciences. Threatened, too, is the belief in the self-regulating capability of the forces of pluralist society. The view was once almost undisputed that political parties created Western-style democracy and that modern democracy would be unthinkable without their commanding presence. That 'party doctrine' has been weakened, however, and with the coming of post-industrial society some might argue that the parties are no longer in a position to shore up traditional parliamentary government. There may be a case for holding that the Federal Republic better meets the requirements of 'party government' and that British difficulties herald a post-industrial future – giving Britain an almost paradigmatic status, while Western Germany, having caught up with the ruling concepts of the past, is now the one-eyed king in the country of the blind.

A negative rendering of parliamentary government in Britain is easily overdrawn, just as it is possible to exaggerate the positive gains made by the Federal Republic. Nonetheless, the extent to which the parliamentary system has become anchored in Western Germany is impressive, not merely in 'catching up with the British' but in adapting the 'Westminster model' to quite different political traditions as well. Besides the legacy of German history – and notably the failure of the one determined effort to implant parliamentary democracy in the constitution of the Weimar Republic – there are also the barriers set by the nature of the German political culture to consider. Clearly, the exact mixture of beliefs, values and attitudes supportive of liberal democracy can show a wide variation, but in the case of Germany the values of the *Obrigkeitsstaat* were pervasive and they constituted a complete authoritarian alternative to the idea of responsible party government.

There could not be a simple emulation of successful parliamentary democracies elsewhere, a straightforward matter of transplanting the requisite institutions and manipulating a 'guided democracy' along the correct path. Doubtless these elements were present in the period after 1945, but a copy-book approach would scarcely have had long-lasting results. The really important point is that the innovations that were made in the Federal Republic proved to be entirely consonant with German traditions, whereas constitutional engineering by itself could have proved an unmitigated disaster.

After 1945 there was a remarkable absence of doctrinal dispute – unlike the experience of the *Paulskirche* in 1848 or in Weimar during 1919 – and a number of assumed obstacles to democratic advance proved not to be impediments after all. Thus the longing for bureaucratic expertise and solutions that had been basic to the anti-party sentiment, as well as the concept of the *Obrigkeitsstaat* as existing above the parties, had both to be overcome after the Second World War. Yet, as it transpired, the parties won an unanticipated advantage through their dissolution in 1933, since so many other institutions were discredited by the Nazi dictatorship. In the period from 1945 to 1946 the parties were first in the field and gained a lead they were not to lose over all other contenders for governing power. In the uniquely German concept of the 'party state', distinct from and even alien to Anglo-American ideas of party government, the parties themselves donned the Emperor's clothes of the German state tradition, successfully diverting the authoritarian heritage into a working liberal democracy.

It is easy to neglect the special features of the German political system and to concentrate more on the strong parallels that can be drawn with Britain. The key concept of 'alternating government' is now a base-point for the study of West German politics, even if twenty years passed before it occurred in the Federal Republic and even though alternation is still largely a question of potential rather than the regular movement of a pendulum. Moreover, the institutional and political correlates of a British-type system are all reproduced. There are marked resemblances in the roles of prime minister and federal chancellor, and it is not quite coincidental that the British version of 'prime-ministerial government' – in opposition to the pure doctrine of the cabinet system and even modifying the idea of parliamentary government – should have enjoyed a vogue remarkably akin to the German formula of 'chancellor democracy'. The parallels can be extended in the clear-cut division that exists in Germany between Government and Opposition. Here again, the rooted German disinclination to accept the role of Opposition as an essential feature of parliamentary life and as a justification for the alternation of power had first to be overcome.

That development depended largely on the evolution of the party system in the Federal Republic towards a two-bloc formation. The rapid move away from a multi-party system has been quite exceptional in Western Europe and, even though coalitions have usually been necessary to produce parliamentary majorities, the presence of only two major contestants, the CDU/CSU on the one side and the SPD (together with the FDP) on the other, supplies the vital ingredient for alternation. Furthermore, the nature of the constituent parties aids the process of parliamentary reconciliation: neither extreme of Right or Left is of any electoral significance, and the parties are forced to compete for the critical margin of votes near the centre of the political spectrum. Their competition is evidence of a broad consensus, and that is an essential complement to a functioning parliamentary system.

Such are the similarities with the supposed ideal form of parliamentary government that the unwary observer might conclude that any deviations are only of minor importance. It could lead to the supposition that, for instance, German federalism is a subordinate factor in the constitutional structure. Yet the federal system has to be regarded as a powerful constraint upon the federal government in almost all of its domestic dealings, and it also acts as a major modification to the working of parliamentary government: the representation of the *Länder* governments in the Bundesrat and the powers of that body in relation to the Bundestag means that legislative authority has to be shared. It follows that a government's working majority in the Bundestag by no means represents unqualified majority rule, nor are comparisons with the battles for Commons supremacy over the Lords of any validity – the federal constraint is a permanent feature of the constitutional equilibrium. It may also be argued that the federal structure is actually inconsistent with parliamentary sovereignty: the outward appearance of the form of party government appears in blatant contradiction to the 'summit diplomacy' enforced on the parties in order to overcome the stalemate that frequently affects federal legislative proposals. The suspicion that the parties are acting in collusion may even adversely affect the legitimacy of the parliamentary system.

A further 'deviation' resides in the philosophy of the constitution itself. Although the Basic Law spells out all the essential requirements of parliamentary government – especially in the provisions for the election and the removal of a chancellor by the Bundestag – it would be dangerous to treat this aspect in isolation from the emphasis that the constitution places on the concept of the *Rechtsstaat*. It is not only that governments have to operate within the framework of the law, they also have to accept the constraints of judicial intervention accorded by the Basic Law to the Federal Constitutional Court which in the scope of its authority rivals the American Supreme Court and which at times verges on becoming a substitute for the political arena. The German *penchant* for legalistic forms should not obscure the fact that the *Rechtsstaat*, as given expression by the Basic Law, imposes powerful legal norms on political behaviour.

These examples may be sufficient to guard against a simplistic transfer of a parliamentary model to German circumstances. A reversed sequence is equally inapplicable, to suppose that the British system could somehow benefit by importing a selection of German 'deviations': a federal solution for regional problems or a bill of rights in a written constitution with the full panoply of judicial review. The objection is not primarily that the innovations would attack the central doctrine of the sovereignty of Parliament, although that sacrifice would of necessity follow, but that in the attempt, say, to incorporate aspects of the German *Rechtsstaat* orientation the result might lead to an unacceptable judicialisation of politics. Far from helping to supply a consensus-building constraint to British politics, a more likely consequence would be to weaken the status of the law.

It is true that the German institutional setting emphasises integration, even to the extent of making untoward developments appear as an 'impending crisis' that could threaten the integrative power of the system, but a widespread social consensus has manifestly evolved in Germany, whereas in Britain there now appears to be a higher degree of polarisation. Yet however the German mixture of social and constitutional practices is dubbed – 'limited pluralism' or 'liberal corporatism' – it does not fit any neat model of government, let alone lend itself to any cut-and-dried parcel of legislative and constitutional refinement. There is no such thing as a 'German model' for export and any attempt to imitate the forms of a German consensus might well destroy what tacit agreement still exists between the competing British elites.

A certain paradox is evident: the smooth running of German parliamentary democracy goes hand-in-hand with a fear that, from one direction or another, a threat could suddenly materialise – most obviously through a fragmentation of the party system from whatever underlying cause. There are possibly two major effects arising from this concern. One is that likely problems are specified well in advance, and a great deal of attention is paid to arriving at rational solutions. The other is that a premium is placed on building up a consensus to meet the challenge: the whole tone of the political style is to avoid fundamental confrontation. That mood is far distant from the doctrinal spirit that imbued the masses, the parties and the elites in the Weimar Republic.

The present system of responsible party government has developed, if not 'unintentionally', then at least contrary to many expectations of those who framed the Basic Law. It is not easily to be justified in terms of a theory of party government, if only because there is no such accepted single theory.

The lack of doctrinal concern in the Basic Law contrasts to the questing democratic spirit that animated the Weimar constitution. It had liberally borrowed institutional devices from successful democracies, and yet it succumbed ignominiously. If it is true that democracy is learned by practice and not on the forms of a political finishing school, then the Federal Republic has done well to take a pragmatic course rather than to strive for an ideal democracy – a hopeless graft on to an undemocratic tradition. If the fault of the Germans was once that 'they reach too high and fall too low', the contrary might now almost be said. Today, the Federal Republic is *par excellence* the home of political pragmatism. On an academic level apart, there is little concern with visions of creating a far better democracy; the points of reference are the less eligible examples, based in German history or on the practice of socialism in the German Democratic Republic.

The apparent sobriety of West German politics, to which the description of a 'cheerless pragmatism' might be attached, has no one cause, nor is there a single 'efficient secret' to be gleaned through a study of the political institutions. The best clue is provided by the 'symmetry' that has emerged between the main features of political culture and post-war institutions. Yet the real puzzle is to explain why a precise fit between the two should have come about. Changes in political culture are not susceptible to conscious moulding in the short term and hardly at all within a liberal-democratic order. The juxtaposition of 'party government and political culture' does, however, imply that there are close interconnections between the two. The existence of institutions affects attitudes and behaviour, and the prevailing culture influences the working of institutions. It is a dynamic interaction, and one of the fascinations in studying the development of the Federal Republic is to analyse the phases – and the levels – of interaction. In this process the parties have occupied a vital place, since they mirror the changing political culture at the same time as operating as formal political institutions. That is true of any liberal democracy, but in Western Germany the formalisation of the role of the parties has been particularly significant, the rendering of the 'party state' has special implications, and to a large extent the problems of explaining the changes in Germany are embodied in the party system itself.

The two labels that one might use to portray the Federal Republic – 'impending crisis' and 'cheerless pragmatism' – both provide insights on the nature of West German democracy. We can appreciate, too, that the one stands in a definite relationship to the other, even though they point to quite different versions of the future. However, neither succeeds in conveying accurately the reality of present-day German politics, in contrast to the earlier years of the republic when self-confidence was lacking and the gains could not be taken for granted. It is still the case that a relaxed attitude towards the voicing of political dissent is often missing, but there is a greater willingness to express dissenting opinions, to become involved in the 'new politics', to reject pragmatism as the sole rationale of judgement. There are differences of viewpoint as to how Western Germany will fare in the future. Some see the partial rejection of 'established politics' as a hint of an ideological re-birth and a return to doctrinaire positions. But another reading of contemporary developments is much more positive: the signs of disaffection should not be over-interpreted, for they are no greater than one would expect in any normally functioning democracy. The difference now, perhaps, in contrast to Germany's past misfortunes, is that opposition operates from within a consensus, not against it.

2 Responsible Party Government in the German Political System

PETER PULZER

'The ministry is really nothing more than the common executive committee of the two Houses, composed of the most prominent and influential members of the majority; but never a force opposed, perhaps even hostile to parliament and derived from the monarch's personal will. A decisive change in the majority changes the ministry, thus there is always harmony between the principal powers in the state, even if the struggle between the majority and the minority can, naturally, be severe. . . .

A second characteristic of the English view of parliament is the arrangement whereby the popular representative assembly by no means has the purely negative role of defending infringements of, or threats to, public liberties and of resistance to illicit power or maladministration, but rather attends to a significant portion of the administration of the state in a direct and positive way. . . .

These are the principal traits of England's magnificent representative political system. We see undisguised party government, in which the government and the majority of the representative institution are always at one, because the direction of public affairs is transferred immediately, and without any disturbance, from the previous holders to those who are recognised in advance as the leaders of their opponents, as soon as the latter have gained a majority of the votes. We see a severe contest between the parties for leadership, but never an assault on the power of the state as such, never an attempt to render this *in principe* impossible by denying it necessary supply. For each party would merely be inflicting wounds on itself, if it made demands and committed acts that would cause it embarrassment and bring it into damaging contradiction with its own past, since it might after all find itself in government any day.'[1]

'A parliament with political responsibility must lead at any rate in the direction of a two-party system. These do not always need to be two specific parties, they can also be coalitions.'[2]

What is surprising about the first quotation is that it dates from the same year as the repeal of the Corn Laws and comes from a German scholar, Robert von Mohl, at a time when most of his liberal contemporaries (e.g. Friedrich Christoph Dahlmann, Georg Gottfried Gervinus and Rudolf von Gneist) still praised Britain for its limited monarchy and mixed constitution. Indeed, given its date it might be regarded as a shrewd prophecy rather than an exact description. Alone among German liberals Robert von Mohl grasped the essentials of the British system as it was then developing: the eclipse of the crown, the fusion of executive and legislature, the duality of governmental majority and oppositional minority. What is interesting about the second, which comes from Hugo Preuss, one of the begetters of the Weimar constitution, is that it forecasts accurately what was to happen half a century later, but for the wrong reason.

THE NATURE OF THE DOCTRINE

Responsible party government is based on programmes and accountability. It requires, in the words of the American Political Science Association's famous commission:

> that the parties are able to bring forth programmes to which they can commit themselves and, second, that the parties possess sufficient internal cohesion to carry out these programmes. . . . The fundamental requirement for accountability is a two-party system in which the opposition party acts as the critic of the party in power, developing, defining and presenting the policy alternatives which are necessary for a true choice in reaching public decisions.[3]

However, it requires a great deal else before it can function in the way desired. A monopoly of effective political decision-making by the parliamentary majority is most easily achieved if there is:

(a) a unitary constitution, ensuring undivided sovereignty and an absence of divergent policy pressures on different levels of the party organisation;

(b) a unicameral legislature, or at any rate one in which the directly elected chamber has a preponderance of power;

(c) an overlap between the executive and legislative functions, so that the political executive can be largely recruited from elected party members.

It will be evident why, in the United States, where the constitution denies each of these three conditions, the kind of party government advocated by the APSA cannot be achieved.[4]

On the other hand, the following conditions hamper the achievement of responsible party government:

(a) a bureaucracy or other branch of the government machine, such as the military or the police, not amenable to effective civilian control;

(b) a professional party machine, whether or not acting on behalf of a mass membership, so strong that it can impose programmes or candidatures on the parliamentary party and subject its members to inquisitorial control;

(c) local caucuses, whether composed of notables or party activists, that can deflect the allegiance of the member from national policy considerations;

(d) a diffusion of issues and electoral considerations that make members primarily constituency ambassadors;

(e) pressure groups or lobbies sufficiently strong to impose candidatures or programmes on parties, or to affect governmental decisions on major policy issues.

For obvious reasons it would be unrealistic to expect this model to correspond with twentieth-century political life; indeed some of its components can be attained only at the expense of others. For instance, effective discipline inside a parliamentary party is unlikely to arise permanently until there is something approaching a mass electorate; but once there is a mass electorate there are bound to be organised extra-parliamentary pressures on parliamentary behaviour. The question is therefore not whether party machines, lobbies or constituency pressures are desirable, but at what point their influences seriously diminish the exercise of responsible party government or the prospect of its attainment. A contrast of British and German conditions in the formative period will illustrate this.

There is no reason to suppose, with Duverger, that 'the two-party system seems to correspond to 'the nature of things',[5] nor that there is a causal connection between the electoral system and the number of political parties, nor that the powers of the legislature determine the behaviour of either legislators or electors in some precisely predictable way. No doubt the single-member constituencies which have prevailed in Britain since the Third Reform Act of 1884 have helped to keep the two-party system alive, but they do not explain the origins. It emerged from a struggle inside parliament to deprive the Crown of its prerogatives, a struggle which would, if successful, result, in the words of David Hume, in 'the Commons . . . assuming by usurpation the whole power of government'.[6] It was this intra-legislative contest rather than 'the nature of things' that led to a bi-polar division of opinion; though existence of party *names* from the late seventeenth century onwards is no guarantee of the existence of a party *system*.

There were, however, a number of other reasons why this contest was able to develop into stable responsible party government with a two-party system by the second half of the nineteenth century. The first was the absence of democracy, which made it relatively independent of external forces. Electoral pressures were intermittent. Ministers might be answerable to members, but it was far from certain to whom members were answerable. Party formation could therefore take place in parliament with little reference to popular opinion, and restrict itself to dividing for or against the government of the day. The second, which arises out of the first, was the lack of a party apparatus. No-one dictated platforms, no-one attempted to impose mandates, members of parliament were not salaried employees, professional propagandists or machine men: they were men who (to employ Max Weber's distinction) lived for rather than off politics.[7]

The third is that members were not primarily constituency representatives. Though the fifteenth-century statute requiring them to be 'dwelling and resident' was not repealed until 1774, it had fallen into disuse long before.[8] Unrestrained by either localism or democracy, MPs tended not to be parochial notables or 'single-minded seekers of re-election', as one recent observer has described US Congressmen.[9] Instead, they could at their best be men of national standing who contributed to the debate on national issues at a national level. Corruption was a great help in this respect. The argument for having twenty-one Cornish boroughs with a total electorate of 1400 is not that they sent a lot of Cornishmen to Westminster, but that they sent a lot of government supporters there. Indeed the existence of such a body of men was a necessary condition for the evolution of parliament as a forum in which regional, local and sectarian issues were at a discount.[10] Indirectly their existence was a precondition for the evolution of national political parties. The fourth is the absence of organised, durable pressure-groups, capable of making demands on parties and candidates, and of imposing conditions in return for financial or agitational support.

This summary should not be seen as an idealisation of the eighteenth- or nineteenth-century British constitution. No doubt many MPs were stupid, greedy, prejudiced or opportunistic. No doubt many electors shared these attributes. The lack of nationally organised lobbies did not mean lack of pressure from specific interests. The obligations to patrons were considerable, but neither universal nor overwhelming. What mattered was that parliamentary business could be conducted without constant reference to extra-parliamentary pressures and this helped to build up a degree of corporate loyalty and commitment to parliament as an institution that is another precondition of successful parliamentary government.

Thus reinforced, British parliamentary government was able to weather the transition to democracy with remarkably little crisis and remarkably few changes of parliamentary form. The leaders of the parliamentary parties have remained the dominant politicians in the country, even though increasingly challenged by constituency caucuses, party machines and pressure groups. The exigencies of distinctive legislative programmes have resulted in increasingly tight back-bench discipline, a development that has strengthened party as an instrument of government; the exigencies of mass electoral campaigning have resulted in extra-parliamentary organisations, but as long as these remain subordinate to the parliamentary leadership they, too, by disciplining the voter, strengthen responsible party government. There is, of course, considerable evidence that all these forces supporting classical parliamentary government have been in decline in Britain, particularly during the 1970s, and if that decline continues the nature of the system will change. But that does not invalidate the proposition that for a century or more the ways of Westminster acted as a model and a norm.

THE IMPERIAL LEGACY

The debate on parliamentary government in Germany is younger than in Britain, but the British experience was inevitably a reference point. The German experience, as it evolved under the Empire, was almost everything that the British was not.

(1) The Reichstag inherited party cleavages from the parliaments of the constituent states. The multi-party system of the Reichstag was made up of 'numerous regional two-party systems existing side-by-side';[11] some of the parties, in particular the Catholic *Zentrum*, operated under self-imposed geographical restrictions. The result was that by 1914 there was only one party that made a point of fighting every constituency, the SPD,

which was also the only party to have a coherent national organisation. However, the *Zentrum* did have a mass base in the *Volksverein für das katholische Deutschland* and the National Liberals and Conservatives were beginning to attempt creating a bureaucratic structure. Election was by single-member constituencies with two ballots. This provided little incentive to reduce the number of parties, but given the regional and state bases of the parties it is doubtful whether, say, the abolition of the second ballot would have changed much.

(2) The constitution of the Empire was federal, which perpetuated a fragmentation of sovereignty. The Empire was a perpetual union (*'ewiger Bund'*) of rulers;[12] the Bundesrat, which comprised the delegations of the state governments, was less an upper house of a legislature than a collegiate executive. That arrangement created a vested interest in opposing any extension of parliamentary prerogative, most of all any moves towards cabinet government and executive responsibility to the Reichstag, which could come about only at the expense of states' rights.

(3) The political system of the Empire rested on the dualism of executive and legislative authority, as generally understood in nineteenth-century continental constitutionalism. In Germany the acceptance of this arrangement was reinforced by the dualism of state and society as expressed in Hegelian doctrine. According to this, political parties were the expression of societal concerns; they were by definition representative and particularistic only. The state, in contrast, was above party and concerned with the general interest; the bureaucracy was an objective, impartial adjudicator of conflicting claims. As long as these assumptions predominated, the status of politicians and parliaments was bound to remain low, and their claims to participation in political responsibility easily resisted.

(4) As long as parliament remained subordinate to the executive, the parties had no role as recruiters of political leadership and no incentive to behave with political responsibility. At any rate in its early years the Reichstag contained a number of eminent men: Rudolf von Gneist, Heinrich von Treitschke, Rudolf Virchow among others. But they did not aim at political office and were not cut out for it. The consequence was a vicious circle. As long as the Reichstag had only a negative role to perform, a parliamentary career would be held in low esteem. As long as parliamentarians were publicly despised, the Emperor Wilhelm II setting the example, few men of outstanding qualities would be attracted to it. There was no prospect of the system bringing forth the caesaristic–plebiscitary element, 'the dictator of the electoral battlefield' that Max

Weber saw as the essential link between a democratic franchise and parliamentary government.[13]

(5) Compared with the stagnation of political parties pressure groups, whether promotional or producer based, developed rapidly and forged close links with the press, the bureaucracy and political parties. This evolution did not displease successive governments or conservative political forces, who had long been playing with notions of an economic parliament and preferred corporatist to parliamentary representation. In the end, however, the government neither set up a *'Wirtschaftsrat'* nor promoted a democratisation of the political structure in which competition for influence could be freely and openly conducted: 'It was a contradiction, when interest groups and agitational bodies like the Navy League, the Pan-German League or the Hansa League could propagate German imperialism without hindrance,' but 'were not required to accept any political responsibility'.[14]

The constitutional practice of Imperial Germany did not stand still. This is not the place to debate whether the Imperial constitution can be characterised, with E. R. Huber, as a viable compromise between absolutist and representative principles, or whether the very existence of a Reichstag and political parties created irresistible forces making for parliamentarisation.[15] But by 1914 important shifts of power had taken place; so had important shifts in the content of the constitutional debate. In the first place the exigencies of modern government meant that governmental functions were transferred from the competence of the individual states and the Bundesrat to that of the Reich and therefore the Reichstag. While the Reichstag's own demands remained frustrated, it was increasingly indispensable for underwriting the government's legislative and financial initiatives. This development reached its climax under Chancellor Bülow who, between 1907 and 1909, created a bloc consisting of the two conservative and two liberal parties for the purpose of reforming the Reich finances The step was viewed with alarm by the state governments; the Bavarian representatives in Berlin reported back that 'we now have a parliamentary and no longer a constitutional system' and that 'the principles that majorities were to be taken where one found them, according to circumstances, was abandoned the moment Prince Bülow identified himself with the bloc'.[16]

The Bavarians' alarm was in many respects premature. Parliamentary majorities continued to be the creations of the executive rather than the outcome of the parties' initiative, even if the executive was increasingly dependent on prior consultations and informal soundings. Above all, there was no consensus among the political parties on the future of the Reichstag or the party system. Almost alone among politicians Friedrich Naumann advocated a two-party system on the grounds that 'political action means the creation of majorities'[17] and he welcomed Bülow's moves in 1907 as 'the dawn of the English system'.[18] Most parties, especially the Catholic *Zentrum*, were unwilling to abandon the bargaining power that the existing constellation gave them.

Those who favoured further 'parliamentarisation' tended to mean by this the answerability of the chancellor and his ministers to parliament. There was little demand for ministers to be recruited from the leaders of the parliamentary parties, if only because most Reichstag members shared the contempt for their colleagues that the members of the bureaucracy constantly expressed. Nor did the Social Democrats strongly press for parliamentary government on British lines. Those among them who remained wedded to the rhetoric of revolution saw it at worst as a distraction, at best as a stepping-stone. For Karl Kautsky, 'a powerful parliament on the English model with a Social Democratic majority' was the achievement of the dictatorship of the proletariat by peaceful means.[19] There is no indication that he recognised as valid one of the main characteristics of the English model, that of alternating majorities. On the other hand the Revisionists in the party who attached greater importance to parliamentary work and an extension of parliamentary powers were aware that there was no realistic prospect of the SPD achieving a majority of its own; they therefore saw no advantage in a two-party system and advocated coalitions with willing Liberals instead.[20] Similarly, when the SPD talked, in its manifesto for the last pre-1914 election, of 'bringing about a different majority',[21] it could do so only in the context of sharing the opposition to the dominant Conservative–*Zentrum* alliance. These debates among the Social Democrats do much to explain the development of the party system after 1918.

On the other hand, Conservative opponents of full parliamentary government were not slow to underline its disadvantages to the practitioners of interest-bargaining in the existing Reichstag. Hans Delbrück pointed out that under the kind of party discipline that the British system required the House of Commons had less say on the Budget than the Reichstag,[22] and Erich Kaufmann argued that during the war Lloyd George exercised a degree of dictatorial power denied to any Imperial Chancellor.[23]

When, therefore, under the impact of military defeat in 1917–18 German parliamentarians were required to share in the country's government, they did so in ways that reflected and, in turn, perpetuated the assumptions of the Imperial constitution. There were two main elements of continuity. The first perpetuated the duality between executive and legislative power. The majority parties in the Reichstag (Social Democrats, left Liberals and *Zentrum*) that had come together in the inter-party caucus (*Interfraktioneller Ausschuss*) could not decide whether they merely wanted a decisive part in the nomination or dismissal of the chancellor or to insist on choosing one of their own number,[24] and in the end abandoned the latter course. The second concerned the independence of the parties *vis-à-vis* their ministers. The members of the IFA regarded those of their deputies who were to be appointed to junior ministerial posts as their nominees and watchdogs within the executive:[25] they were to be the ambassadors of parties in hostile territory, not popular representatives bearing collective responsibility.

THE LEGACY OF WEIMAR

These usages continued under the Weimar constitution. The Chancellor was now the appointee of the President, dismissible by him.[26] The rest of the cabinet consisted either of non-partisan experts – an echo of the Imperial notion that governments should be above parties – or of the nominees of parties. One-third of Weimar Chancellors and three-eighths of cabinet ministers had not previously been Reichstag members.[27] The interests of the parties represented in the cabinet was monitored by a 'majority caucus' (*Mehrheitsausschuss*); this body, part governmental rank-and-file, part opposition, undermined the authority of ministers within their parties and of the Chancellor over his ministers. In some parties, notably the SPD, any member of the party executive joining a government was required to resign his executive position.[28] This provision, derived from the doctrine that Socialist parliamentarians were simply the delegates of the working class[29] and hence designed to safeguard the independence of the extra-parliamentary party, deprived the latter of a further incentive to support its own ministers. A further diminution of the Chancellor's governmental authority and his responsibility to parliament, and one that has frequently been pointed out as one of the major inconsistencies of the Weimar constitution, was the popular election of the President, which gave that office a legitimacy that rivalled that of the Reichstag.

All these continuities with pre-Republican practices inhibited the growth of responsible party government. There was, however, one major break which had the same effect, namely the change to proportional representation. This innovation, so contentious in retrospect, was scarcely controversial at the time. Only Friedrich Naumann, consistent with his pre-war stand, insisted that, 'Proportional representation and parliamentary government are mutually exclusive. If we want to govern ourselves according to the English two-party system, we have to accept the English electoral system.'[30]

There were numerous reasons why he failed to gain support. In the first place most politicians simply took it for granted that a parliament designed to reflect opinions and interests should do so with mathematical justice, the more so since German parties were instinctively drawn towards ideological self-sufficiency and to defensive tactics in the upheavals of the revolution. More specifically, the SPD was committed to proportional representation, although in the conditions of 1919 it would almost certainly have got the absolute majority under first-past-the-post that proportional representation denied it. So strongly was it taken for granted that democracy entailed proportional representation that the matter was barely debated by the Provisional Government.[31]

One immediate reason for the SPD's advocacy was the experience of the gerrymander of the Imperial constituencies, whose boundaries remained unchanged after 1871. But a more profound reason, which accounted for the party's attachment to proportional representation from its very beginnings and the inclusion of proportional representation in the 1891 Erfurt programme, was its attitude to elections. These were to be treated as an ideological plebiscite from which constituency campaigning and negotiations for run-offs were distractions.[32] Since, moreover, parliamentary government was to be seen as an interlude rather than an end in itself there was no virtue in adapting to its requirements, even when these were acknowledged. If anything, advocacy of proportional representation reduced the price of collaboration with other parties: an SPD motion in favour of the reform had been turned down by the Reichstag by only one vote, in 1913.[33] It is therefore not surprising that in the debates on the republican constitution – which provided for proportional representation for the states as well as the Reich[34] – and on the electoral law the SPD should defend proportional representation, along with female suffrage, as 'the common property of the people' and 'one of the achievements of the revolution'.[35]

However, proportional representation received equally strong support from non-Socialists. In particular those liberal German scholars who were within the historicist tradition emphasised that precisely because the party structure was 'the necessary product of present-day German society', it should be respected.[36] Max Weber thought that the existence of four or five parties would be a permanent feature of German politics, if only because of the religious division; indeed that in Britain a two-party system had been possible only under aristocratic dominance and that modern industrial conditions, as well as the rise of Labour, would make for multi-partism there. (He may yet be proved right.)[37] But above all an electoral system which enforced coalition-based consensus and strengthened moderate parties had its obvious attractions to any liberal living through the gunfire of the post-war years. A two-party system, after all, required parties both of which accepted the rules of the parliamentary game. Under German conditions, Ernst Troeltsch insisted, polarisation would mean that 'blood would flow': but for the 'great coalition' of the two mass-based parties (Social Democrats and *Zentrum*), order would have broken down.[38]

That the polarisation of politics was a risk Germany could not afford to take in the aftermath of the world war is probably true: it would have led, as Troeltsch feared, to civil war and not, as Naumann hoped, to the British parliamentary system. However, there is no denying that in other respects the introduction of proportional representation was dysfunctional to the development of parliamentary government. While there is no evidence that proportional representation as such encourages the proliferation or fragmentation of parties, it can certainly perpetuate it and is indeed frequently invoked in order to achieve this result.

What the German party list system of proportional representation in large multi-member constituencies did encourage was a further shift in the balance of political power away from the Reichstag. It strengthened party machines, it favoured party functionaries and bureaucrats in the adoption of candidates, and it encouraged interest groups to compete for places on the lists on behalf of their representatives. Yet coalition government requires stronger centripetal forces than single-party government and can afford less dependence on external constraints. The bureaucratisation of the parties, and the diffusion of responsibility under coalition government, may well have affected the type of person attracted to a political career. The great majority were colourless and uninspiring. Only one of the party leaders, Gustav Stresemann, could be regarded as a 'chancellor-candidate' of the type that post-1945 German political parties have been efficient at producing. Weimar parties therefore failed to perform one of the most important functions of a responsible party system: the selection and promotion of ministerial talent.

There was no shortage of critics of parliamentary government as it evolved in the Weimar Republic, but few of their remedies pointed in the direction of responsible party government. Critics on the Right preferred to strengthen the presidency at the expense of the Reichstag, especially after the election of Hindenburg in 1925. Many in the centre sought to reduce the number of parties and to strengthen the individual deputy's links with his electors by reducing the size of constituencies. Moderate multi-partism no doubt makes coalition management easier than extreme multi-partism, but it is doubtful whether deputies dependent on caucuses of local notables are any more likely to contribute to a British-style parliamentary system than deputies dependent on impersonal party machines. Even those who advocated single-member constituencies, such as the youthful F. A. Hermens, did so at this stage less because they saw it as the way to a two-party system than because they thought it would favour moderate candidates.[39] There were, however, few grounds for believing that the deepest cleavage in Weimar politics was between moderate and extreme rather than between Left and Right, or for assuming that the unattached voter is by definition moderate. Those younger Social Democrats, like Carl Mierendorff and Julius Leber, who began, in the late twenties, to preach where Friedrich Naumann had left off,[40] were probably unrealistic. Little had changed since Stresemann's lament in 1925 that Germany lacked a 'statesman-like opposition'; his solution was to enforce responsible behaviour on all parties through a great coalition.[41]

In the end the Republic was not saved, and those who survived it in opposition, exile or post-war occupation tried to construct new models of political machinery from the lessons of past failure on the examples of other states. The ideas of many resisters, in particular the conservative circles round Carl Goerdeler, moved away from any reformed parliamentarism towards a monarchical constitution, a more clearly defined dualism of executive and legislature and a functionally representative chamber (*Reichsständehaus*) beside a Reichstag one half of which was to be indirectly elected.[42] The Kreisau Circle round Count Helmuth von Moltke did not want a directly elected Reichstag at all.[43] Illuminating though these notions are of the German 'trauma of the helplessness of parliament',[44] they are diversions from our theme. More germane to it are the thoughts of politicians in exile or after liberation on the future of the party structure.

Within the SPD there was a move away from unthinking attachment to PR, already signalled before 1932. SPD exiles tended to reflect the political norms of their countries of refuge. Those in Britain, despite their shabby treatment by the Foreign Office and the Labour Party, could not help being impressed by their hosts' political practice. The youthful Erich Ollenhauer commented as early as 1941:

> The new German democracy cannot and ought not to be the democracy of Weimar. . . . Splinter parties must be abolished by law and democratic rights should be constitutionally protected, so that democracy can no longer be destroyed under the guise of democratic freedom. We German

Social Democrats must put into practice the experiences of British democracy . . . by adopting smaller constituencies and abolishing electoral
lists.[45]

It is therefore not surprising that the constitutional proposals of the London-
based SPD, published in late 1945, should come down in favour of single-
member constituencies, with some compensatory representation for
minorities,[46] nor that American-based exiles like Albert Grzezinski, the
former Prussian Minister of the Interior, thought similarly.[47] The Swiss-
based exiles, on the other hand, who included non-Social Democrats,
preferred federalism, local self-government, referendums, popular initiatives and a collegiate federal executive.[48] There was more emphasis on
electoral systems than on parties in all these proposals. The cart had as yet no
horses.

TOWARDS THE FEDERAL REPUBLIC

Between these early discussions and the adoption of the Basic Law a great
deal of water flowed under many bridges. In particular, three developments
had taken place in the western occupation zones that influenced the context
of the debates in the Parliamentary Council in 1948–9. The first was the
existence of the *Länder*, established by the Allied occupation authorities.
These, with their elected governments, represented irremovable vested
interests. They ensured, if nothing else did, that the new state would be
federal like its predecessors. The second was the emergence of a new party
system, of which the most significant feature was the creation of the Christian Democratic Union, displacing the old *Zentrum* and much of the Protestant and secular centre–right. An aggregation of the *Landtag* elections of
1946–7 gives the following totals

CDU/CSU	38.5%
SPD	35.7%
FDP	8.2%
KPD	9.3%
Others	8.3%

These party strengths were reflected in the composition of the Parliamentary
Council where CDU and SPD had twenty-seven members each, the FDP
five, and *Zentrum*, the Communists and the right-wing German Party (DP)
two each.

The third development, whose import was least evident at the time, was the creation of the Bizonal Economic Council in the British and American zones in 1947. Its fifty-two members represented Landtag party strengths and from them a five-member executive was to be drawn. Given the prevalence of 'great coalitions' in the *Länder* there was strong support for a similar arrangement in the Economic Council. Kurt Schumacher, the leader of the SPD, was, however, opposed to this; the outcome therefore was a 'small coalition' of CDU, FDP and DP, with Ludwig Erhard as its economic director, and the SPD in opposition. The pattern for the next nineteen years was thus set.

It would be misleading to conclude from this crucial episode that Schumacher and the SPD were now dedicated to the creation of a government–opposition duality in the party system. His principal concern was to avoid power-sharing on unfavourable terms, something from which the SPD had suffered in the Weimar Republic. He discounted the possibility of a two-party system on the same grounds as Max Weber: he regarded the ideological and religious fragmentation of the German people as too deeply rooted, and his own unremitting anti-clericalism did nothing to change this alignment.[49]

By the time the Parliamentary Council met the signals for the evolution of the party and parliamentary system were distinctly contradictory. The *Länder* parliaments had all been elected by proportional representation of various kinds, in some cases with an admixture of directly elected members. (Six of the *Länder* originally had purely proportional systems, viz. Baden, Bavaria, Bremen, Hesse, Württemberg–Baden and Württemberg–Hohenzollern. The remaining five had mixed systems.) The consequence of this was that in six of the eleven *Länder* no party had an absolute majority and in none were fewer than three parties represented. This was, however, not the only reason for the universality of coalition governments: the pressures for maximising democratic consensus and the expressed preferences of the Allies mattered more. In contrast, at the supra-*Land* level the pressures against consensus were, as we have seen, stronger and a 'bourgeois bloc' with Socialist opposition came into being. Given the adoption of PR, minor parties emerged in all the *Länder* despite the declared policy of the Allied occupation authorities to ration the licensing of parties and the efforts of politicians to keep their number down. (In the first regular Landtage, i.e. excluding constituent assemblies: the KPD in all except Bavaria and Schleswig-Holstein, the *Zentrum* in two, the DP in two and other groups in two.) This fragmentation was reflected in the Parliamentary Council, where the smaller parties held the balance and constituted a block against any move to create a majoritarian system.

The evolution of party strengths also affected the attitudes of the major parties to the electoral system to be adopted. The CDU's earliest pronouncement, dating from April 1946, reflected the uncertainty about its prospects: it demanded proportional representation 'with remedies for past shortcomings'.[50] By 1948–9, given its electoral successes and the example of the viability of an anti-Socialist majority in the Economic Council, it had moved away from that position. Within the SPD, on the other hand, the same factors, as well as the personal preferences of Schumacher, pointed away from the exiles' desire for a radical break.

In the end the Parliamentary Council decided against specifying the electoral system in the Basic Law, in contrast with some of the *Land* constitutions (e.g. Bavaria, Article 14.1; Rhineland-Palatinate, Article 80.1; also the later constitutions of Baden–Württemberg and Saar). That the electoral system adopted by the first Bundestag should be a mixture of single-member constituencies and proportionality, with proportionality as the dominant element, should not surprise us. It reflected German political tradition and the practice of the *Länder* as well as the party composition of the Bundestag. What is remarkable is that in spite of this, and in spite of a Basic Law that was not designed to provide for a purely parliamentary system of government, the Federal Republic has moved a long way towards responsible party government.

The contribution of the Basic Law to this development is mixed. On the one hand it does not re-enact some of the Weimar provisions that militated against it. There is no effective head of state and no referendum at the federal level. (There are, however, provisions for popular initiatives and referendums in the majority of *Land* constitutions.[51]) On the other hand it does not provide for the omnipotence of parliament. The founding fathers showed their distrust not only of executive prerogative and electoral hysteria but also of parliamentary irresponsibility.

Article 67 lays down the 'constructive vote of no confidence' which obliges the Bundestag to elect a new Chancellor by a majority of members before it can dismiss an incumbent. The assumption behind this proposal was that:

> Negative and destructive majorities do not suffice for a vote of no confidence, but that an opposition which overthrows the government must be willing and able to assume governmental responsibility itself [52]

This argument rests on a major conceptual confusion. It presupposes either a multi-party legislature or one in which party discipline has broken down, these being the pre-conditions for 'negative majorities'. But talk of 'an opposition' presupposes a two-party or at least bi-polar system, under which negative majorities do not normally arise. The only occasion on which Article 67 has been invoked (27 April 1972) was one on which membership of the pro- and anti-government parties was exactly equal, a statistically improbable circumstance and one that Article 67 had not been designed to meet. The other disadvantage of Article 67 is that it ignores the principle that cabinets need majorities not merely to survive but to govern and legislate. By making the overthrow of cabinets difficult, it threatens to encourage lame-duck chancellors.

On balance, the system of government envisaged by the Basic Law resembled that of German tradition more than the Westminster model:

(1) Like all previous German constitutions, with the exception of that of the Third Reich, it was federal. The reasons for this have been indicated. But the federalism was diluted, compared with that of the USA and Canada or the Bismarckian Empire. The principal division of functions is not vertical (in which the smaller units largely replicate the institutions of the central government) but horizontal (in which the subordinate units are predominantly the executants of centrally determined policy norms).[53] Sovereignty nevertheless remains divided and *Land* governments give politicians and parties independent power bases.

(2) Although there is no collective cabinet responsibility, the relationship between executive and legislature is much less dualistic than under previous constitutions and the composition and term of office of an administration depends more directly on the composition of parliament than under previous German regimes.

(3) As under previous constitutions there is a Bundesrat which represents the *Land* governments. Like them, however, it is partisan in composition; it is both a legislature with powers equal to those of the Bundestag on specified topics and the guardian of states' rights.

(4) The most revolutionary innovation is the creation of the Federal Constitutional Court, with power, *inter alia*, to rule on the compatibility of *Land* or federal laws with the Basic Law.[54] This is, of course, a major constraint on the sovereignty of the legislature and the freedom of action of political parties.

(5) Though the Basic Law is silent on the question of the electoral system, the adoption of modified proportional representation was predictable; so, given what was known about relative party strengths, was a multi-party Bundestag in 1949. In any case, those articles of the Basic Law that dealt with executive–legislative relations (in particular Article 67) assume the continuation of multi-partism, or at any rate the absence, as a

normal state of affairs, of absolute single-party majorities in the Bundestag.

THE CHANGE IN CONVENTIONS

Thirty years later the Federal Republic is much closer to responsible party government. Changes in the character of the parties have been the principal cause of this transformation, changes in the character of elections the principal consequence.

The parties transformed themselves at an uneven rate. The first stage of this process, and the crucial one, was the evolution of the CDU into what some of its founders had always intended it to be, a catch-all party capable of forming a government. It would be difficult to think of this changed role without the personality of Konrad Adenauer. Adenauer's authoritarian and paternalistic style, his secretiveness and his supra-partisan approach to elections have earned him the criticism of most liberal commentators.[55] Yet he made a significant positive contribution: he was undoubtedly one of Max Weber's dictators of the electoral battlefield, and as such forged the connection between electoral choice and government formation.[56] Adenauer's insistence on combining the office of party chairman and chancellor strengthened the link between party and executive responsibility. In the short term the semi-competitive chancellor-plebiscites may have inhibited the German citizen's growth of democratic self-confidence; in the long run the conventions of present-day German politics would be unthinkable without the first decade of 'Chancellor democracy'.

The SPD's development did not run parallel with that of the CDU. Though Schumacher prevailed, after the party's defeat in the first federal election of 1949, over those of his party colleagues who favoured entry into a coalition government, he did so, as in 1947 when the Economic Council was formed, more because he wanted to maintain the purity and integrity of his party than because he was a convert to the principle of alternating majorities. What is rather more significant is that the SPD did not move towards the acceptance of this principle even after it had transformed itself into a catch-all party at Bad Godesberg in 1959 and entered the electoral battlefield on the CDU's terms in 1961 with the nomination of Willy Brandt as chancellor candidate.

One reason for this was the predilection, which survived Schumacher's adversary style, for broadly based government. The SPD had come round to proportional representation in 1948–9 not only for reasons of self-preservation but because it believed, in the words of Carlo Schmid, that 'the risks should be carried by more numerous and broader shoulders'.[57] More specifically, the election defeats had undermined the SPD's confidence in its ability to compete effectively. Once more type-cast as the natural party of opposition, it became more anxious than ever to acquire legitimacy by power-sharing and an 'historic compromise'. When at the 1961 election, at the height of the Berlin crisis, the SPD halved the gap between itself and the CDU, its leaders responded by demanding 'a government of national concentration';[58] two years later the Free Democratic leader Erich Mende mocked the SPD for being not an opposition but 'a coalition partner in reserve'.[59] The formation of the Great Coalition in 1966 was therefore in many respects the culmination not only of the SPD's aspirations since 1945 but of the party's reformation in 1959. The deliberate reduction of the ideological gap between the two major parties was designed to make the SPD a more eligible partner, not a more eligible competitor.

It was, moreover, characteristic of the SPD's coalition behaviour that it rejected the offer made by the CDU to change the electoral system to single-member constituencies. Here again more than one motive was at work: for some sections of the party, especially at *Land* level, an alternative coalition with the FDP was attractive; above all, the party's own polling organisation, *Infas*, came up with highly unfavourable forecasts of its chances under a single-member system.[60] This ran counter to the arguments elaborated by the 'Cologne school' of political scientists, inspired by F. A. Hermens, who argued not only that electoral reform alone would make alternations of power possible, but that the structure of the German electorate was changing sufficiently to give the SPD an equal chance with the CDU.[61] Once the SPD had decided that it was not interested in a change of electoral system the topic lost any political salience; paradoxically, both the reformers' and the anti-reformers' prognostications were falsified by events. A change of power did take place in 1969, when an SPD/FDP government replaced the Great Coalition, even though the electoral system had not been changed. In the same election the SPD won 127 of the constituency seats, compared with the CDU/CSU's 121, *Infas* notwithstanding.

It was the first alternation of power in the history of the Federal Republic and, so far, the only one. It was not, strictly speaking, conducted according to the rules of responsible party government. Though an SPD–FDP government became more and more likely as the campaign went on, assuming that the outcome permitted it, neither party was committed to such a coalition in advance. Its formation was not certain, even after the election results were known, until the negotiations between the parties were complete.[62] It appeared to be the outcome of post-electoral bargaining, not of electoral mandate. Once established, however, the 'social–liberal' coalition proved durable. Its re-election in 1972, 1976 and 1980 was preceded by its members' commitment to its continuation. As after 1949, the new opposition was slower than the new government to adapt itself to its role. Lacking experience and organisation, and resentful at having been manoeuvred out of office, the CDU hesitated between opposition *à l'outrance* and constructive moderation, between provoking new elections that would return it to its rightful place and re-entering a government coalition by negotiation.[63] Only after its second defeat in 1972 did it seriously set about organising itself as an opposition.

Beginning with the 1970s, therefore, we have seen a direct link between electoral verdict and government formation, one of the hallmarks of responsible party government. Hugo Preuss' forecast in 1919 that German parliamentary government was bound to create bi-polarity, if necessary by stable coalitions, seems to have been borne out. To what extent he could have foreseen the circumstances under which the decline of both the religious cleavages and the ideological domination of the working-class movement would make such a development possible is another question: there is a strong case for claiming that the political history of the Federal Republic constitutes a new, independent variable without which the prophecy could not have been validated.

One feature of the change in the spectrum of opinion, without which the polarisation could not have come about, is the position of the FDP. Although it had, on occasion, coalesced with the SPD in *Land* governments before 1966[64] it was not at the federal level a genuinely pivotal party equally available as a partner to both major parties. Indeed, until the late 1960s it was perceived by most SPD supporters as being to the right of the CDU. In surveys before the 1961, 1965 and 1969 elections twice as many SPD respondents gave their second preference to the CDU than the FDP. The crucial switch took place immediately after the formation of the 'social–liberal' coalition, when the 1969 panel's second preferences for the FDP rose from 35 to 55 per cent. In 1972 and 1976 they were higher still. The FDP supporters' conversion took place earlier: three-to-one leads for the CDU in 1961 and 1965 gave way to equal preferences in 1969 and SPD leads in 1972 and 1976.[65] The same pattern is revealed by the constituency votes of electors who give their list vote to the FDP and who tend to split their vote

TABLE 2.1 *Constituency vote of FDP list voters, 1965–76*[66] *(percentages)*

Constituency vote to	1965	1969	1972	1976
CDU/CSU	20.9	10.6	7.9	8.0
SPD	6.7	24.8	52.9	29.9
FDP	70.3	62.0	38.2	60.7

more than major-party supporters. The explanation for this earlier move in the FDP is that those who disapproved of the party's leftward shift had deserted it by 1969. This transformation of the party's following was an integral part of the new polarisation.

Another pointer to the implantation of the norms of responsible party government is the changed recruitment of political leadership. Of three 'chancellor-successors' two (Erhard, 1963 and Schmidt, 1974) were prominent members of the preceding cabinet; the third (Kiesinger, 1966) was a *Land* prime minister but with a previous Bonn career. Of the four oppositional 'chancellor candidates' one (Willy Brandt) kept his *Land* political base in 1961 and 1965 but was a leading cabinet minister at his third try in 1969; one (Barzel, 1972) was already the CDU's parliamentary leader; one (Helmut Kohl, 1976) was a *Land* prime minister who felt obliged to vacate his provincial base after his election defeat and move to Bonn in order to continue as leader of the opposition; the fourth (Strauss, 1980), though a *Land* prime minister, is essentially a Bonn figure who has sat in several federal cabinets. The non-partisan 'expert minister', a frequent feature of Weimar cabinets, has all but disappeared from the political scene. The career politician has taken over.

CONSTITUTIONAL PRACTICE IN THE SEVENTIES

Against this evidence from electoral behaviour and the structure of the party system, we have to consider institutional factors that militate against the full exercise of responsible party government and also raise the question of how durable this development is. Some of these factors are common to all liberal industrialised states: chiefly the power of interest groups and of the bureaucracy. As we have noted, the unavoidable existence of these bodies raises the question of the degree of their influence over politicians.

West German pressure groups are nominally non-partisan, but many of their functionaries also hold office in political parties and the large *Land* lists from which half the Bundestag is elected facilitate the placing of pressure group nominees. Moreover the predominant role of specialist committees in the work of the Bundestag encourages the close relationship of deputies with lobbies even where this did not exist already.[67] While the parties, in their electoral interest, no doubt try to maximise their 'aggregative' function, there is little doubt that they are one of the main channels for the transmission of organised group interest.

The predominant place of the bureaucracy in all German political systems, and the high status enjoyed by the civil servant, are commonplaces of all textbooks. Given the present-day extensive role of the bureaucracy in all welfare-state mixed economies, it is difficult to distinguish myth from fact in the emphasis on the special case. What is peculiar (though not unique) to the Federal Republic is the heavy interpenetration of party and bureaucracy. This operates in two directions. On the one hand, appointment and promotion in the administration, especially at municipal and *Land* level, frequently depends on party affiliation, which in turn means that public sector employees of one kind or another are a large and increasing contingent of party membership.[68] In both the SPD and the CDU one member in five is a public employee; the proportion of public employees to all fully employed members is one in three in the SPD and one in two in the CDU. On the other hand, a high proportion of elected politicians are also members of the public service, there never having been any incompatibility between the two careers. In 1975, 49 per cent of the members of the Bundestag were public servants (or 41 per cent if present and past government ministers are ignored).[69] While it could be argued that party patronage facilitates the control of elected representatives over administrative policy, there is no doubt that the large-scale membership of parties and legislatures by public servants provides a large and ever-open back door for the presentation of their professional and administrative interests.

In addition to the influence of pressure-groups and the bureaucracy, there are limitations on the exercise of responsible party government that are more specific to German conditions. The first relates to intra-party democracy and the organisation of public opinion. 'Party responsibility', the APSA committee asserted, 'includes also the responsibility of party leaders to the party membership as enforced in primaries, caucuses and conventions'.[70] The Basic Law, probably more concerned to outlaw *Führer*-dominated parties than to encourage participation, requires that the internal organisation of parties 'must correspond with democratic principles' (Article 21(1)). A moment's reflection, and indeed a modicum of familiarity with classical writings at least as old as the century, will reveal that answerability to party activists must come at the expense of answerability to parliament or the electorate at large. No doubt modern democratic politics cannot be conceived without mass-membership parties, any more than without pressure groups or bureaucracy. The questions they raise are, therefore, as with pressure groups and the bureaucracy: how much power can they wield before the necessary parliamentary base of responsible party government is eroded? The power of the 'convention' or 'caucus' can evolve in two general directions. It can undermine the authority of the party leadership and so disintegrate the party. As Henry Jones Ford observed at the time of American party reform in the 1890s:

Structure and function are correlative and the notion that administrative capacity and corporate responsibility would somehow survive in parties after the extirpation of the organic structure with which they are associated, finds no parallel except in the case of the Cheshire cat, whose grin remained after the cat had disappeared.[71]

Or it can become a king's guard, with which the party leader can crush parliamentary dissidence, which is Ostrogorski's thesis.[72]

West German experience supports Ostrogorski rather than Ford. Party conferences do not impose policies or personalities on the parliamentary leadership. In the early seventies about one-third of delegates to SPD conferences belonged to the Left opposition, but the leadership made few policy concessions to them; in the later seventies the question of nuclear energy has been the only one to divide a substantial body of rank-and-file opinion from the leadership. The Young Socialists, though vocal, have exercised little power inside the party. Within the CDU the picture is different. Since going into opposition the party has been divided between conciliators and hard-liners, the latter gathered round Franz-Josef Strauss and his Bavarian power base. The division here is, however, between groups of leaders, not between leaders and rank-and-file, and is exacerbated by the CSU's status as a separate party which forms a joint parliamentary group with the CDU. The effect of Article 21(1) on German political reality has been negligible.

A more significant recent development has been the development of citizens' initiative groups, mainly on environmental questions, whose total membership probably exceeds that of the political parties.[73] Their existence raises a number of difficulties. Some at least are led by people who publicly express a fundamental lack of faith in the existing social and political order. All are, almost by definition, concerned with a particular grievance, often local. The proliferation of single-issue organisations is a challenge to the parties in their efforts to aggregate interests and maximise votes. On the other hand, in so far as the existence of these groups constitutes a vote of no confidence in existing institutions, it remains to be seen whether their continued activities will have the effect of re-integrating alienated citizens and restoring the legitimacy of institutions to whose defects they owe their origins.

A further specifically German feature that qualifies the operation of responsible party government is the surviving tradition of intra-parliamentary co-operation. When, at the beginning of the Federal Republic's life, Kurt Schumacher declared that, 'The essence of opposition is the permanent attempt to force the positive, creative will of the opposition in concrete instances and with concrete propositions on to the government and its parties',[74] he showed a better understanding of the practice of past German parliaments than of the doctrine of the responsible opposition. Despite the rhetorical antagonism of the two major parties during the 1950s, the SPD behaved more in the manner of a 'co-operative' than a 'competitive' opposition.[75] In the first Bundestag it opposed only 14 per cent of bills at their third reading,[76] a pattern set for all subsequent legislative periods. The opportunities presented by the Bundestag's committees, whose amendments, often based on cross-bench consensus, were rarely overturned,[77] were too tempting; they in any case corresponded with the habits the Social Democrats had acquired during the Empire and the Weimar Republic.

Throughout the life of the Federal Republic the Bundestag has acted more in the manner of a working parliament (*Arbeitsparlament*) than a debating parliament (*Rednerparlament*).[78] When the CDU found itself excluded from office in 1969 it displayed the same mixture of adversary rhetoric and legislative responsibility as the SPD twenty years earlier. Rainer Barzel, the opposition leader, who had promised 'four times 365 days' opposition' also claimed that the CDU had said 'No' to only eleven bills in the first two parliamentary sessions.[79]

Even more important in its effect, and overlapping with the collaborative style of parliamentary business is federalism. It not only splits the party system but removes important areas of decision-making from the control of the national parties altogether.

The effect on the party system is two-fold. *Land* elections do not coincide with federal. Different issues and personalities, and different party constellations, could and did lead to *Land* coalitions inconsistent with those in office in Bonn. Immediately after the end of the war great coalitions were universal in the *Länder*, and *Land* prime ministers of both parties pleaded for one in Bonn in 1949 in the hope of preserving theirs. In the course of the 1950s *Land* great coalitions became a rarity: the last, in Baden-Württemberg, ended in 1960. But other *Land* coalitions that crossed the government–opposition divide in Bonn continued in being, and did not come to an end until the CDU after 1969 adopted an explicit policy of ensuring this, preferably by 'catapulting' the FDP out of the *Landtage*.[80] Only between 1972 and 1976 did *Land* coalitions completely reflect party relationships in Bonn. In 1976 CDU/FDP coalitions were formed to solve deadlocks in Lower Saxony and Saarland. Except in these two *Länder* and Baden-Württemberg, the FDP pledged itself in election campaigns to coalesce only with the SPD.

The reason for the CDU's changed line in 1969 is to be found in the legislative competence of the Bundesrat. Initially created to preserve states' rights and counteract the primacy of 'party politics',[81] the Bundesrat quickly established its claim to equal partnership in legislation. Nevertheless in the first twenty years conflicts between the two houses were rare and generally confined to technical or particularist issues. The dominance of the CDU in both houses for most of the period may have concealed the possibilities of deadlock, though the parties did not ignore it altogether.[82] In 1969, however, the SPD/FDP majority in the Bundestag faced a CDU majority in the Bundesrat. The CDU was therefore able to use the Bundesrat both as an additional opposition platform and as a means either of obstructing government legislation or of imposing amendments on it. Between 1969 and 1976 the conciliation commission of the two houses was summoned 137 times, compared with 267 times between 1949 and 1969.[83]

In addition to bringing into question the locus of parliamentary sovereignty and the cohesiveness of the party system, federalism establishes areas of policy-making with strong bureaucratic dominance. Though the *Länder* are designed to protect local peculiarities, the exigencies of modern government, as well as the precedents of previous regimes, impose a strong drive towards voluntary co-ordination in the forms and standards of public services, most notably in education. This 'co-operative federalism' is institutionalised in the *Land* prime ministers' conference, but much of the day-to-day work is in the hands of largely autonomous bureaucratic committees.[84] Both the administrative and the party political experience of West German federalism underline the proposition that only under unitary government and the dominance of the directly elected chamber can responsible party government of the pure type flourish. It is difficult to dissent from Gerhard Lehmbruch's judgement that under the present distribution of competences 'political responsibility tends to be diluted in a tangle impenetrable to the wider public'.[85]

PROSPECTS

The 1980 federal election was the third in succession in which West German electors were faced with a straight choice between an incumbent government and an opposition, and the third in succession in which the participant parties declared in advance what coalitions they would be willing to enter into. This bi-polar, competitive party structure is a long way from what the founding fathers of the Federal Republic envisaged or what those who hoped for such an evolution thought feasible. Though there is considerable evidence that the majority of politicians and electors accept this configuration, there are some doubts about its permanence.

The re-emergence of a 'split' party system since 1976 is one reason for them. A possible change in the party system is another: the re-emergence of minor parties, the submersion of the FDP or a declaration of independence by the CSU. A third is the continuing influence of liberal CDU politicians who see their best hope in the principle that 'our system is fundamentally dependent on coalitions' and that parties are 'mutually available for coalitions'.[86] There are, in addition, structural factors that undermine its functioning. Some are common to all liberal states with advanced economies: the power of the bureaucracy, the bargaining strength of lobbies, the policy-making ambitions of extra-parliamentary caucuses. Some are attributable to special German traditions: this applies in particular to the ambiguous relationship between civil servants and parties, the co-operative style of parliamentary procedure and a sovereignty doubly divided by the existence of the *Länder* and the Bundesrat. In one way or another, therefore, unambiguous majorities in the Bundestag will continue to need the support of other concurrent majorities.

NOTES

1. Robert von Mohl, 'Über die verschiedene Auffassung des repräsentativen Systems in England, Frankreich und Deutschland', *Staatsrecht, Völkerrecht und Politik*, vol. I (Tübingen, 1860) pp. 33–5.
2. Hugo Preuss, *Verhandlungen der verfassunggebenden deutschen Nationalversammlung*, 8. Ausschuss (4 April 1919) vol. 336, p. 243.
3. *Toward a More Responsible Two Party System. A Report of the Committee on Political Parties* (American Political Science Association, 1950) p. 18.
4. See the arguments of Austin Ranney, *The Doctrine of Responsible Party Government* (Urbana, 1962) esp. pp. 21–2.
5. Maurice Duverger, *Political Parties. Their Organisation and Activity in the Modern State* (London, 1954) p. 215.
6. David Hume, 'Of the Coalition of Parties' (1748), *Essays Moral, Political and Literary*. In F. Watkins (ed), *Hume, Theory of Politics* (Edinburgh, 1951) p. 224.
7. Max Weber, 'Parlament und Regierung im neugeordneten Deutschland' (1918), *Gesammelte Politische Schriften* (2nd edn., Tübingen, 1958) p. 352.
8. E. and A. G. Porritt, *The Unreformed House of Commons. Parliamentary Representation before 1832* (Cambridge, 1903) vol. I, p. 122; Sir John Neale, *The Elizabethan House of Commons* (London, 1949) p. 31.
9. David R. Mayhew, *Congress, The Electoral Connection* (New Haven, 1974) p. 5.
10. Sir Lewis Namier, *The Structure of Politics at the Accession of George III* (2nd edn, London, 1957) pp. 63–4.
11. Manfred Fenske, *Wahlrecht und Parteiensystem. Ein Beitrag zur deutschen Parteiengeschichte* (Frankfurt-am-Main, 1972) p. 366.

12. Preamble, *Verfassung des Deutschen Reiches*, 1871.
13. Max Weber, 'Politik als Beruf', *op. cit.*, pp. 523, 532. The examples Weber had in mind were Gladstone and Abraham Lincoln.
14. Wolfram Fischer, 'Staatsverwaltung und Interessenverbände im Deutschen Reich, 1871–1914'. In Fischer (ed.), *Wirtschaft und Gesellschaft im Zeitalter der Industrialisierung* (Göttingen, 1972) pp. 212–13.
15. Ernst Rudolf Huber, *Deutsche Verfassungsgeschichte seit 1789*, vol. III (Stuttgart, 1963) pp. 4, 11, 20. The state of the debate is summarised by Gerhard A. Ritter, 'Entwicklungsprobleme des deutschen Parlamentarismus'. In Ritter (ed.), *Gesellschaft, Parlament und Regierung. Zur Geschichte des Parlamentarismus im Deutschland* (Düsseldorf, 1974) pp. 11–14.
16. Quoted in Manfred Rauh, *Föderalismus und Parlamentarismus im Wilhelminischen Reich* (Düsseldorf, 1973) pp. 252–3.
17. Cit. Dieter Grosser, *Vom monarchischen Konstitutionalismus zur parlamentarischen Demokratie* (The Hague, 1970) p. 63; also Naumann, F., *Die politischen Parteien* (Berlin, 1910) pp. 48–9, 106.
18. Grosser, *op. cit.*, p. 27, n. 21.
19. Letter to Franz Mehring, 8 July 1893; cit. Grosser, *op. cit.*, p. 34; similarly Kautsky, K., *Parlamentarismus und Demokratie*, 2nd edn (Stuttgart, 1911) p. 121.
20. Eduard Bernstein, 'Vom Parlament und Parlamentarismus', *Sozialistische Monatshefte* vol. XVIII/2 (1912) pp. 654–6; 'Regierung und Sozialisten', *op. cit.*, vol. XIX/2 (1913) pp. 838–43.
21. *Protokoll über die Verhandlungen des Parteitages der Sozialdemokratischen Partei Deutschlands, abgehalten in Chemnitz vom 15. bis 21. September 1912* (Berlin, 1912) pp. 23–5.
22. Hans Delbrück, *Regierung und Volkswille. Eine akademische Vorlesung* (Berlin, 1914) pp. 84–6.
23. Erich Kaufmann, *Bismarcks Erbe in der Reichsverfassung* (Berlin, 1917) p. 81.
24. Udo Bermbach, *Vorformen parlamentarischer Kabinettsbildung in Deutschland* (Cologne–Opladen, 1967) pp. 100–4.
25. *Ibid.*, pp. 117–18, 125–8.
26. *Die Verfassung des Deutschen Reiches vom 11. August 1919*, Article 53.
27. G. Loewenberg, *Parliament in the German Political System* (Ithaca, NY, 1967) p. 244.
28. Gerhard A. Ritter, 'Kontinuität und Umformung des deutschen Parteiensystems 1918–1920', in Ritter, *Arbeiterbewegung, Parteien und Parlamentarismus* (Göttingen, 1976) p. 123, n. 23.
29. Kautsky, *op. cit.*, p. 114.
30. *Verhandlungen der Verfassunggebenden Deutschen Nationalversammlung*, 8. Ausschuss (4 April 1919), vol. 336, p. 242.
31. *Die Regierung der Volksbeauftragten 1918/9* (intro. Erich Matthias), 26 November 1918 (Düsseldorf, 1969), vol. I, pp. 219–23.
32. Friedrich Schäfer, 'Sozialdemokratie und Wahlrecht. Der Beitrag der Sozialdemokratie zur Gestaltung des Wahlrechts in Deutschland', *Verfassung und Verfassungswirklichkeit*, vol. II (1967), pp. 165–7.
33. 17 April 1913. *Stenographische Berichte der Verhandlungen des Deutschen Reichstages*, vol. 289, pp. 4837–8.
34. *Die Verfassung des Deutschen Reiches vom 11. August 1919*, Articles 17, 22.

35. Richard Schmidt, 22 April 1920. *Verhandlungen* . . . , vol. 333, p. 5336. The quite illogical connection of proportional representation with female suffrage had a venerable lineage; cf. August Bebel, *Die Sozialdemokratic und das Allgemeine Stimmrecht. Mit besonderer Berücksichtigung des Frauen-Stimmrechts und des Proportional-Wahlsystems* (Berlin, 1895).
36. Ernst Troeltsch, *Spektator-Briefe. Aufsätze über die deutsche Revolution und die Weltpolitik, 1918–22* (Tübingen, 1924), p. 115.
37. Max Weber, 'Parlament und Regierung . . .', *op. cit.*, pp. 371–2.
38. Troeltsch, *op cit.*, pp. 206, 208, 211.
39. F. A. Hermens, *Demokratie und Wahlrecht: Eine wahlrechtssoziologische Untersuchung zur Krise der parlamentarischen Regierungsbildung* (Paderborn, 1933) pp. 148–65; *Democracy or Anarchy?* (Notre Dame, 1941) pp. 19–21; *Mehrheitswahlrecht oder Verhältniswahlrecht?* (Berlin–Munich, 1949) pp. 29–30. Cf. his statement that a two-party system 'cannot be created by organisational measures', *Demokratie und Wahlrecht*, p. 50.
40. E.g. Julius Leber, *Ein Mann geht seinen Weg. Schriften, Reden und Briefe* (Berlin–Frankfurt, 1952) pp. 104–5.
41. Public speech in Berlin, 10 December 1925. Gustav Stresemann, *Vermächtnis* (ed. Henry Bernard) (Berlin, 1932–3) vol. II, p. 379.
42. 'Über den künftigen inneren Zustand Deutschlands', Gerhard Ritter, *Carl Goerdeler und die deutsche Widerstandsbewegung* (dtv-edition, Munich, 1964) pp. 539–45.
43. 'Grundsätze für die Neuordnung', 9 August 1943. Ger van Roon, *German Resistance to Hitler. Count von Moltke and the Kreisau Circle* (London, 1971) pp. 347–54.
44. The phrase is Gerhard A. Ritter's. *Gesellschaft, Parlament und Regierung*, p. 18.
45. At an executive committee meeting of 'Union deutscher sozialistischer Organisationen in Grossbritannien', 11 May 1941; cit. Anthony P. Glees, 'The SPD, the Labour Party and the Foreign Office: A Study of Exile Politics' (unpublished dissertation, Oxford, 1979) p. 125.
46. 'Richtlinien für eine deutsche Staatsverfassung', Wolfgang Benz (ed.), *Bewegt von der Hoffnung aller Deutschen. Zur Geschichte des Grundgesetzes. Entwürfe und Diskussionen 1941–1949* (Munich, 1979) p. 122.
47. 'Die staatliche Neugestaltung Deutschlands', *ibid.*, pp. 84–8.
48. 'Grundsätze und Richtlinien für den Wiederaufbau Deutschlands', *ibid.*, pp. 104–20.
49. Lewis J. Edinger, *Kurt Schumacher: A Study in Personality and Political Behaviour* (Stanford, 1965) p. 196.
50. 'Verfassungsrechtliche Thesen', 23 April 1946. Benz, *op. cit.*, pp. 321–3.
51. Baden-Württemberg, Article 60; Bavaria, Articles 72–5; Bremen, Articles 69–70; Hesse, Article 124; North Rhine-Westphalia, Article 90; Rhineland-Palatinate, Article 109; Saar, Article 101.
52. Adolf Süsterhenn, 8 September 1948, *Stenographische Berichte über die Sitzungen des Parlamentarisches Rates über das Grundgesetz* (Bonn, 1948–9) p. 22.
53. As elucidated in Nevil Johnson, *Government in the Federal Republic of Germany: The Executive at Work* (Oxford, 1973) pp. 100–5.
54. *Grundgesetz für die Bundesrepublik Deutschland*, Article 77(1)2.

55. Cf. Kurt Sontheimer's judgement that 'Adenauer made few concessions to the spirit of democratic co-operation', *The Government and Politics of West Germany* (London, 1972) p. 139.

56. On the contentious question of the 'Chancellor effect' in elections during the 1950s, see Arnold J. Heidenheimer, 'Der starke Regierungschef und das Parteiensystem: Der "Kanzler-Effekt" in der Bundesrepublik', *Politische Vierteljahresschrift*, vol. 2 (1961) pp. 241–62.

57. *Parlamentarischer Rat*, 24 February 1949, *op. cit.* (see note 52), p. 131. Schmid himself hoped that in calmer times Germany would be able to go over to a system of alternating majorities. See Carlo Schmid, *Erinnerungen* (Bern, 1979) pp. 396–7.

58. Heribert Knorr, 'Die Grosse Koalition in der parlamentarischen Diskussion der Bundesrepublik, 1949–65'. *Aus Politik und Zeitgeschichte*, B 33/74 (17 August 1974) p. 33.

59. *Stenographische Berichte der Verhandlungen des Deutschen Bundestages*, 7 February 1963, p. 2610D.

60. David P. Conradt, 'Electoral Law and Politics in West Germany', *Political Studies*, September 1970, pp. 349–55.

61. In particular Rudolf Wildenmann, Werner Kaltefleiter and Uwe Schleth, 'Auswirkungen von Wahlsystemen auf das Parteien- und Regierungssystem der Bundesrepublik Deutschland', *Kölner Zeitschrift für Soziologie und Sozialpsychologie*, Sonderheft 9 (1965). Hermens' final thoughts on the subject may be read in *Demokratie oder Anarchie? Untersuchungen über die Verhältniswahl* (2nd edn, Cologne, 1968).

62. For details, see Udo Bermbach, 'Stationen der Regierungsbildung', *Zeitschrift für Parlamentsfragen*, vol. I (1970) pp. 415–16.

63. See Geoffrey Pridham, *Christian Democracy in Western Germany: The CDU/CSU in Government and Opposition, 1949–1976* (London, 1977), ch. 5.

64. For details see Peter Merkl, 'Coalition Politics in West Germany', in Sven Groennings *et al.* (eds.), *The Study of Coalition Behaviour* (New York, 1970) pp. 17–19.

65. Helmut Norpoth, 'The Parties Come to Order. Dimensions of Preferential Choice in the West German Electorate'. *American Political Science Review*, vol. 73 (1979), pp. 727–30.

66. Statistisches Bundesamt, *Die Wahl zum 7. Deutschen Bundestag am 19. November 1972* (200800–720008) pp. 64–6; *Die Wahl zum 8. Deutschen Bundestag am 3. Oktober 1976* (2012008–76900) p. 22.

67. On the relationship between lobbies and parliamentary committees, see Loewenberg, *op. cit.*, pp. 191–202, and Gerhard Braunthal, *The West German Legislative Process: A Case Study of Two Transportation Bills* (Ithaca, NY, 1972) pp. 157–77.

68. See Kenneth H. F. Dyson, *Party, State and Bureaucracy in Western Germany* (Beverly Hills–London, 1977).

69. Adalbert Hess, 'Statistische Daten und Trends zur "Verbeamtung der Parlamente" in Bund und Ländern', *Zeitschrift für Parlamentsfragen*, vol. 7 (1976), pp. 34–42; Horst Schmollinger, 'Abhängig Beschäftigte in den Parteien der Bundesrepublik: Einflussmöglichkeit von Arbeitern, Angestellten und Beamten', *op. cit.*, vol. 5 (1974) pp. 58–60.

70. *Op. cit.* p. 23; also pp. 65–70.

71. Henry James Ford, Review of Frank J. Goodnow, *Politics and Administration* (1898), *cit.* Ranney, *op. cit.*, p. 79.
72. Moïse I. Ostrogorski, *Democracy and the Organisation of Political Parties* (London, 1902) vol. I, pp. 210, 217, 607–8.
73. Udo Bermbach, 'On Civic Initiative Groups'. In Max Kaase and Klaus von Beyme (eds.), *Elections and Parties: Socio-Political Change and Participation in the West German Federal Election of 1976. German Political Studies*, vol. 3 (London–Beverly Hills, 1978) p. 227.
74. *Bundestag . . .*, 20 September 1949, p. 32.
75. As defined by Robert A. Dahl in Dahl (ed.), *Political Oppositions in Western Democracies* (New Haven–London, 1966) pp. 336–8.
76. Walter Kralewski and Karlheinz Neunreither, *Oppositionelles Verhalten im ersten deutschen Bundestag, 1949–1953* (Cologne, 1963) p. 92.
77. Michael Hereth, *Die parlamentarische Opposition in der Bundesrepublik Deutschland* (Munich–Vienna, 1969) p. 59.
78. As distinguished by Winfried Steffani, 'Amerikanischer Kongress und deutscher Bundestag'. In Kurt Kluxen (ed.), *Parlamentarismus* (Cologne, 1967) pp. 236–7.
79. Peter Pulzer, 'Responsible Party Government and Stable Coalition: The Case of the German Federal Republic', *Political Studies*, vol. 26 (1978) p. 190.
80. For the evolution of coalition patterns in the *Landtage*, see Gerhard Lehmbruch, *Parteienwettbewerb im Bundesstaat* (Stuttgart, 1976) pp. 29–32, 125–34, and Geoffrey Pridham, 'A "Nationalisation" Process? Federal Politics and State Elections in West Germany', *Government and Opposition*, vol. 8 (1973) pp. 455–72.
81. Lehmbruch, *op. cit.*, pp. 66–7.
82. For instance, see Arnold J. Heidenheimer, 'Federalism and the Party System: The Case of West Germany', *American Political Science Review*, vol. 52 (1958), pp. 812–15, 818–24.
83. Tabulation in *Zeitschrift für Parlamentsfragen*, vol. 8 (1977), p. 156.
84. For a detailed account of the procedures, see Fritz W. Scharpf (ed.), *Politikverflechtung: Theorie und Empirie des kooperativen Föderalismus in der Bundesrepublik*, vol. I (Kronberg, 1976).
85. Gerhard Lehmbruch, 'Party and Federation in Germany: A Developmental Dilemma', *Government and Opposition*, vol. 13 (1978) p. 171.
86. Helmut Kohl, 'Ich bin ein Mann der Mitte', *Die Zeit*, 16 July 1976, p. 3.

3 The Rebirth of Democracy: Political Parties in Germany, 1945–49

MARTIN McCAULEY

Uncertainty about the capacity of existing political institutions to cope with the problems of the contemporary world is widespread and West Germany is no exception. Rapid material advance papered over for many years the cracks in the German political edifice. It is worthwhile, therefore, to examine again the foundations of the Federal Republic and to look anew at the conditions which gave birth to a successful parliamentary democratic German state.

The decision by the Allies to impose on Germany the onerous burden of unconditional surrender meant that after defeat there was no political group which could legitimately speak in the name of the German nation. The Allies intended to ban all political activity in the immediate aftermath of defeat. There was a widespread fear in all four occupation zones that a Nazi resistance would emerge. However on this issue the Soviet Union, the United States, the United Kingdom and France were quite wrong. Germans everywhere sought to adjust as rapidly as possible to the new circumstances. The self-confessed Nazi became difficult to find. This led to a rapid change in Soviet policy, and the licensing of political parties and democratic organisations in June 1945 re-established party-political politics. The Western Allies, not consulted on this issue, followed suit after the Potsdam Conference. Was the new political order a resurrection of the Weimar system or did it represent a new departure in German political life? It was clear that in the Soviet zone, renamed the German Democratic Republic in 1949, something quite different had come into being; but what of the Federal Republic? Likewise the economic system which emerged in the GDR was a radical departure from the pre-1945 and pre-1933 order of things. Was capitalism restored in the Federal Republic after 1945 or was it radically changed by war, destruction and the efforts at decartellisation? May one regard the years 1945–49 as decisive and formative in the evolution of West Germany, or were the 1950s of greater significance? In the period under review economic misery was widespread in all occupation zones, communities were poor and almost everyone underfed. There were ten million refugees in the West and about eight million dwellings for fourteen million families. Does this explain why the Germans exhibited such a capacity to adjust to the realities of occupation? Political parties also moved in the direction favoured by the occupying powers. Since the goals of the Soviet Union were totally different from those of the Western Allies a gulf developed between the Soviet and Western zones. Had most of the Social Democrats and Communists who had spent the Nazi years in Germany had their way a united party of the Left would have emerged in the East in 1945 and would have enjoyed considerable all-German support. Nevertheless separate Social Democratic (SPD) and Communist (KPD) parties were set up. The SPD was an ardent suitor in the summer of 1945 but its enthusiasm for a united party cooled as it grew in influence. This brought it into conflict with the KPD which was attempting to recruit from the same milieu. Then the KPD changed course and began to promote unity. The fusion of the two parties in April 1946 is the most important political event in Germany over the years 1945–49. A significant proportion of the SPD leadership opposed fusion and a poll taken in West Berlin revealed that a majority of Social Democrats did not favour an immediate fusion. Kurt Schumacher, the most influential Social Democrat in the West, strongly opposed the submergence of the Eastern SPD in the SED. He would not hear of the same happening in the West. The fusion ended co-operation between Communists and Social Democrats in the West and seriously weakened the KPD. The creation of the SED made it the dominant party in the East and limited the options open to the other political parties. It also narrowed options in the West. Originally the SED was seen as a middle way between Communism and Social Democracy, but this course was soon dropped as the SED gradually took on the appearance of a Marxist–Leninist party. This development estranged Communists and Social Democrats in West Germany even more. Nevertheless the SED was a strong political threat in Germany and its sister party the KPD was feared. All the other parties had an interest in improving socioeconomic conditions in order to restrict the appeal of communism. The policies and tactics which the Western parties adopted were all calculated to counter the attractiveness of the SED and to make West Germany safe for parliamentary democracy. The SED was often its own worst enemy and its espousal of Marxism–Leninism harmed the prospects of socialism, Marxist and non-Marxist alike, in the Western zones. Since it was connected in the public imagination with economic planning, socialisation, land reform and so on, these measures became less and less attractive to the West Germans; also the stream of refugees and the increasing number of members of East German political parties moving westward kept alive and vivid the pattern of events in the East. Paradoxically the West, although numerically and economically potentially stronger, found itself under the eastern shadow. It was this threat more than anything else which welded the parties together. They either all sank together or swam together. How different from the days of Weimar. It is now appropriate to examine this transformation.

THE SITUATION IN 1945

The Joint Chiefs of Staff Directive No. 1067, dated April 1945, prohibited all political activity in the areas falling within their jurisdiction. The arrest of Admiral Dönitz and his cabinet at the end of May paved the way for the Allied statement of 5 June 1945 – that they were formally taking over responsibility for governing Germany. This meant that all the anti-fascist organisations, the National Committee for a Free Germany as well as all other spontaneous political formations had to dissolve. All occupying powers were agreed on this move, including the Soviets. They also thought that political parties should not come into being in the foreseeable future. What was envisaged was a slow process of normalisation, with political activists who enjoyed the confidence of the occupying powers leading the way. In the Soviet zone mass organisations, embracing communists and non-communists, were seen as the best approach to re-educate politically the German population. Moscow quickly changed its mind and issued Order No. 2 of 10 June 1945 permitting political parties and other democratic organisations to come into being. The KPD appeared the following day, soon followed by the SPD, CDU and LDPD. In order to underline their commitment to democracy they were invited to form an anti-fascist democratic bloc. All decisions of the bloc were to be unanimous. Democratic forces, it was underlined, must hold together to resist the reappearance of Nazism. The bloc also ensured that coalition politics would not be practised, and this removed the risk that the other parties would form a coalition against the KPD. The great weakness of Weimar had been that parties had fought one another to the benefit of fascism. This must never happen again. Hence the nature of party politics in the Soviet Zone was different from Weimar from the very beginning.

The Western Allies were rather taken aback by this move since they had not been consulted. They had expected the Potsdam conference to decide such matters. The Soviets moved quickly in other directions as well. They also established a central German administration before the conference. The aim was to provide the nucleus for a future all-German administration. Again the Allies were not consulted. The Potsdam Agreement envisaged the establishment of central all-German administrations but the French veto prevented its realisation. Since the Soviets had been making capital out of the fact that democracy was being re-forged in their zone while political parties were forbidden in the West, the Allies were obliged to license parties in their zones as well. A declaration was duly made at Potsdam on 2 August 1945 which stated that 'all democratic parties shall be allowed and permitted throughout Germany'.

The French were the least pleased with having to permit them, and prevaricated as long as possible. Basically the Americans were the most forthcoming. Since each political party had to obtain a licence to begin a legal existence the relevant occupying power could decide which political persuasions it wanted and which it wished to suppress. All occupying powers were nervous about a Nazi renaissance and tended to favour parties of the centre and left. It is striking how many parties included the word 'Democratic' in their title. Right wing parties were licensed in the Western zones only from 1948 onwards. Needless to say no such party appeared in the East.

When the occupying powers arrived they found that the whole structure of German administration had collapsed. They therefore found themselves organising activities at a much lower level than anticipated. They had to appoint politicians who were non-Nazis and find competent officials. The Americans tended to take the advice of the clergy in Catholic areas but not that of pastors in Protestant areas, relying on academics and intellectuals. The British often sought the counsel of trade unionists, reflecting the influence of the Labour Party, then in power. When it came to accepting political leaders, the Western powers tended to rely on those who had been politically active before 1933. Political life in the Western zones was organised along quite different lines from that in the East. In the West political activity was initially restricted to the local level so as to prove that grass roots' support existed. Only gradually was activity on a *Kreis*, then a *Land* basis, and then on a zonal level permitted. In the East political activity was organised from the centre downwards. The parties were to be active not only in Berlin but throughout the whole of the Soviet zone; indeed the four parties set up in the summer of 1945 were conceived of as all-German parties, all of them included the word Germany in their names. This neatly illustrates Soviet and Western views of democracy. The Soviets saw it as a process in which democratic centralism predominates, key decision-making is restricted to a small central group, then decisions are communicated to members, and meetings take the form of acclamation and declamation of already agreed decisions. Of course democratic centralism is supposed to be a two-way process, but given the acceptance of the collective guilt of all Germans for the National Socialist era there was little likelihood of local opinion which conflicted with the centre being tolerated for long. The non-socialist parties were neatly tied into this arrangement through the 'anti-fascist democratic bloc'. The Allied view of democracy saw local activity as very important, and once the new rules of the game had been mastered political activity could be extended higher and higher until it embraced the whole of the zone. Inherent in this view was the acceptance of a plurality of legitimate views and acceptance of the fact that conflict and opposition were creative. The Soviets did not share this predilection for creative debate: they tended to arrive at a position and then expect the political parties to legitimise it. All occupying powers in 1945 found it very difficult to transmit their interpretation of democracy. They were all required to engage in denazification, democratisation and demilitarisation, and it was the second of these which caused the greatest difficulties.

THE APPEAL OF SOCIALISM

Socialist solutions were in the air in 1945. Capitalism had failed and it was held by many to have been in some way responsible for the rise of fascism. The destruction meant that economic life could be refashioned and made more responsive to the needs of the average person. Communists and Social Democrats, among others, had suffered grievously in concentration camps and prisons during the National Socialist era, and this experience forged a new community of interest. One of the lessons drawn from the Weimar period was that democracy was fragile. If the proponents of democracy did not unite the enemies of democracy might again reassert themselves. A united party of the Left was the goal, but it had to be different from the KPD and SPD of yore. This conviction was especially strong among Social Democrats. Hermann Brill, head of the SPD in Thuringia, for example, while in Buchenwald had been a fervent apostle of the unity of the Left.[2] He had signed the Buchenwald Manifesto which had proposed the socialisation of the economy, the rule of law and the unity of socialism. Since Germany was in such confusion he was in favour of authoritarian democracy. He even opposed the reconstitution of the SPD in Thuringia. However he had to concede that it took two to create the unity of socialism, and in the summer of 1945 the KPD leadership was not interested.

Socialism appeared attractive to some members of the middle class as well. This attraction was especially strong in the CDU in Berlin, and Jacob Kaiser was the most forceful advocate.[3] He stated that the age of bourgeois society was over, it had gone the way of feudalism: 'We are now in the era of the working people'. The CDU appeal, issued in Berlin after the founding of the party, favoured the socialisation of industry and the transfer of the large landed estates to the peasants. The concept of Christian socialism emerged in the Rhineland, influenced by Roman Catholic social thinking. This found expression in the Cologne Guidelines of June 1945 which advocated 'real Christian socialism'.[4] State ownership of natural resources and ' key monopoly industries', eliminating all large-scale capitalist enterprises, was favoured. The Frankfurt Guidelines spoke of 'socialism founded on Christian responsibility'. The high point of this trend was the Ahlen programme of the British Zone CDU in February 1947. It proposed the abolition of the capitalist system, the promotion of a new economic and social order, co-determination in industry, the expropriation of large landed estates and industrial enterprises as well as the introduction of economic and social planning. The onset of the Cold War sounded the death knell for such ideas, it all sounded too reminiscent of what the SED was advocating in the East. The Dusseldorf programme of 1949 threw most of the socialism overboard in time for the first Bundestag elections.

Three of the four parties licensed in the East and in the West between 1945 and 1948 favoured socialism of one hue or another. The odd one out was the Liberal Party. In the East the LDPD did not share the prevailing enthusiasm and defended the market economy and private property. In the West the FDP expressed similar views.

The main reason why so little came of these ideas was the policy of the occupying powers. In the East security was uppermost in Soviet minds. In 1945 there was no certainty that the Soviet Union would be maintaining a physical presence in Germany, so her policy had to be circumspect. The Soviets wished to create optimal conditions for the success of the KPD. Since they did not expect the CDU and the LDPD, representing a minority of the population of the zone, to prove too much of a problem, they concentrated on wooing the SPD. Had they so wished they could have had a united socialist party in June 1945 and this party would have dominated Soviet zone politics. It could then have been extended to the Western zones. Communists would have worked within an all-German framework and there would have been little the Western Allies could have done to stop them extending their influence. The main reason why SMAD did not permit this to happen, to the relief of the Americans especially, was that the KPD would not have been in complete control. The KPD had to be refounded to reassert the dominance of the pro-Moscow faction in the party leadership. Only two of those who signed the KPD appeal in June 1945 had spent the Nazi era in Germany, no-one from the West signed it at all. No key functionary moved to the West to work after returning from exile in the Soviet Union. Hence Berlin and the East held the key. Walter Ulbricht spoke of achieving 'ideological clarification' in the party before the SPD's offer of fusion could be considered seriously. He had in mind 'Left sectarians' such as the heirs of the Schumann–Engert–Kresse group in Leipzig.[5] They wanted the Soviet Army to carry on advancing to Cape Finistère and sweep the Americans out of Europe. Then the socialist revolution could be initiated. Twelve years of National Socialism had confused the workers. Ulbricht's solution was expressed in a letter to Wilhelm Pieck, the nominal head of the party, dated 17 May 1945; 'We must bear in mind that the majority of our comrades have sectarian views and so the composition of the party must be altered as soon as possible by drawing in active anti-fascists who are now proving themselves in the work they are doing.'[6] Hence the KPD was to be refashioned by leaders who had just returned from exile and, like them, their ideas had come from without.

THE KPD CHANGES COURSE AND PROPOSES FUSION WITH THE SPD

In order to garner support and to espouse policies on which there was as much agreement as possible, the KPD set in motion industrial, land, school and judicial reforms. This, to the KPD's and SMAD's surprise, led to a head-on clash with the CDU which was unwilling to back fully the land reform which involved expropriation without compensation. So Andreas Hermes and Walther Schreiber were dismissed in December 1945 by Colonel S. I. Tyulpanov, the key SMAD political official. CDU influence was evidently proving an embarrassment and SMAD must have been rattled to take such drastic action, a course which could only increase the unpopularity of the Soviets.

'Unity of action' with Social Democrats did not produce the results the KPD was hoping for so a switch in policy was announced. From September 1945 onwards the Communists started courting the SPD with the intention of achieving a union. But the SPD was no longer the enamoured suitor of the summer months. Otto Grotewohl, not famous for taking a hard line policy towards the KPD, even started talking about Social Democracy as a 'middle way' between Left and Right.

A conference of sixty – thirty members from each party – met in Berlin in December 1945 and passed a resolution which stated that the prelude to political and organisational fusion of the KPD and the SPD would be the deepening and broadening of inter-party co-operation. Wilhelm Pieck, the head of the KPD, made it clear that the KPD was not thinking of fusion before the end of 1946. The SPD thought it had won a breathing space, but the KPD and the Soviet military authorities, SMAD, began energetically to promote fusion at local level even before the decision had been taken at *Land* or national level. In Thuringia the opponent of rapid fusion, Hermann Brill, was manoeuvred into resigning and was replaced by Heinrich Hoffmann, the man favoured by SMAD. The KPD kept the SPD under pressure, seeking a firm commitment to unity in the immediate future. The Social Democratic position was weakened by the hostile reception which the December conference had received in the British and American zones. Kurt Schumacher would hear nothing of an all-German congress to discuss the matter. The East SPD *Zentralausschuss* split on the issue. Otto Grotewohl reluctantly accepted fusion in January 1946 but other members, such as Gustav Dahrendorf and Gustav Klingelhöfer, were bitterly opposed. The Berlin organisation arranged a poll of members on 31 March 1946. In the end only those SPD members in the Western sectors were allowed to vote. Just over 82 per cent were opposed to immediate fusion with the KPD but 62 per cent were in favour of a pact with the Communists which would eliminate strife between the two parties.[7]

The fusion of the KPD and the SPD produced a new type of German political party, the SED. However in forcing through unification in April 1946 SMAD seriously damaged the prospects of the Left throughout Germany. Since the Social Democratic rank and file were more radical than their leaders it is possible that a majority was in favour of fusion in April 1946, if the Soviet zone as a whole is taken. What is certain is that those Social Democrats who were in favour thought that a new-style party was coming into existence. They were not in favour of the SED becoming a carbon copy of the old KPD. The acrimonious debate in the East affected the West in a tangible way. Those SPD leaders who were strongly against fusion went West and in doing so moved to the Right. Hermann Lüdemann went from the Mecklenburg SPD to the Schleswig-Holstein SPD, Gustav Dahrendorf went from Berlin to Hamburg and Hermann Brill moved to the US zone, to name only three. Those who left East Germany had had bitter experience of Soviet and Communist behaviour and influenced the evolution of Social Democracy in the Western zones. The same goes for those CDU and LDPD politicians who found they could no longer work in the Soviet zone but wished to continue their political careers. They exercised an important influence on West German political life.

The concept of a special German road to socialism, articulated by Anton Ackermann, and the assertion that the SED would be different from the KPD and the SPD, convinced many waverers in the East. Parity was to be observed in all appointments. Many former Social Democrats were in favour of a rapidly expanding membership since they saw this as redounding to their advantage.

THE KPD IN THE WESTERN ZONES

The fusion of the KPD and SPD was intended to be an all-German phenomenon. However the KPD was at a disadvantage in the West. It was still founding its basic organisations in early 1946 and moreover the Western Allies did not favour all-German parties. There was much 'unity of action', joint action committees which carried out communal, charity and social work and joint demonstrations and meetings were held. KPD and SPD leaders from the Soviet zone travelled to the British and American zones to promote unity. Often a considerable minority in the SPD was in favour. For example, in Augsburg about 30 per cent were for fusion. The main target of KPD propaganda was Kurt Schumacher who dismissed talk of unity by declaring that Germany already had a united party of the Left, the SPD. The KPD tried to split the ranks of the SPD and to fuse with the more radical elements. The movement for unity was particularly strong in the Ruhr and here the British authorities supported opposition, even providing British lecturers to point out the dangers inherent in amalgamation. In the US zone there were some strong advocates of fusion among American personnel. In Ludwigsburg, for example, the responsible Americans were active in their support and had it not been for the vigorous opposition of Wilhelm Keil, a Schumacher supporter, they would have carried the day.[8] In Baden, in the French zone, Communists and Social Democrats set up their own committee in March 1946 to bring about unity, but it collapsed shortly afterwards.

On the whole, the KPD was too optimistic about its level of support in the Western zones. In April 1946, party membership was still about 25 per cent below that of 1933. The party just failed to set in motion the debate which was needed to sway uncommitted Social Democrats.

KPD delegates from the Western zones attended the founding of the SED in April 1946 and thereafter the KPD was bound by all SED decisions. KPD members occupied twenty of the eighty places on the SED *Parteivorstand*. This arrangement continued until January 1949 when the KPD again became a separate party. The fusion was a turning-point in all four zones. Henceforth close, equal co-operation between Communists and Social Democrats was impossible. SED/KPD abuse of Schumacher and all those opposed to fusion increased and widened once again the gulf between the two parties of the Left. The main beneficiary of this state of affairs was the SPD. Those delegates who had attended the 40th SPD Congress which had voted for fusion were regarded as having 'placed themselves outside the SPD'. The most active were expelled. As the KPD became more and more linked to Soviet interests it lost support in the West. This was demonstrated in the various elections in 1946. In the British and French zones the KPD did not secure its pre-1933 level of support, and in Bavaria it could not get a single deputy elected.

Since the KPD could not split the SPD in open conflict it decided to rename itself the SED and attempt to attract Social Democrats in that way. In May 1947 OMGUS in Berlin refused the request but the Communists countered by saying that they were not just changing their name, they wished to join the SED.[9] The British authorities also refused to allow it, stating that it could only be permitted if the SPD or a majority of SPD members were in favour. The French followed suit. At the same time discussions had been taking place in the East with a view to re-establishing the SPD there. Had the SPD reappeared again, the Western Allies would have found it very difficult to ban the SED. American attitudes to the KPD in their zone hardened perceptibly in 1947 with some Communists being imprisoned and others leaving their posts in the media.[10] General Clay rejected co-determination and socialisation as well.

THE EAST MOVES TOWARDS A PEOPLE'S DEMOCRACY

By the summer of 1947 Christian Democrats and Liberal Democrats had secured quite a favourable position for themselves in the East. In the 1946 *Kreis* and *Land* elections support for the CDU and LDPD had been slightly greater than that for the SED. In Jacob Kaiser the CDU had a determined and vociferous leader, and the Liberals had actually been able to link up with the FDP and form the Liberal Democratic Party of Germany in Rothenburg in March 1947 – the first and last all-German party. It fell victim, however, to the gathering Cold War and withered away in November 1947.

The establishment of the Economic Council in Frankfurt-am-Main followed by its counterpart in the East, the German Economic Commission (DWK), was another turning point. The DWK was the first institution in which the parity principle was ignored by the Communists; its top personnel were almost all Communists.

The DWK gradually acquired more and more responsibility for the economic and social life of the zone and undermined the position of the non-socialist parties. The SED began to espouse an increasingly pro-Soviet position. An important element in this shift was the change in Otto Grotewohl's thinking. In April 1947 he had argued at the Bavarian Congress of the KPD that the Soviet Union alone was pursuing policies which corresponded to the genuine interests of Germany, and at the Second SED Congress in September 1947 he dropped his interpretation of the SED as a middle way between Communism and Social Democracy and pointed to Lenin and Stalin as models to be followed. The founding of the Cominform in September 1947 and Zhdanov's division of the world into two camps, with countries such as Indonesia and India outside, increased the pressures to imitate the CPSU. The failure of the Munich conference of ministers-president revealed how unwilling the SED leadership was to enter into a compromise on German unity with other political parties. The failure of the Moscow and London conferences of foreign ministers in 1947 brought home to the USSR that little economic help would be forthcoming from the Western zones. This led to the economy of the Soviet zone being restructured, with the Soviet planned economy as the model, so as to increase the flow of goods to the Soviet Union. From this time onwards the Soviet authorities paid less and less attention to the effects their policies would have in the West. The dismissal of Jacob Kaiser and Ernst Lemmer from their positions as leaders of the CDU in December 1947 fits this pattern. The political ground-rules were being changed in the East, and when the DWK was given legislative powers which exceeded those of the *Landtage* in February 1948 the parliamentary system was effectively at an end. Whereas previously the *Landtage* had legislated for a local area the situation now was that the DWK and the German People's Council could legislate for the whole zone. The devolution of the immediate post-war years was over and the zone was a centralised entity once again.

The non-socialist parties were outmanoeuvred in the 'anti-fascist democratic bloc' by the creation of two new parties, the NDPD and the DBD, as well as by the expansion of the functions of the mass organisations. Until then only non-contentious legislation could be piloted through the bloc, but the SED could no longer be baulked as it moved towards its goal of transforming the zone into a people's democracy.

Hence the ground-rules in the Soviet zone were changed dramatically in 1947–48. KPD/SED policy was decisively influenced by Walter Ulbricht. Although Wilhelm Pieck was the nominal head of the party, the guiding force was Ulbricht. In order to assert his authority within the SED he had to establish close contacts with the Soviet military and with Colonel S. I.

Tyulpanov in particular. He did this very effectively and gradually cut his colleagues off from direct contact with SMAD. Ulbricht favoured a Soviet orientation for the KPD/SED and did not share the predilections of such men as Anton Ackermann who wanted a 'German road to socialism' to be devised. Ulbricht was usually ready to sacrifice all-German goals for advance in the Soviet zone. He was pleased at the failure of the Munich conference which marked the end of serious attempts to reunite Germany. Personal political ambitions doubtlessly played a part in forming his views, but he played a not inconsiderable role in bringing the division of Germany about. Ulbricht could argue that a KPD/SED which was akin to the CPSU – and this meant making it into a state party, a party which dominated government, the administration and the economy – was in the best interests of Moscow. He was a strong advocate of fusion with the SPD since he recognised the dangerous attractiveness of that party in the second half of 1945. This led to a bitter feud between him and the SPD headed by Kurt Schumacher. It is striking that the Soviet zone is the only territory on which the fusion of the Communist and Social Democratic parties took place in 1946; elsewhere in Eastern Europe it came about in 1948. The Soviet zone was used as a sounding board by Stalin. Land-reform and the nationalisation of enterprises belonging to former Nazis and their supporters, initiated without consulting the Western Allies, were carried through without incident. If the Allies would countenance reform in the Soviet zone, leading to creeping sovietisation, then they would permit the same in Eastern Europe. The same applied to the political parties. Coercion, chicanery and discrimination could be practised without producing an armed confrontation. Ulbricht and the KPD/SED gained from this. There was considerable opposition, which lasted until the late 1950s, within the KPD/SED leadership, to the course Ulbricht was charting but he always had SMAD at his back.

THE WEST MOVES TOWARDS A FEDERAL REPUBLIC

In contrast to the parties in the East those in the West were afforded the opportunity, in the Parliamentary Council, of drawing up the political ground-rules in consultation with the military governors.

The parties in the Parliamentary Council believed themselves to be drafting a Basic Law which was provisional but which should not prejudice the shape of the future all-German constitution. They set out to avoid head-on clashes and the passing of clauses by small majorities. Their aim was to achieve as great a consensus as possible, 80 per cent if it proved attainable.[11] The spirit of compromise ran through the whole proceedings. The party leaders were especially keen to avoid the pitfalls of the Weimar era. They agreed that the parties had a collective responsibility to ensure that parliamentary democracy worked. The flight from responsibility had been one of the greatest weaknesses of the pre-1933 days. The Basic Law presented the parties for the first time with the opportunity of playing a decisive role in the government of the new state. Political parties had never decisively shaped government policy before 1945.

Since the USA, for one, strongly favoured a federal state, it was up to the parties to decide the lines of competence between the federal and the *Land* governments. A strong centralised state, due to the bitter experience of the past, was ruled out. There was considerable disagreement on how strong the *Land* governments should be and this was mirrored in the differing views of CDU/CSU delegates from north and south Germany. The KPD opposed a federal state and Kurt Schumacher was not originally in favour. In cultural and educational affairs the military governors made it clear that the federal government should have no authority.

The parties were considerably influenced by their experience at *Land* level and the constitutions which had been adopted in 1946–47 gave them insights into the functioning of a democratic system.

The parties compromised on economic goals in the Basic Law. The SPD knew that it could not achieve a majority for socialisation measures since the FDP was opposed. It reasoned that the federal government should have the legislative power to create conditions conducive to economic and social justice. This would be more effective than anchoring economic and social goals in the constitution. One of the reasons why the SPD was so ready to compromise on this vital issue was its desire to see the deliberations come to a speedy end so that the elections to the first Bundestag could be held. The SPD did not think that time was on its side. As it turned out the party was over-sanguine about its prospects and the market economy reasserted itself as early as 1948–49.

Parliamentary democracy was favoured. The federal government gained wide-ranging powers, while the *Länder* parliaments were limited essentially to legislating on cultural, police and communal affairs. This amounted to a strengthening of the central parliament. In direct contrast to the provisions of the Basic Law, all the *Länder* constitutions contained articles expressing social and economic goals.

Hence the role of the political parties was enhanced, democracy was to be further developed by means of parliamentary majorities. Competitive, pluralistic democracy was accepted as the way to achieve the new society. Democracy was to be capable of defending itself and not to permit its enemies to destroy it, as in the Weimar Republic. Militant democracy could declare certain activities illegal.[12]

The electoral system was decisively influenced by the occupying powers in East and West Germany. In the East the elections of 1946 had been on a party basis, and the unwelcome results (for the Communists) convinced SMAD and the SED that a united list would be preferable in future. Henceforth electors were not given a choice of parties but could either vote for or against a list of candidates drawn from all parties. In the West the proportional representative system was favoured but the British objected. They preferred the single-member constituency principle, the person coming top of the poll, irrespective of the size of his majority, being elected. The result was that the Basic Law incorporated both approaches.[13]

The first electoral law passed by the Parliamentary Council contained no reference to a minimum level of support before a party could be represented in parliament. The military governors stepped in and approached the ministers-president since the Parliamentary Council was no longer in session. The latter made various proposals including one which ruled out representation in parliament if the party did not secure 5 per cent of the votes in any one *Land*, or victory in one constituency. The ministers-president then enacted the revised legislation with the military governors taking full responsibility – since they possessed supreme authority.

Before 1949 the regional associations of the various parties possessed the power in the West. The KPD was the only exception. The CDU/CSU was a coalition of interests recognising Konrad Adenauer as leader. The SPD was led by Kurt Schumacher but there was a great diversity of views within the party. The occupying powers were very wary of active trade union activity, and it was only in 1948 that a unified trade union movement, the DGB, came into being.

THE ROLES PLAYED BY SCHUMACHER AND ADENAUER

Two men played a key role in shaping the policy of their parties in the immediate post-war years, Kurt Schumacher and Konrad Adenauer. Kurt Schumacher was both a nationalist and a socialist. Marx only contributed some of the strands which made up his *Weltanschauung*. He saw the restoration of the nation as a primary goal. The formation of a classless society would then become a possibility. Hence he regarded the interests of the workers as being co-terminous with those of the nation. 'The unity of Germany means the unity of Europe. A divided Germany would only result in a disunited Europe.' For him the key to a socialist Europe was Germany.

Consequently he denounced all policies which he judged would lead to a splitting of Germany. The CDU, the KPD, the occupying powers, the Marshall Plan and the Schumann Plan were all attacked. Not surprisingly, the Americans became very suspicious of his policies. Schumacher thought that the SPD had a moral right to rule and could expect excellent relations with the occupying powers, especially Great Britain. Personal differences between him and Otto Grotewohl surfaced very early. They were already apparent at the first conference of Social Democrats from all occupation zones at Wenningsen, near Hanover, in October 1945. No agreement was reached on establishing an all-German SPD or even on convening an all-German conference. The *Zentralausschuss* in Berlin was recognised as the SPD leadership in the Soviet zone and Schumacher was acknowledged as the leader in the three Western zones. Grotewohl and Schumacher were to co-operate. However, as early as October 1945 Schumacher sent a letter to the party committees in the Western zones warning them against attempts to establish a united party of the Left. This was a direct criticism of the Berlin *Zentralausschuss*. Then Schumacher interpreted an agreement to exchange speakers to mean that only Grotewohl was welcome to speak at Social Democratic meetings in the West.[14] His vehement opposition to the fusion of the KPD and the SPD exacerbated the already strained relations with Otto Grotewohl. Unlike most other Social Democrats he had not grown nearer to the Communists in prison; he had in fact avoided political involvement there completely. Grotewohl felt let down in early 1946 when the Western SPD showed little understanding for his predicament. Schumacher's advice to Grotewohl to dissolve the SPD, rather than join with the Communists, was not very realistic or helpful. His attacks on Soviet policy made Grotewohl's position in Berlin even more difficult. There was little rapport between the two leaders of German Social Democracy. Schumacher refused to move to Berlin, preferring Hanover. Here again personal political ambitions were involved. An all-German SPD might have preferred Grotewohl as leader.

Schumacher's attitude made life easy for Ulbricht. The latter could almost be certain that any compromise on German unity would be turned down, and this knowledge permitted the SED to step up its propaganda, claiming that it was the only party with a coherent all-German programme as well as being the only one with the true interests of everyone in Germany at heart. Schumacher's singular devotion to German unity, seen exclusively from a Social Democratic point of view, paradoxically deepened the division of Germany.

Konrad Adenauer was a skilled, flexible politician. Basically conservative, he was never attracted to the goals of Christian socialism. However, he was astute enough to swim with the tide while pointing out that the bourgeois virtues were the foundation of democracy and freedom. As chairman of the Parliamentary Council, he gained national exposure. Such was his concern at the strength of Marxist socialism that he was willing to split Germany if this ensured that the Western zones would be free of communism. There was little point in being a conservative in 1945, there was precious little to conserve, but the CDU/CSU was the most successful at building up a programme of what it did not want. The opposite of what was happening in the East may sound rather unappealing, but it was manna to all the refugees and dispossessed. Adenauer and his party became more attractive as time passed. Ironically the SED was of considerable help to the CDU in this respect; but CDU/CSU policy was exclusively for West German ears. It could be objected that they had an all-German policy but that all it amounted to was expelling the Soviets from their zone and incorporating Eastern Germany in the Western body politic. Adenauer here is on a par with Ulbricht; both of them had a pretty shrewd idea that neither would be at the head of an all-German state.

CONTINUITY OR A NEW DEPARTURE IN THE WEST?

It is quite clear that 1945 marked a turning point in Eastern Germany, but what of the West?[15] It did not appear in 1944 that capitalism would survive. Impending defeat and disaster meant that the industrial monopolies and Junkers had been brought crashing down. What would take their places? The Junkers, a privileged aristocratic class, had played an important role in developing capitalist society but they almost disappeared, since practically all of their estates had been in the East or in the lost territories. Militarism was no longer a problem; the army's mystique had gone for ever. Since the occupying powers had supreme authority, it would be they who would decide if and when a professional army reappeared.

Denazification removed many Nazis from their posts between 1945 and 1947. There were more changes at the top in the economy, state and administration than in 1933 or 1918. Only the churches remained almost untouched. The National Socialist elite therefore lost power. The bourgeoisie came into its own for the first time in German history. Moreover, the upper classes, or what was left of them, and the top civil servants accepted the democratic rules of the new state. The lower middle classes, the artisans, shopkeepers and the like, wanted protection from the rigours of a market economy. The gulf between the white- and blue-collar workers closed quickly as the market economy got under way. Prosperity after 1949 made them socially homogeneous.

Common suffering brought believers together during the National Socialist era, irrespective of denominational distinctions. Roman Catholics were completely outnumbered in the East but not in West Germany. The flood of refugees and the destruction of segregated living quarters broke up the old patterns of religious demography. This all had a very important impact on the formation of political parties. The formation of the CDU was a conscious attempt to bridge the confessional divide and form a party which could challenge the Marxist parties of the Left. A purely Catholic party, such as the *Zentrum*, could not hope to become a leading party. The CDU deliberately set out to become a *Volkspartei* and it was rewarded with success at the first Bundestag elections. The Social Democrats also broadened their support base but it was only in 1959 that they set out also to become a *Volkspartei*. Schumacher was convinced that large sections of the middle classes had been proletarianised, and if they could be attracted to the SPD then it would become the dominant party. The Communists and the Liberals also gained from the shaking up of the social structure. These four parties were the only ones licensed by the authorities before 1948 and this advantage gave them a head start which, with the exception of the Communists, they never lost. Table 3.1 shows the pattern of voting at *Land* elections over the period 1946–48. The dominance of the CDU/CSU and SPD is striking.

A democratic parliamentary system was entrenched for the first time in Germany. In the Weimar Republic there had been several important parties which rejected the republic.[16] The West German state's most influential anti-system party was the KPD but its appeal faded after 1947. Anti-system parties of the Right enjoyed little popularity. Hence the Bundestag was composed of those who accepted the republic, and this contributed to the stability of the new system, something Germans desperately sought after 1945. The new parliamentary regime was not held responsible for the *débâcle* of 1945; it would be judged on its ability to respond to the aspirations of the population. One criticism of the Basic Law might be that its framers had not understood the implications of the scientific technical revolution.

All things considered, the political order was a new departure. West Germany gradually began to resemble other advanced industrial societies and to seek solutions to its problems in the same way as its allies. However National Socialism and war were a high price to pay for social and political modernisation. Germany's role in the world changed dramatically. A divided country, it was no longer a leading power and not even one possessing complete sovereignty. This may as time passes be seen as a blessing in disguise.

On the other hand, there are continuities with the period before 1945.

TABLE 3.1   Land elections, 1946–48 (percentage of votes received)

	CDU/CSU	SPD	KPD	FDP
Bavaria (30 June 1946)	58.3	28.8	5.3	2.5
Hesse (30 June 1946)	37.3	44.3	9.7	8.1 (LDP)
Württemberg-Baden				
(30 June 1946)	40.9	32.3	10.0	–
Hamburg (13 October 1946)	26.7	43.1	10.4	18.2
West Berlin (20 October 1946)	24.3	51.7	13.7 (SED)	10.3 (LDPD)
Württemberg-Baden				
(24 November 1946)	38.4	31.9	10.2	–
Bavaria (1 December 1946)	52.3	28.6	6.1	5.6
Hesse (1 December 1946)	30.9	42.7	10.7	15.7 (LDP)
Lower Saxony (20 April 1947)	19.9	43.4	5.6	8.8
North Rhine-Westphalia				
(20 April 1947)	37.6	32.0	14.0	5.9
Schleswig-Holstein				
(20 April 1947)	34.1	43.8	4.7	5.0
Rheinland-Pfalz (18 May 1947)	47.2	34.3	8.7	9.8
Württemberg-Hohenzollern				
(18 May 1947)	54.2	20.8	7.3	–
Saarland (5 October 1947)	51.2 (CVP)	32.8	8.4	–
Bremen (12 October 1947)	22.0	41.7	8.8	5.5
West Berlin (5 December 1948)	19.4	64.5	–	16.1 (LDPD)
Soviet zone (20 October 1946)	24.5	–	47.5 (SED)	24.6 (LDPD)

SOURCES: Heino Kaack, *Geschichte und Struktur des deutschen Parteiensystems* (Opladen, 1971) pp. 182–7. Ekkehart Krippendorff, *Die Liberal-Demokratische Partei Deutschlands in der Sowjetischen Besatzungszone 1945/48* (Düsseldorf, 1961) p. 99.

Capitalism and the bureaucratic order survived. Hence the question of whether capitalism was restored in 1945 is misleading. It carried on, but in a new guise. All the Western Allies favoured a market economy and sought to improve the efficiency of the German economy. Decartellisation, if it promoted competition and efficiency, was to be supported. The currency reform of 1948 favoured the owners of capital and put labour at a disadvantage. The social and economic transformation which the SPD hoped to inaugurate did not occur since the SPD remained in opposition until the late 1960s. The occupying powers did sweep most Nazis from their positions but this purge was largely negated after 1947 when the search for competent officials began in earnest. Even in the Soviet zone technical expertise was sufficient to blot out NSDAP membership provided that it had not been active membership. The goal of resuscitating the West German economy took precedence over everything else after 1948. The military governors had initially only been willing to license those parties they could be sure would not resurrect National Socialism. This had led to a safety-first policy, none the more so when it came to nominating trade union leaders. Indeed, in trade union affairs the occupying powers played a decisive role. A unified, industry-wide trade union movement came into existence despite strong German support for regionally based unions.

Given their dependence on the occupying powers, the German politicians could not demand that socialisation and land reform, as provisions in some of the *Land* constitutions, be put into effect. General Clay opposed socialisation and co-determination in the American zone, and the British had to bow to US pressure and drop the socialisation of the coal, iron and steel industries in the Ruhr in the summer of 1947. The Americans were of the opinion that such a move could reduce the efficiency of the Ruhr at the very moment when industrial recovery was vital. Nevertheless, the German politicians could have achieved more had they been willing to apply consistent pressure. General Clay was sensitive to German public opinion and did not want to be seen to be in open conflict with the parties. However, since many of the people involved had not been active in the resistance to Hitler, it is unreasonable to expect them to be strong and vigorous opponents of the occupying powers. Since Hitler had not been overthrown by Germans there was no party which could claim a legitimate right to have a decisive influence on policy after 1945. The parties knew that if they opposed the military governors the only beneficiary would be the masters of East Germany. If they wanted a viable democratic parliamentary system to evolve in West Germany then they had to work together and defer to the Allied authorities. They were not very demanding. Perhaps the fact that everything was considered to be provisional and a preliminary to the establishment of an all-German state provides the main clue as to why the behaviour of the German politicians was so moderate.

CONCLUSION

The fusion of the KPD and SPD narrowed options in both East and West Germany. It led to the rekindling of the market economy in the West. West Germany had to become economically strong so as not to be a burden on the Western Allies but also to win back East Germany. The belief surfaced that a resurgent West German economy could act as a magnet and attract the East away from the planned economy. Efficiency thus became of paramount importance and economic and social experimentation was frozen out in such a climate. Bourgeois values reasserted themselves and increasing prosperity was seen as justifying them. The Social Democrats, under Kurt Schumacher, knew that they had to break out of the working-class ghetto if they were to conquer power. Tactically the CDU proved more skilful than the SPD. The decision by the SPD to 'drop out' of the Economic Council was a mistake. It simply added to the prominence of CDU views on the economy. However Schumacher was sensitive to the fact that time was not on the side of the SPD in 1948 and 1949 and was prepared to compromise over many issues in order to speed up the passing of the Basic Law.

West Germany really only had one option: remain neutral or become part of the Western alliance system. Since it had no army and feared the military and political power of the East, the choice was easy to make. The Social Democrats were eventually forced to agree with the other parties on this evaluation. The key decisions pointing the way ahead were taken over the years 1945–49, but one could argue that the 1950s were decisive in forging the West German state as it exists today. Then it became palpably clear that Bonn was not Weimar.

NOTES

1. Gerhard Loewenberg 'The Remaking of the German Party System', in Mattei Dogan and Richard Rose (eds), *European Politics: A Reader* (New York, 1971) p. 267.
2. Frank Moraw, *Die Parole der 'Einheit' und die Sozialdemokratie* (Bonn–Bad Godesberg, 1973) pp. 66–9.
3. Werner Conze, *Jacob Kaiser. Politiker zwischen Ost und West, 1945–1949* (Stuttgart, 1969).
4. Geoffrey Pridham, *Christian Democracy in Western Germany. The CDU/CSU in Government and Opposition 1945-1976* (London, 1977); Helmut Pütz, *Die CDU. Entwicklung, Aufbau und Politik der Christlich Demokratischen Union Deutschlands* (Düsseldorf, 1978). It should be stressed that only parts of the CDU were in favour of a form of socialism. In fact the CDU decided in Stuttgart on 3 April 1946 that Christian socialism was an inappropriate term. Adenauer was to inform Kaiser of this decision. At the same time it was decided that the CDU headquarters should not be in Berlin but in the Main–Rhine area. Karlheinz Niclauss, *Demokratiegründung in Westdeutschland: Die Entstehung der Bundesrepublik von 1945–1949* (Munich, 1974) p. 46.
5. Horst W. Schmollinger, 'Das Bezirkskomitee Freies Deutschland in Leipzig'. In Lutz Niethammer *et al.* (eds.), *Arbeiterinitiative 1945* (Wuppertal, 1976) pp. 224–7.
6. Walter Ulbricht, *Zur Geschichte der deutschen Arbeiterbewegung*, Band II, *1933–1946*, I. Zusatzband (Berlin, DDR, 1966) p. 205. Martin McCauley, *Marxism–Leninism in the German Democratic Republic: The Socialist Unity Party (SED)* (London, 1979) p. 43.
7. Moraw, *op. cit.*, pp. 160–1, The results of the elections to the *Gross-Berlin* city

council on 20 October 1946 underline the opposition still felt by Social Democrats to the fusion. The SPD received 48.7 per cent of the votes, the CDU 22.2 per cent, the SED 19.8 per cent and the LDPD 9.3 per cent. In the Western sectors the SPD received 51.7 per cent and the SED 13.7 per cent. *Ibid.*, p. 197.

8. Werner Müller, *Die KPD und die 'Einheit der Arbeiterklasse'* (Frankfurt-am-Main, 1979) p. 264.
9. *Ibid.*, p. 336.
10. *Ibid.*, p. 366.
11. Niclauss, *op. cit.*, p. 220.
12. *Ibid.*, p. 113.
13. Loewenberg, *op. cit.*, p. 271.
14. Moraw, *op. cit.*, 124–7.
15. The main source for the view that the old order was restored is E. Kogon, *Die unvollendete Erneuerung. Deutschland im Kräftefeld 1945–1963* (Frankfurt-am-Main, 1964); for the opposing view see R. Dahrendorf, *Gesellschaft und Demokratie in Deutschland* (Munich, 1968). See also Jürgen Kocka, '1945: Neubeginn oder Restauration?', in Carola Stern and Heinrich A. Winkler (eds), *Wendepunkte deutscher Geschichte 1848–1945* (Frankfurt-am-Main 1979) pp. 141–68.
16. Reinhard Schwickert and Michael Wolffsohn, 'Das Weimarer und das Bonner Parteiensystem', *Zeitschrift für Parlamentsfragen* (1978), vol. 4, p. 537.

4 The German *Volkspartei* and the Career of the Catch-All Concept

GORDON SMITH

Against all apparent odds, the party system that emerged in Western Germany after 1945 avoided the fateful *Zersplitterung*, the fragmentation of parties and interests, which had contributed to the downfall of the Weimar Republic. The former centrifugal style of politics was abandoned, but the new republic also moved swiftly and decisively away from a multi-party system towards a stable form of majoritarian government. The almost dramatic alteration of the party system – its mutation even – can be traced to the phenomenon of the *Volkspartei*: the inescapable starting-point for an analysis of political development in the Federal Republic is its dominating presence.[1] It is not too much to say that the limited polarisation maintained by the two self-confessed *Volksparteien* encapsulates the political life of present-day Western Germany.

The *Volkspartei* represents one way of ensuring mass attachment to the political system, of securing a 'democratic integration'. In its claim to be 'a party of the whole people', the *Volkspartei* was a radical departure from the parties of the Weimar Republic. Those parties were variously based: in the representation of particular classes or sectional interests, through the promotion of a distinctive ideology or at least drawing on the commitment to a shared *Weltanschauung*. In their place, the new type of party sought to override class differences, to subsume competing interests, and to avoid presenting a divisive ideology.[2] The contrast with the party system in the Weimar Republic is startling, and it may seem as if the arrival of the German *Volkspartei* is the sole secret of the post-war metamorphosis. In a sense that is true because the parties have been the most obvious agents of political change, but they were also dependent on wider changes in German society.

Therein lies a major problem: the difficulty is that so many relevant features can be included under the rubric of 'social change', and especially for Germany there are a number of candidates with convincing claims. Thus should attention be paid exclusively to the structural changes in German society? And, if so, what were the really important ones and when did they occur? Are they to be located in the period prior to 1945 as a side-effect of National Socialism – the unintended consequence of the Nazi 'social revolution' – which paved the way for the modernisation of Germany's lagging pre-industrial society? Or is the emphasis to be placed on developments taking place after 1945? If it is, should the examination be restricted to what happened in Germany or must the account be rendered as part of a wider European movement reflecting alterations in the nature of industrial society?

Quite apart from an analysis couched in terms of a changing social structure, the successive shocks administered to the political system are a factor in their own right. The rupture of 1933 was compounded by the equally sharp break in 1945, and both effects were intensified by the impact of allied occupation and the division of Germany. Should not those discontinuities in the political system figure most prominently in an explanation?

The shock treatment alone might be regarded as a good reason for wishing to avoid a return to the *status quo ante* of the Weimar Republic, and with it the fear of a repeated cycle of catastrophe. Yet avoidance was not entirely a matter of exercising political will or of displaying good intentions. Determined political leadership was important and so also were the constitutional provisions which set the rules and limits for political competition. But can the contribution of a few outstanding party leaders, along with a set of institutional devices, furnish an adequate explanation?[3] A similar reservation applies to the parties themselves. To an extent they were autonomous agents, but would not the *Volksparteien* have succumbed to a re-birth of ideological politics?

An ideological renaissance did not occur, and to explain why it did not take place reference has to be made to changes in the German political culture. Without a basic reorientation in the minds of the people, the efforts of the *Volkspartei* would have come to nothing. Is it not reasonable to argue that the fundamental changes were a direct result of a transformation of the political culture? There are, nevertheless, difficulties in using this concept as an all-purpose key of explanation, and its ingredients were scarcely amenable to instant change: German political traditions were nurtured over a long period and could not simply be discarded; it is difficult to imagine that central values could have been altered at will or that rooted attitudes and prejudices were erased overnight. The events from 1933 until 1945 did amount to a political–cultural shock, but was it sufficient to obliterate the old authoritarian style? It would be strange if, in addition, a new political culture had immediately arisen, nicely attuned to the requirements of a stable, liberal democracy.

Interpretations of West German political development – including an assessment of the exact nature and role of the *Volkspartei* – can easily be frustrated in the attempt to balance the competing explanations.[4] In some way the various approaches have to be combined, for the problem is not to be resolved by making difficult choices, let alone by casting around for entirely new areas of explanation. The method proposed here is to group the relevant factors in the form of two explanatory models. The first is of general application because it draws on arguments concerning social change, political competition, and the nature of parties which are applicable to a number of countries. The second is specific in that it relates entirely to the conditions which have applied in Germany. These perspectives differ sharply from one another, and the question is whether or not they can be combined. If there is a conflict, then the explanation of the changes in Germany remains elusive as ever, but if they are compatible – as the following presentation may show – then the two models buttress one another. That conclusion would help explain certain peculiarities in the evolution of the German party system.

APPLYING A GENERAL MODEL

An answer to the problem of accounting for the new look of West German politics is to be found in the writings of Otto Kirchheimer. One of his central themes was the transformation of West European party systems, and although his arguments were generally based, they are immediately relevant to Germany. The evidence Kirchheimer considered pointed to a radical change in the nature of political competition and with it to a basic restructuring of party systems, away from the predominance of exclusive 'ideological' parties towards new ones, pragmatic and with a broad popular appeal. These 'catch-all' parties were best suited to respond to the changing conditions in Western Europe.

Kirchheimer located the trigger for a political realignment in the economic and social developments in Europe consequent upon the Second World War. The upheaval of that conflict had accelerated underlying changes in European society, and they were further advanced by rapid economic progress in the post-war years: 'One may justifiably say that diminished social polarisation and diminished political polarisation are going hand in hand.'[5] In this condition of flux, old political loyalties were dissolved, and the parties were forced to compete on new terms, as Kirchheimer put it: '. . . the acceptance of the law of the political market became inevitable in the major Western European countries'.[6] The 'political market' was a direct expression of the character of changing industrialised societies, and it had a pervasive effect on existing parties: 'Under present conditions of spreading secular and mass-consumer goods orientation with shifting and less obtrusive class lines, the former class–mass parties and the denominational mass parties are both under pressure to become catch-all people's parties.'[7] The old-type parties of mass integration cohered around a strongly-held *Weltanschauung* and they fulfilled a vital 'expressive function' for their particular clienteles. Yet once the social changes had become apparent, an existing mass party was encouraged to respond in kind: 'Abandoning attempts at the intellectual and moral *encadrement* of the masses, it is turning more fully to the electoral scene, trying to exchange effectiveness in depth for a wider audience and more immediate electoral success.'[8]

Parties reacted to the challenge in different ways. Whilst some embraced their new role, others sought a compromise position or else ignored the challenge entirely. However, as Kirchheimer argued, 'Conversion to catch-all parties is a competitive phenomenon. A party is apt to accommodate to its competitor's successful style.'[9] One can appreciate the pressure on a party to emulate the success of a rival by seeking to adopt its formula. Once one party had established itself on the new basis, it could win a commanding electoral position by making an appeal across established class and denominational lines, in contrast with those parties that still concentrated their attention on a narrow or at least restricted section of the electorate – with the probability that those bastions would gradually be whittled away. For such parties the prospect could not be encouraging: the victorious catch-all party could be in a position to govern alone and indefinitely, whilst they would be forced to languish in permanent opposition.

This partial summary of Kirchheimer's 'transformation' thesis is sufficient in its main drift to set against the actual course of development in Western Germany. What will be at once apparent is just how closely the model fits: the mere substitution of the *Volkspartei* for the catch-all label allows an exact translation of the general trend to a German equivalent. In the first place, the formation and rise of the CDU corresponds to the catch-all party as a prototype for post-war Germany. Turning its back on the ideology of the Weimar predecessors, the CDU precisely exchanged 'effectiveness in depth for a wider audience', and the party was then well placed to reap the electoral benefit of German economic recovery in the 1950s. The 'economic miracle' completed the transformation of West German society, and it could be argued that the Federal Republic was *par excellence* the representative of the new consumer-oriented society.

The applicability of the model to the SPD and its fortunes is just as striking. Whilst, as Kirchheimer pointed out, the CDU had 'less to de-ideologise' from the outset,[10] the SPD was bound by its history and by its formal commitment to a socialist ideology which stemmed from a theory of the 'class struggle'. Thus the SPD stood as a *Klassenpartei*, the very antithesis of the new-style *Volkspartei*, and it therefore had to make a definite break. The successes of the CDU and its dominating electoral position forced a conversion on the SPD. With a static share of the vote, without faith in its ideological position, unable to present fundamental alternatives to CDU policies, the SPD was in sterile opposition. The power of the catch-all party as a 'competitive phenomenon' was then displayed: the 1959 Godesberg Programme of the SPD deliberately extinguished any sharp or distinctive ideology and explicitly rejected a 'class' label for the party. The SPD adopted a strategy of *Annäherung* towards the ruling CDU, a self-conscious emulation of Christian Democracy, even if seen through a left-wing mirror.[11]

What transpired is simply an addendum to Kirchheimer's main thrust of argument. The smaller parties went to the wall – only the Free Democrats perilously surviving – for all were subjected to the new rules of political Darwinism. The catch-all party system arrived in Western Germany: the CDU and the SPD successfully monopolised the 'wider audience' between them, emphasising the personal qualities of their rival contenders for the chancellor's office, paying attention to a wide variety of group interests, displaying their near-identical wares in the modern political market-place.

The essential correspondence between the stages of the model and West German reality does carry conviction. Against that, Kirchheimer's formulations were intended to have a much wider application, and the general model has first to be related to the actual course of development within Western Europe as a whole. Only then is it fruitful to scrutinise the case of the Federal Republic.

One strength of Kirchheimer's perspective is the emphasis it places on significant changes in the character of advanced societies and the consequences they would have for the parties. The old ideological parties were founded – even frozen – on the terms and issues affecting the initial mass entry to politics during the primary wave of political mobilisation in Western Europe: 'Continental European parties are the remnants of intellectual and social movements of the nineteenth century. They have remained glued to the spots where the ebbing energy of such movements deposited them some decades ago'.[12] Although parties proved remarkably resistant to external influences once they had anchored themselves in the party system, ultimately they could not be immune. Clearly, a radical restructuring of party systems became ever more likely, but what direction would it take?

It is in his answer to this question that Kirchheimer is less convincing. Along with many others in the late fifties and early sixties, Kirchheimer was caught up in the 'end of ideology' debate and was representative in believing that affluent 'consumerism' represented a monolithic social consensus.[13] From a later standpoint that view appears to be at least an oversimplification. Although the form of ideological contest has changed, it has by no means reached an end, nor have old class divisions been entirely submerged even if they are less prominent. Above all, it would be an error to assume that political cleavages would become 'simple' as well as less pronounced. One result of the declining intensity of old cleavages *may* be the catch-all party, but it is not a necessary consequence. An alternative is that sections of the electorate, far from turning to the large catch-all party, will lend their support to movements and parties that better meet their 'expressive' demands.

This latter interpretation at least accords much better with the actual state of party competition in Western Europe. Of course, it is extremely difficult to devise adequate tests which would measure the nature of inter-party competition, the extent of ideological difference, whether in fact the political market-place was supreme in Western Europe. Some measures – of electoral volatility, of diminishing social-class and religious differences in party support – may give some support to Kirchheimer's contentions, although far from conclusively. But a leading implication of Kirchheimer's findings is that there should be a definite contraction in party systems, that the number of successfully competing parties should decline. Ultimately, catch-all politics requires the survival of only two significant parties, each able to win power solely for itself. Yet, taking the experience of Western Europe as a whole, that development has failed to occur. Most multi-party systems have remained intact, others have even expanded. Empirical tests applied to several West European party systems to measure their degree of 'fragmentation' over several years show no evidence of contraction.[14] Certainly polarisation has become less acute, as the decline or adaptation of anti-system parties indicates, but old disputes remain and new parties, new sources of cleavage, ensure that political vitality is retained.

Kirchheimer did qualify his arguments in various ways. Thus he made a distinction between the larger and the smaller West European states, and he was inclined to treat the latter, especially those that have become known as the 'consociational' democracies, as special cases.[15] However, it is doubtful whether exceptions on such a scale are acceptable, for in principle all the countries are open to the same influences and have reached a comparable level of economic development. Even if consideration is restricted to the larger states – Britain, France, Italy and West Germany – there is little enough to confirm the existence of a common trend. The British two-party system has the requisite form, but its historical position had nothing to do with contemporary factors, nor on most forms of reckoning has its polarisation declined. Moreover, the sudden if transient upsurge of Scottish and Welsh nationalism in the 1970s, together with the impact of a large protest vote for the Liberals, brought Britain to the brink of a multi-party system.[16]

Both France and Italy have by far the largest Communist parties in Western Europe, and even though neither can be treated as ideologically strong, they each offer a radical alternative to the existing capitalist system. The French Fifth Republic does present a different picture from the fragmented and unstable Fourth Republic, but the present concentration of the parties in a two-bloc system owes more to the form of presidential rule and election than it does to societal change. That presidentialism imposes constraints, rather than there having been a natural evolution, is shown by the uneasy, even hostile, relationship of the members of the respective 'blocs': Giscardians with or against Gaullists, Socialists with or against Communists.[17] In Italy, the antagonisms of 'polarised pluralism' have become muted, but it is still an accurate enough description of the opposing worldviews of Catholic Christian Democracy and Italian Communism, and in Italy the potential following of the extremes of Left and Right is a 'reserve force' if the two major contenders should show an inclination to move closer together.[18]

Pointing to all these 'exceptions' may make any general model seem rather threadbare – or even invite the charge of flogging a dead horse – but it is also possible to conclude that Kirchheimer was partly right and partly wrong: correct in drawing attention to the pressures for change, incorrect in his forecasts of how parties and voters would react. Yet in the present context the real problem is different. If it were the case that Kirchheimer's thesis was substantiated throughout Western Europe, then Germany would have been well in the mainstream. But as the general model remains unconfirmed, a curious situation arises: what should have been a normal and general development, on closer inspection leaves Western Germany as a partial anomaly, a somewhat abnormal normality.

Some pertinent questions arise. Why should Western Germany have taken the road of the catch-all party so early and so decisively? Why also should she have continued to conform to the model in an exemplary fashion when it is inapplicable in many countries? These questions raise important issues. After all, if the keystone of the transformation thesis is the 'unfreezing' of political cleavages through the thawing effects of economic progress and material affluence, it is remarkable that post-war Germany – faced with a shattered economy and the tasks of rebuilding – should have been so soon susceptible to the changing political determinants, and it is strange that the movement affected her rather than other societies which at the outset were economically far better placed. A similar puzzle surrounds later development: if the catch-all phenomenon was at most partial and transient, why has it been so complete and resilient in the Federal Republic? It is worth posing a final question to summarise the disparities. Can the German *Volkspartei* really be equated with the catch-all concept or are the similarities misleading?

AN ALTERNATIVE EXPLANATION: POLITICAL CENTRALITY

At least in its full application, the career of the catch-all concept has been less than illustrious. The catch-all party has failed to carry all before it: there is no party equivalent of Gresham's Law. The only surprise is that it applies so well to the West German party system, but that must surely mean that the correspondence can only be explained by specifically German factors – not by general ones – and in particular by referring to the nature of the *Volkspartei*.

The problem is to account for the apparent centripetal *effects* on the West German party system, but to do so by finding an alternative set of causes. The general explanation is founded on the presence of a strong positive consensus, even though the political market-place is a rather mundane arena. The strength of that consensus generates a powerful centripetal drive in the electorate, with the parties willy-nilly following suit, so that political competition is concentrated over a narrow part of the spectrum. Can that concentration be reproduced by other means?

A moment's reflection will show that the same type of clustering could come about in the absence of the positive attraction if there were sufficient barriers to the extension of party competition, a 'negative consensus' rather than a positive one. The shape of the party system would be the same in both cases: the extremes of Left and Right would be unimportant either way and regardless of the quality of the ruling consensus. If there is a centripetal movement, we should expect the ideological spectrum to peter out on both Left and Right, a natural abbreviation and a gradual attenuation. But the alternative negative consensus is distinguished by the sharp break in the continuum, a truncation of the extremes.

We can apply the term 'political centrality' to this latter situation, so as to preserve the 'centralising' quality, but making a contrast with the quite dissimilar process underlying the centripetal drive. The basis of political centrality is not primarily a competitive stance, but actually a restriction on competition. In contrast, the 'market-place' is supremely a competitive phenomenon: the parties compete on the same terms for a substantially similar cross-section of the electorate.

The theme of political centrality – the negative consensus, the rejection of ideology rather than its decay – applies convincingly to post-war Germany. It would anyway be difficult to find traces of a positive consensus in the immediate wake of the dictactorship. All the signs were negative: a country divided, without its own government, subject to the dictates of the occupying powers, a population demoralised and disoriented after the collapse of the Nazi regime in the crushing defeat of Germany. Nor is it possible to make use of modernisation theory to take a positive view. The argument that National Socialism in furthering an unintended social revolution served 'to create the basis of liberal modernity' may be largely acceptable,[19] but the enforced social modernisation only established the preconditions for later development, not a consensus on 'liberal modernity' itself.

As a description of a significant strand in post-war politics, 'political centrality' can first be related to the party system. Was it in any way 'truncated'? The argument presented here is that it was and that, despite the entirely different factors at work, there are parallels in the positions of the Left and Right in German politics. Both flanks were deeply affected by what can best be termed as an 'ideological trauma'. In the case of the German Right the trauma was directly attributable to National Socialism, whilst for the Left it was brought to a head by the division of Germany and the circumstances of the division. Neither wound was easily healed.

After the experience of the Third Reich, any wide identification with the values of National Socialism has been politically impossible: no aspect of the regime has been rehabilitated. But it was more than a break affecting the potential of right-wing extremism. National Socialism had made a successful appeal to a number of living German traditions: nationalism, militarism, anti-semitism, mystical romanticism, the authoritarian state. Winning coherence through the unifying presence of the Führer, Nazi ideology was free to borrow extensively from the armoury of the more conventional expressions of right-wing ideology. The important point is that, in casting its net widely, the National Socialist creed tainted even those values which had no necessary connection with the totalitarian system and its excesses. Thus even orthodox conservatism was tinged with the colour of 'reaction' in the German context. It is easier with this background to appreciate the reasons both for the foundation of Christian Democracy and its prolonged success. The adoption of the 'Christian' label offered a political haven to a large section of the electorate which otherwise might have found a more congenial home in a right-wing party. In earlier times such a party could have sported the *'Volkspartei'* tag in its title, but with an emphasis on its popular-national basis and its opposition to the class parties of the Left.[20] The CDU version was entirely different, for it emphasised the quality of 'democratic collection' not that of being an ideological rally. The CDU deliberately sheared itself from all the traditions of Germany's immediate past, but it did not mean that the old values were thereby eradicated, rather that they were preserved as undercurrents in the party, as tendencies which, if conditions permitted, could take Christian Democracy on a more conservative course. Yet the Right suffers from the disability that its distinctive symbols – to a large extent rooted in the Wilhelmine era – were discredited, if not entirely destroyed, by the 'German Catastrophe'.

Handicaps of a quite different character have faced the Left. Its 'disabilities' did not stem from a single cause but from an accumulation. German Social Democracy – far more than related movements elsewhere in Western Europe – experienced denigration and exclusion because of its alleged anti-national commitments and un-German inspiration. This historical anti-Left sentiment had a significant influence on the post-1945 development of the SPD, for the party then reacted by following a policy of national identification, a refutation of the 'anti-national' charge. That movement on the part of the SPD has to be seen in relation to a wider pattern which originated in the circumstances of the division of Germany and the loss of the eastern territories and which took its full shape in the creation of the rival socialist state in East Germany. The national commitment of the SPD was also an ideological commitment, since it involved a clear-cut rejection of any association with the Communist Left. That rejection was made explicit in the SPD's refusal to unite in common cause with the KPD in 1946.[21] Thus the existence of the German Democratic Republic represents an ideological as well as a national divide, and for the SPD the ideological *Abgrenzung*, which began as a reaction to the policies pursued by the Soviet Union in Eastern Germany, has continued to be a major factor in determining the party's outlook.

Seen from this point of view, the very early post-war history of the SPD was the truly decisive phase, and – in its implications – the party's reaction to the situation of Germany amounted to an 'ideological rejection'.[22] It may also be mistaken to concentrate attention on the party's later and formal emergence as a *Volkspartei* – and thus to treat the SPD's conversion as a 'competitive phenomenon'. The adoption of the Godesberg Programme confirmed a change that had taken place much earlier, one which had its basis in ideological confrontation, not all-purpose reconciliation.

Political centrality does help to explain important aspects of post-war development, especially in drawing attention to the specific features of the German *Volkspartei*. But the idea of centrality has a wider application, and the parties themselves were subject to influences other than those that determined their precise ideological character. It is here that reference should be made to certain German political-cultural traditions, for they have a definite relevance to the centrality argument. There are, firstly, the general descriptions which underline the difficulties of anchoring 'democratic political competition' in Germany. They are encapsulated in such formulations as, for example, that Germans show a 'desire for synthesis', seek an 'avoidance of conflict', and display a 'dislike of politics'. They all point to elements in the political culture which are antithetical to party competition and more attuned to an authoritarian style, even in keeping with the old *Obrigkeitsstaat*. Party democracy in Germany was also weakened by the strength of the state tradition and the sharp dichotomy of 'state' and 'society'. The order, unity and permanence of the state should be insulated from the partial, transient and divisive forces of society – with the parties being particular culprits.

Whatever reservations may be expressed concerning general statements of a political culture, in the German case there is widespread agreement: the parties first had to overcome an endemic suspicion, and that mistrust was confirmed by the failure of party democracy in the Weimar Republic. The consolidation of the political system after 1945 therefore depended in part on a change in the nature of the parties, and that change is the principal component of the new-type *Volkspartei*, only distantly related to its catch-all cousin. In the first place, it required a shift from parties geared to sectional and class interests, divisive forces, to ones claiming to speak 'for the whole people'. In the second place, the parties had to make the vital connection with the state, to accept responsibility for it, to become *staatserhaltend*. In this sense, the parties became *Staatsparteien* just as much as *Volksparteien*, not merely bland, vote-winning engines, but forced into a common mould by the German state tradition.

Thus far, the content of political centrality has been presented in terms of cultural and ideological factors specific to Germany, but they were reinforced by structural features of the political system. Some of these date from the period of occupation when the allies were in a position to dictate both the mode and the extent of political competition. The force of the structural constraints they imposed are adequately summed up in the expression 'democracy under licence'. The parties that were the most successful in adapting themselves to the conditions set by the Western powers were also the ones that continued to be successful thereafter.[23]

That 'pre-constitutional' period of the occupation regime was followed by the regulation achieved by the Basic Law. Most generally the Basic Law succeeded in making the *Rechtsstaat* an institutional component of the political system. That elevation had the consequence of affecting the content of political decision-making and thereby restricting the area of freedom for the parties. In a most particular fashion, the Basic Law also succeeds in epitomising the idea of political centrality in Article 21: the provision for declaring parties unconstitutional that undermine the free democratic basic order or that endangered the existence of the Federal Republic. The use of the clause in the 1950s, to ban the extreme right-wing SRP and then the KPD, was perhaps of no great practical importance since the parties concerned were electorally insignificant, but the restriction neatly symbolises the potency of structural factors.

Political centrality usefully brings together the various strands of history, culture and institutions to a focal point in the conditions affecting the growth of a new party system. Its attraction is increased through providing an explanation based entirely on German circumstances. But does that mean that a more general account is made superfluous? At this point we should put the two approaches side by side to see not only whether there is a compatibility but, more importantly, whether the two are mutually supportive.

THE TWO FACES OF THE *VOLKSPARTEI*

Compared with the development of other party systems in Western Europe, the progression in Germany stands out as an anomaly: where multi-party systems existed in the past, they continue to do so, except in the Federal Republic. The discrepancy can be expressed by referring to the 'general transformation' argument: Why should it have come about that Kirchheimer's model, which at least appears so triumphantly correct for Germany, should be of such limited application elsewhere?[24]

The answer to this question can be made fairly direct. Unlike other countries, Western Germany was subjected to two types of pressure, one emanating from the special features of her own political system, while the other expressed the changes common to advanced, industrialised societies. Neither influence by itself would perhaps have been decisive. If the factors leading to political centrality had been the only ones at work, then their effect would not have been permanent. It is evident too – judging by the experience of other party systems – that the consequences of societal change do not ineluctably point to a refashioning of party competition.

The conclusion then follows: to explain what happened in Germany it is necessary to superimpose one type of explanation on the other. The result is a 'dual model', and its leading characteristic is the mutual reinforcement that takes place between the two sets of effect. We are, in fact, presented with a potentially powerful explanatory tool, one which can clarify the three puzzling aspects of German post-war development: why the change in the West German party system came about so early, why that change proved to be somewhat exceptional, and why the new shape of the party system has proved to be so persistent.

There are two particular strands in this argument that have to be taken up if the presentation is to be convincing. One concerns the degree to which the two 'sets of effect' are truly distinctive and act independently of one another. The other relates to the question of their 'mutually reinforcing' character. To face the problem squarely: Are there really two separate types of explanation, or is one merely an extension of the other?

The first issue has already been touched upon at various points in examining the alternative approaches, but it is as well to summarise the reasons for saying that they both have an independent status. In the first place, political centrality is composed of purely national elements, such as political culture, which owe nothing to any transnational forces. Secondly, it is largely an expression of inherited, historical traits. Thirdly, there were important ideological impulses at work in shaping 'centrality', even if they took a negative rather than a positive form. Fourthly, the conditions of political centrality act to restrict competition among the parties: they amount to an imposition and not to an electoral strategy. Even without further amplification, the contrast with the centripetal position is stark. The latter is based precisely on the generality of social change affecting a large number of countries, and it places their individual characteristics in a subordinate category. Furthermore, it is based entirely on the evidence of contemporary economic and social changes and their political ramifications: the catch-all party is a product of today's world. The movement of the parties also depends on their loss of ideology, a 'freedom from' rather than a debilitating weakness. Finally, the centripetal model is focused completely on the maximisation of competition between parties: ultimately only electoral strategies remain.

These four areas of contrast show fairly conclusively that there can be very little overlap between the two explanations, nor for that matter is there likely to be much interaction: in theory they could go their separate ways, but – and that leads us to the second issue – in Germany their effects were convergent. To argue the case for a mutual reinforcement between political centrality and the centripetal forces does not require that they should have been equally prominent throughout the whole of the post-war period; on the contrary, it is more likely that their influence has varied considerably and that the balance between them has shifted. It is reasonable to assume that Western Germany was not at first very much prone to the pressures making for centripetal competition – after all, those pressures, as we have seen earlier, reach a peak in the conditions of an affluent society and only when the inherited class structure has already been substantially eroded. If anything, it is to be expected that the weight of national and historical factors would have been predominant at the outset. Later, at some stage during the 1950s, the solvent processes of the West German economy took effect, and they proved to be especially potent, acting as they did on a society which was poised on the brink of modernity. It was during the 1950s that the Federal Republic was remarkable for the pace-setting way in which the party system was transformed.[25] Over the past two decades that system has become consolidated, but its present inertia is quite compatible with the view that there has also been a long-term decline in the importance of political centrality.

That decline was to be expected. It would anyway have been rather surprising if the nature of German political culture had not fundamentally altered from the picture of the immediate post-war years and earlier. The change in popular attitudes means that the stereotypes of the uneasy German relationship to politics have had to be abandoned. The legitimacy of the republic and its institutions have also become more firmly rooted, and it is hardly sensible still to refer to a continually hovering 'crisis of legitimacy'. This growth of political self-reliance has had the side-effect of releasing the political extremes, even if their following remains negligible: expressions of right-wing sympathy have become detached from the negative aura of the past, and the Left no longer suffers special handicaps – for one thing the division of Germany is now an accepted historical fact.[26] The symbols of an 'ideological truncation' have withered, and the plethora of new groups, the rise of 'alternative politics', and the remarkable growth of the *Bürgerinitiativen* – these are all indications of a decreasing willingness to conform.[27]

Yet it is also true that the decline of political centrality has only recently begun to stir the party system: the hold of the major parties over the electorate is unshaken. That inertia could be explained purely in terms of the competitive success of the catch-all parties. Their place was initially secured by the peculiarities of German political life in the earlier post-war period;

subsequently they were able to hold their own position. Thus, it is possible to delineate a changing balance between the influences, centralising and centripetal, and to appreciate their reinforcing capabilities.

This examination of the issues involved in using the two approaches leads to the conclusion that both have credentials as entirely independent explanations of party system change and that for Germany they both happened to act in the same direction. The result was to enable the *Volkspartei* to reign supreme, to give it an almost unchallengeable authority. So much can be admitted, but the fact of its high electoral status leaves unclear what kind of a party dominates the Federal Republic at the present time.

The modern *Volkspartei* has two faces: one still expresses German political traditions, while the other represents a society that is typical of many other West European countries. It would be wrong to suppose that the traditions are only vestiges of the past, just as it would be to believe that the *Volkspartei* was born in an ideological vacuum and that in some way it had become ideologically neutral.[28] The distinctive quality of party traditions is evident: both Social and Christian Democracy belong to wider European families, both provide a critical perspective on modern society, each has its own bulwark of support in the electorate together with a relatively high party membership.[29] Neither party is free from ideological tension, and the limited polarisation between the SPD and the CDU should not obscure the fact that it is based firmly on the Left–Right axis, and both parties are free to rediscover their ideological roots.

This is not to deny the force of the catch-all qualities of the party system, its other face, but a Downsian-like picture of party competition is suspect because it neglects the qualities of the individual parties by a one-sided concentration on systemic properties – an attempt to relegate the *Volkspartei* only to shopping for votes in the market-place. Far from treating the German *Volkspartei* as the most advanced European version of the catch-all type, it would be more accurate to see it as properly representative of West European party traditions. The emphasis can be made more pronounced: in its combination of the old and the new, the *Volkspartei* is the predominant West European form, not a German deviation.

NOTES

1. The leading theoretical discussion of the *Volkspartei* is H. Kaste and J. Raschke, 'Zur Politik der Volkspartei', in W-D. Narr (ed.), *Auf dem Weg zum Einparteienstaat* (Opladen, 1977). See also M-Ch. Zauzich, *Parteien im Wandel: Von der Weltanschauungspartei zur Volkspartei* (Munich, 1976).
2. These characteristics may, however, be unevenly represented. Thus H. Scheer,

Parteien kontra Bürger? Die Zukunft der Parteiendemokratie (Munich, 1979) pp. 130–1, gives four possible competing versions of the *Volkspartei*.

3. Besides the power of the Constitutional Court to ban 'undemocratic parties', the most important institutional device is the electoral system, in the '5 per cent' clause of the electoral law modifying the proportional principle. However, its effect on the representation of smaller parties may have been marginal – but perhaps critical in the case of the extreme right NPD which obtained 4.3 per cent in 1969. See M. Rowold, *Im Schatten der Macht: Zur Oppositionsrolle der nicht-etablierten Parteien in der Bundesrepublik* (Düsseldorf, 1974).

4. For an integrative approach to the problem of 'competing explanations', see F. L. Wilson, 'Sources of Party Transformation: The Case of France', In P. H. Merkl (ed.), *Western European Party Systems* (New York, 1980). In principle, Wilson's model could be used for the German case.

5. O. Kirchheimer, 'The Waning of Opposition in Parliamentary Regimes', in R. C. Macridis and B. E. Brown (eds), *Comparative Politics* (Homewood, Ill., 1964), p. 287. Kirchheimer's major articles have been collected in F. S. Burin and K. Shell (eds), *Politics, Law and Social Change: Selected Essays of Otto Kirchheimer* (New York, 1969).

6. O. Kirchheimer, 'The Transformation of Western European Party Systems', in J. LaPalombara and M. Weiner (eds), *Political Parties and Political Development* (Princeton, New Jersey, 1966) p. 184.

7. Kirchheimer, 'The Transformation . . .', p. 190.

8. *Ibid.*, p. 184.

9. *Ibid.*, p. 188.

10. *Ibid.*, p. 187.

11. The condition of the SPD in the early 1960s was portrayed by Kirchheimer thus: 'The SPD now shuns the very idea of an opposition role and multiplies both demands and offers of unconditional participation.', 'Germany: The Vanishing Opposition', in R. A. Dahl (ed.), *Political Oppositions in Western Democracies* (New Haven, Conn., 1966) p. 255.

12. Kirchheimer, 'The Waning of Opposition in Parliamentary Regimes', p. 286.

13. The rendering of the end of ideology in party system terms was also made by S. M. Lipset, 'The Changing Class Strucutre and Contemporary European Politics', in *Revolution and Counterrevolution: Change and Persistence in Social Structures* (London, 1969); also L. Epstein, *Political Parties in Western Democracies* (New York, 1967).

14. See S. B. Wolinetz, 'The Transformation of Western European Party Systems Revisited', *West European Politics*, vol. 2/1, January 1979. Wolinetz concludes: 'We can expect either continued fragmentation, or more likely, alternation between periods of fragmentation and periods of consolidation.' Another attempt to put Kirchheimer's theory to the test has been made by L. Mayer, 'A Note on the Fragmentation of Party Systems', in P. H. Merkl, *op. cit.*, Mayer uses an 'obverse' index of aggregation and finds that in seventeen of the eighteen Western-type party systems – the exception is Austria – the level of aggregation fell between 1965 and 1973. His comment – 'a result that seems to refute any reasonable interpretation of Kirchheimer's thesis' (p. 519) – applies to the 'simplifying' process but not to whether cleavages become less pronounced, for which an index of polarisation would be required.

15. After excluding from catch-all contagion single-claim parties and those with a

specific clientele, Kirchheimer adds: 'Nor is the catch-all performance in vogue or even sought among the majority of the larger parties in small democracies. . . . It seems easier to stabilise political relations on the basis of strictly circumscribed competition (Switzerland, for instance) than to change over to the more aleatory form of catch-all competition.' 'The Transformation . . .', p. 188.

16. In 1979 there was a reversion to a straight two-party system in Britain in terms of seats won and a clear governing majority, but the Conservative/Labour share of the vote remained relatively low at about 80 per cent in comparison with the last 'normal' year, almost 90 per cent in 1970.

17. Frank Wilson (*op. cit.*, pp. 545–6) argues that the key factors promoting change in the French party system were 'the competitive situation and the role of leaders'. It seems that he treats the presidential election as a change in the 'competitive situation', although that appears to be a straight institutional concomitant.

18. Apart from the extremist potential of the MSI on the one side and the Democratic Proletarians on the other, plus the Radical Party as an unknown quantity, the aggregate vote of the DC and PCI is relatively modest, and there is no consistent upward trend: the two shared about 69 per cent of the vote in 1979 compared with 73 per cent in 1976.

19. R. Dahrendorf, *Society and Democracy in Germany*, (London, 1968) p. 412.

20. The implication of the *Volkspartei* appellation differs according to the historical period. In the nineteenth century it had a liberal-progressive connotation, but after the First World War it signified opposition to the class-based parties of the Left, with the *Deutschnationale Volkspartei* the main protagonist. Significantly the Centre Party called itself the 'Christliche Volkspartei' for the 1919 election only. See Kaste and Raschke, *op. cit.*, p. 26.

21. The bitterness of the struggle between the SPD and KPD is well documented by K. P. Schulz, *Auftakt zum kalten Krieg: Der Freiheitskampf der SPD in Berlin, 1945–6* (Berlin, 1965).

22. It is worth noting that Kirchheimer did recognise the impact of 'centrality' in post-war Germany, yet without accommodating it to his centripetal theme: 'While deviant opinion is to some extent tolerated, legitimacy is not easily granted to movements and parties moving outside recognised channels. . . . Prevalent legitimacy notions have a tendency to narrow down the radius of action left for legal, but extraparliamentary opposition.' 'Germany: The Vanishing Opposition', p. 259

23. It is important to note that the constraints of the occupation period were not simply restrictive. Thus Loewenberg maintains that: 'The establishment of new ground rules for party competition by the occupation regime *permitted social change to work its political effect.*' G. Loewenberg, 'The Remaking of the German Party System', in M. Dogan and R. Rose (eds), *European Politics* (London, 1971) p. 279 (italics added). In other words, the 'ground rules' of occupation were in tune with the longer-term changes in German society.

24. A leading example of Kirchheimer's model holding good is Austria. Although Kirchheimer generally excluded the smaller European democracies, he made an exception for Austrian Social Democracy: 'It is becoming an eager and rather successful member of the catch-all club' ('The Transformation . . .', p. 188). But the competitive position of the Socialist Party and the People's Party has been quite different from that of other party systems, since there was a

quasi-two-party system in existence even prior to the fall of the first republic, although at that time the polarisation was intense.

25. An intensive regional study of the process of party change is contained in H. Kühr (ed.), *Vom Milieu zur Volkspartei: Funktionen und Wandlungen der Parteien im kommunalen und regionalen Bereich* (Königstein/Ts, 1979). One conclusion is that, although the macro-trend to the *Volkspartei* was quickly evident, important sub-cultures – *milieux* – persisted until the 1960s.

26. The 'acceptance' of the division of Germany has led to a decline in an all-German national consciousness and hence to a loss of party-political relevance. See G. Schweigler, 'Whatever happened to Germany?', in E. Krippendorff and V. Rittberger (eds), *The Foreign Policy of West Germany* (New York, 1980).

27. The tensions between the parliamentary/party system and the various forms of action groups are examined in B. Guggenberger and U. Kempf (eds), *Bürgerinitiativen und repräsentatives System*, (Opladen, 1978). See, in particular, P. Haungs, 'Bürgerinitiativen und Probleme der parlamentarischen Demokratie', and T. Schiller, 'Bürgerinitiativen und die Funktionskrise der Volksparteien', in that book.

28. The rooted ideological character of the *Volkspartei* is not really open to question, since it is the assumptions – social, economic and political – on which the party is based that are relevant, not just the visible features of its competitive stance. Kaste and Raschke (*op. cit.*, p. 26) go further in arguing that the *Volkspartei* always was – and still is – a '*Kampfbegriff*'. But where the *Volkspartei* is the dominant form, the view that the representative parties are engaged in a 'struggle' becomes less easy to sustain.

29. The parties represented in the Bundestag have between them about two million individual members, a member-voter ratio of about 1:20. A significant feature in recent years has been a lowering of the average age of party members. For a critique of catch-all theory implications for party membership, especially as put forward by Lewis Epstein, see P. Haungs, 'Über politische Parteien in westlichen Demokratien: Bemerkungen zur neueren Literatur', in P. Haungs (ed.), *Res Publica: Studien zum Verfassungswesen – Dolf Sternberger zum 70. Geburtstag* (Munich, 1977).

5 Party Government and Party State

KENNETH DYSON

Attempts to explore the party politics of a particular country, or to compare the party politics of different countries, often fail to reveal the more intimate, internal features of that politics. They depend too much on overly schematic approaches, such as rational theories of coalition formation or sociological analysis of cross-cutting and reinforcing cleavages.

Such an opening statement is not intended as a condemnation of these approaches. It is the prelude to the claim that much of the variety and complexity, and consequently openness, of the texture of party politics stems from the character and diversity of ideas about the role of parties which are present within the political culture. There is a temptation, which is encouraged by formal theories and by political sociology, to perceive these ideas and the reality of party politics as different worlds. Ideas are held to represent little more than an elevated language or smokescreen for self-interested proposals. Of course, ideas about party are in part tools or weapons of partisan political argument. They are manipulated in processes of politicking as interests seek satisfaction of their wants. Ideas about party are also in part a reflex of political conduct. They reflect changes in political practice, for example the attempts of the parties themselves to give legitimacy to their activities or the efforts of other longer-established institutions to limit or discredit the activities of the parties. One reason for exploring such ideas, and especially changes of these ideas, is in order to reveal underlying shifts in political practice. However, the full relevance of ideas about party emerges only when it is recognised that political actors are prisoners as well as manipulators of received ideas. Ideas can take on a life of their own, and perceptions of political reality are structured by the momentum of inherited conceptions. In other words, ideas about party are in part constitutive of the reality of party politics.

PARTY GOVERNMENT IN BRITAIN AND GERMANY

It is a commonplace of German political history to emphasise that political ideas, which have been so much the product of a bureaucratic and militaristic tradition, have denied political authority to the parties. The parties were viewed as divisive, parochially self-interested in outlook and unable to provide that unity-of-direction and creative energy which is required of government and essential to the stability and effectiveness of the state itself. If the parties embodied the fragmentation which was held to be characteristic of civil society, government was part of a wider, universal and ethical community, the state, and acted with reference to the idea of a public interest which transcended the rivalries of groups. As a consequence, and in contrast to Britain, the legitimacy of party government has been a protracted problem. For example, during the Weimar Republic *Parteienstaat* (party state) was primarily a pejorative term which offered an explanation of political crisis. The effective functioning of the state was being prevented by the presence of party outlooks in government and administration, the two central areas of the state.

In Britain political activity and reflection focused upon Parliament and in particular the complex 'balanced' unity of Crown-in-Parliament which had been victorious in the seventeenth century over the claims of monarchs that their prerogative constituted a sovereign power. In large part because the seventeenth-century settlement had confirmed the political importance of civil society which was represented in Parliament, it was difficult to entertain imported ideas of, or to sustain a native tradition of belief in, a realm of public affairs that was, and ought to be, emancipated from civil society. Political activity involved a complicated, changing struggle for power within the framework of Crown-in-Parliament. Although political reflection was chiefly concerned with representation and the conditions of representative government, it did not completely abandon the Crown, as the writings of Bolingbroke and later Tories indicate. Nevertheless, the concept of the Crown was theoretically undeveloped and did not merge into a larger concept of the state.[1] The notion of a realm of 'high' politics remained, but it was increasingly restricted to matters of security and to foreign affairs, both areas in which Britain had some sense of 'stateness'. Parliament drew the Crown, in the form of ministers, firmly into its orbit, for it was an institution with a superior self-confidence that sprang from its sense of historical legitimacy. In turn, Parliament was the political expression of civil society, from which its members were drawn and to which they were accountable. Hence the realities of post-seventeenth-century politics focused attention on the questions of representativeness of civil society and of how to provide responsible government, one which was to be responsive to public opinion, pursue prudent and consistent policies and, above all, be accountable.[2] Representation became the key concept of political thought and the source of the major theoretical disputes.

During the nineteenth century the model of the balanced constitution (which the Americans had earlier adapted) gave way gradually to that of responsible party government. The notion of party became increasingly important, developing from its eighteenth-century association with shifting parliamentary factions to its association, especially after 1867, with government itself. In practice party provided a more stable and effective linking-pin between government and Parliament. Governments were elected on the basis of party programmes, were sustained in Parliament by organised majorities and were responsible directly to the electorate for their record. The comparative ease with which the idea of party government took root is to be explained, in part, by a freedom from foreign invasion, religious bigotry and racial tension and contrasts with the internal conflicts and external vulnerability of the new German Empire after 1871. In addition, this transformation reflected the receptiveness of a parliamentary tradition of rule to party organisation, for this tradition rested on a moral faith in a spirit and practice of civic humanism. Party involved a difficult transformation of ideas of representation, but it did not have to contend with a political tradition in which such ideas were less central. Indeed, despite changes in name, in issues and in the franchise party politics continued to manifest itself in the parliamentary arena during the last 300 years.[3] The pressure for party unity stemmed mainly from the need to maintain a government in that arena.

Till now attention has been given to the historical features of British political development which did not generate or support the idea of the state as the institution of rule and which make the German debate about *Parteienstaat* so difficult for the British observer to comprehend. Quite simply, the seventeenth-century settlement represented a confirmation of a feudal heritage of flexible institutions rather than an attempt to secure political order by offering a rationalist defence of public authority. In particular, England had not experienced 'the Reception'. In the sixteenth century England was 'modern' in the sense that under the Tudors it experienced the religious Reformation and the development of a Renaissance monarchy. However, common law and Parliament together stood in the way of a rationalist and systematic conception of law and institutions, specifically of the Roman-law conception of an integrated 'public power'. This public power refers to a coherent arrangement of organs of state; they embody public authority, are devoted to the public interest and implement the law. In both legal and political ideas the feudal heritage was strong. This heritage supported the notion of consent in law; whether the tacit consent of a common law which expressed established conventions of conduct or the explicit consent of statute which made law by counsel. Roman law was intimately associated with the canon law of the Church and a medieval theocratic conception of kingship. Hence the common law and Parliament saw the political threat which its wholesale reception entailed. In addition, precisely because English medieval society was comparatively well integrated, it had little need of an elaborate integrative theory of law on the Roman model.

By contrast, during the nineteenth century Roman law began to affect intimately the German conception of public authority and its component institutions by endowing them with a superiority, distinctiveness and even mystique. It provides the background against which the state tradition of thought about rule is to be understood. The Roman-law emphasis on coherence and consistency has always provided a legitimating formula for the role of the administrator as the diviner and representative of the public interest, a role which had in turn been encouraged by the ambitions of centralising monarchs. Correspondingly, party became peripheral or external to the public power. It was not identified with the unity and superiority of the state. Legal theories of the state have, therefore, always been a barometer for the condition of the parties, in large part because the powerful law faculties of the universities were the chief source of recruitment to public-service office and trained students for the state examinations which remain the major passport to a public-service career. Of central importance to the theme of this chapter has been the way in which these theories, with some notable exceptions, have come to use *Parteienstaat* as a legitimating rather than pejorative concept in the post-war period.[4]

The legitimacy of party proved easier to establish in Britain where great political faith was placed in the creative nature and resilience of civil society and in the practice of civility as the source of standards in public life. In its functional sense government became increasingly an instrumental concept. It was seen as an instrument of civil society on whose consent its capacity for leadership depended. By contrast, in Germany government (*Regierung*) was viewed, from the nineteenth century onwards, as an organ of the state, as the political aspect of the public power which, unlike administration (*Verwaltung*), provided leadership and control. It was not a key concept of political thought. Instead its function within a wider collectivity, the state, was considered. State was a concept of a universalist character, one which endowed the public power with a unique mission and stressed the interdependency and integration of its constituent organs with reference to this mission. 'Party government' was, therefore, always a threat to the unity of the state and its association with the public interest and with the authoritative exercise of public power. This aspect of the problem of party government was only a part of the larger problem of legitimation of the *Parteienstaat*. The legitimacy of party had to be established in broader terms for a German audience than for a British one. Party had to be reconciled with the state tradition, to be seen as forming a part of an ongoing mode of thought about political rule: and this tradition was an element of continuity which was disrupted by the Third Reich but restored by the Bonn Republic. The intellectual problem for party was to make the shift from a narrow identification with civil society, whose weaknesses were a preoccupation of political reflection, to the wider functions and organisational responsibilities which were associated with the state.

The resolution of this intellectual problem of party was dependent on an initial and major transformation in political reality itself. Pressure to adapt theories of the state came from two sources: first, from the need to take account of those formal changes in the political structure and in the guiding principles of that structure which paved the way for responsible party government based on organised majorities; and second, from the consequences for the practice of party politics of social, economic and international developments as these affected the new Federal Republic. However, it is important to emphasise that these practical changes of a constitutional and extra-constitutional nature took place within, and were interpreted with reference to, a tradition of thought about rule.

In the first place, the Basic Law sought to design a new form of state which was both to be radically different from the totalitarian order of the Third Reich which had preceded it and to contrast with the failed Weimar Republic. Above all, the constitutional character of the state was different. It was a *Rechtsstaat* in the material sense, that is founded on a commitment to certain substantive principles which were to be advanced and protected by the new Federal Constitutional Court as well as by the traditional, and now strengthened, administrative courts. It was also a *Bundesstaat* which was more decentralised than its Weimar predecessor and enabled the state (*Land*) governments to exercise a powerful role within the federal legislative process through the upper chamber, the Bundesrat. In order to provide for more stable government executive–legislative relations were redesigned by stressing the authority of the Federal Chancellor within the federal government (Article 65); and by a special restrictive provision for votes of no confidence (Article 67) which required the Bundestag to express its lack of confidence in the Federal Chancellor only by electing a successor by a majority of its members.

Of particular importance, novelty and relevance to this chapter was

Article 21, according to which 'the political parties shall participate in the formation of the political will of the people'. As commentators emphasised, this article was the first which dealt with the political institutions of the new republic: its priority reflected the fact that party representatives had drafted the constitution. From Article 21 the constitutional theorist and long-serving judge on the Constitutional Court Gerhard Leibholz concluded that 'from an ideal–typical perspective the parties are the organised people'. The *Parteienstaat* character of the new regime was derived in this manner from Article 21 rather than given clear expression in the constitution like the *Rechtsstaat* and *Bundesstaat*. Nevertheless, whatever arguments might be advanced about the constitutional weakness of the *Parteienstaat*, it was increasingly recognised as an important attempt to bring political and legal theories into line with the realities of post-war Germany. The major disputes revolved more and more around the meaning of the concept, a meaning which was clouded rather than illuminated by the polemics that accompanied its first major theoretical elaboration by Leibholz. Leibholz offered a dogmatic view of a 'democratic party state' of 'instructed' party delegates which was replacing 'liberal parliamentarianism'. The Basic Law legitimated the function of parties as 'the surrogate of direct democracy in the modern territorial state'. Such a conception invited criticism not only on empirical grounds (for example, that the parliamentary parties enjoy considerable independence) but also on normative grounds that this thesis of the *Parteienstaat* devalued representative democracy and parliamentary institutions.

The Basic Law facilitated the legitimation of party not only by its provisions on the constitutional nature of the state but also by its characterisation of the state as an association. It was 'a democratic and social federal state' and 'all state authority emanates from the people' (Article 20). The idea of the *Sozialstaat* was derived from the depiction of the Federal Republic as a *sozialer Rechtsstaat* in Articles 20 and 28. *Sozialstaat* was interpreted to mean that the state had the function of promoting the welfare of its citizens by its policies. However, unlike the welfare state (*Wohlfahrtsstaat*) of the past, it implied the participation of social interests in the state and the mutual dependence of state and society. Nevertheless, these important formal changes in the constitutional nature of the state and in its character as an association did not simply mean that the English-language concept of party government could be easily adopted and take root. The idea of public authority itself remained unchanged, and the conception of party had to take account of its unified, inviolable and sovereign nature. The conception of party could not simply refer to the function of providing responsible government which was based on organised majorities in parliament. It had also to refer to the function of party within the state, that wide collectivity of institutions which comprise the public power.

Legal and political theories had, in addition, to adapt to a variety of other practical, extra-constitutional changes which combined to facilitate the integration of the ideas of party and state on a scale not achieved during the Weimar Republic. Quite simply, and as the constitution had intended, post-war politics developed in a manner different from that of its Weimar predecessor. This different pattern of development owed a great deal to external circumstances which included Allied aid, membership of the Western alliance system, West European integration (notably the rapprochement with France) and, speeding up all these processes, the Cold War. The new republic did not remain an outsider in the international community, was not burdened by reparations and, moreover, was able to benefit from an expanding and buoyant international economy. Comparatively benign economic and social circumstances, and the security that was provided by treaty arrangements, were crucial to the emergence of responsible party government and its corollary, the displacement of a fragmented party system which reflected deep ideological and regional divisions. Of course, changes that were internal to the political system were also important to the emergence of reponsible party government. It was the success of the Adenauer governments in encouraging and exploiting international and economic developments which enabled the Christian Democratic Union, in alliance with its Bavarian counterpart the Christian Social Union, to emerge as a cohesive majority party of government using a broadly defined ideology to attract a maximum range of support. Faced by the continuing electoral success of the CDU/CSU, by the disfranchisement of the Soviet zone where it could be expected to do well, and by the effects of the East on the popular credibility of left-wing alternatives, the Social Democrats opted in the late 1950s to adapt to the model of the 'catch-all' party (*Volkspartei*). They took on board, with modifications, the new consensus, especially about economic policy, that had been created by CDU-dominated governments. International developments, government policy and adaptation by the opposition contributed to the prosperity and security upon which social peace and readiness to compromise depend. In the early 1950s it was very possible that a fragmented and polarised party system, like that which had made the formation of stable governing majorities so difficult during the Weimar Republic, could have emerged. However, the share of the vote that was captured by the two major parties continued to climb – to over 90 per cent in 1976.

By the early 1970s, and indeed earlier, observers were speaking with confidence about a more concentrated party system that provided the conditions for responsible party government. The Grand Coalition (1966–9)

blocs.

between CDU/CSU and SPD had been an important step in this process; it demonstrated that both major parties were capable of governing. After 1969 there emerged a 'two-bloc' party system (the social–liberal coalition of SPD with the Free Democratic Party versus the CDU/CSU) which created a more direct link between the electors' party choice and the formation of a government. This ability of the parties to form effective and responsible party government was, of course, essential to the growing acceptance of the larger idea that the parties were the source of direction to the public power as a whole because they participated 'in the formation of the political will of the people'; and that in order to perform this wider function they must occupy the leading posts within the state apparatus.

PARTY STATE IN GERMANY

In order to gain a fuller understanding of the changing reality of German party politics it is necessary to go back beyond the developments of the 1950s and 1960s to the peculiar circumstances of the origin of the new republic. Following the Second World War party leaders found themselves in a situation different from that of their Weimar predecessors. The reality of military defeat was more vivid because it was experienced on German soil; surrender could not be attributed to a 'stab in the back' by democrats. Moreover, party leaders had the Weimar experience in mind as they considered their courses of action. The striking feature of their situation was a power vacuum which had been created by the collapse of traditional elites, notably of the army corps under the Nazis and of the Junkers whose estates were concentrated in the East, and by the discredit of traditional state institutions such as the bureaucracy by guilt of association with the Nazi period. On this occasion, licensed and supported by the Allied occupation powers, the parties moved pre-emptively to forestall the rise of the counter-elites whose presence had always threatened the Weimar Republic. They presided actively over post-war reconstruction, including constitution-making at state and federal levels and, even if on traditional lines, the reconstitution of the bureaucracy. The parties were the special instruments of democracy; the grip of democratic ideas was secured by party penetration of other institutions.

The importance of party membership as a major criterion of career advancement in public institutions was confirmed from the beginning. *Parteibuch* (party membership) was a measure, indeed the easiest and perhaps best available measure, of loyalty to the state itself as well as to the particular priorities of the party in power. It served a dual role: as an indicator of moral reliability (party as a guarantor of the democratic state and of an end to the *Obrigkeitsstaat* outlook); and as an instrument for more effective party government as greater organisational depth was given to party views. The parties dominated political and administrative life. They were in effect, although not intendedly, licensed by the Allies to participate in the patronage game, a game the legitimacy of which was established in terms of the parties' sense of being responsible for, and identified with, the 'free democratic basic order'. Integration of the ideas of state and democracy was given its practical expression in the party politicisation of public institutions. The parties placed their members, or members of organisations which were known to be very sympathetic to the party, in key positions and attempted to keep out those whose party connections made them unreliable.[5] Party patronage became intertwined with 'religious patronage' (furthered by the close links between the Catholic Church and the CDU/CSU) and 'interest-group patronage' (an example of which was the close connections between the CDU/CSU and the *Bauernverband* or farmers' association at the state level). Patronage was a complex phenomenon because of the variety of motives which guided it. Such motives included reward for good party work, the search for control, concessions to groups which were electorally significant for the party and compensation for Nazi persecution (in the case, for example, of Catholics and trade unionists). Patronage was further encouraged by the situation of social and economic distress that had been produced by the physical destruction and immense population displacement associated with the circumstances of defeat.

To a far greater extent than their British equivalents parties were able to offer their members valuable material services. There was, in other words, a material incentive to belong to a party. Figures for party membership would suggest an element of job opportunism which reflects a wide recognition amongst officials that extra-administrative criteria play an important complementary role to technical criteria in public-service careers. For example, in the traditional SPD state of Hamburg only 7.4 per cent of CDU members were *Beamte* in 1975 compared to 16.7 per cent in the traditional CDU state of Rhineland-Palatinate. The proportion of *Beamte* in the FDP dropped from 15 per cent in 1965 when it was a coalition partner in the federal government to 8 per cent in 1967 when it was in opposition and rose again by 1971 to the extraordinarily high proportion of 19.6 per cent.[6] The social structure of a party's membership shows a marked shift towards public servants when it is a traditional party of government like the SPD in Hamburg and West Berlin.

A striking difference between British and German party politics, and indicative of very different conceptions of party in the two countries, was in the politicisation of public administration, the broadcasting corporations and educational institutions in the Federal Republic. By 1972 over half of senior officials interviewed at federal and state levels were party members.[7] This process of party politicisation extended down below the legal category of 'political' officials and, moreover, was associated with a marked rejuvenation in age terms of these levels as well as a new variety of previous career backgrounds.[8] At the federal level just over 15 per cent of political officials interviewed (30.8 per cent of state secretaries) had had political careers. Such an openness of career patterns implied a decline of the traditional autonomy of the public service and a greater interest in, and tolerance for, politics amongst many of its members. Party rivalries over appointments and promotions surfaced internally in the deliberations of the personnel councils of ministries about the ministers' recommendations and externally in the computer bank of 'sympathetic' officials at CDU party headquarters. At the federal level after 1966 the SPD relied heavily at first on new planning staffs and planning divisions as a method of offsetting the possibility of bureaucratic opposition from a Bonn administration which was the legacy of seventeen years of CDU/CSU domination.[9] Over time, the limitations of this device became apparent and the SPD had greater opportunity to place its supporters in key posts. Of course, the nature and intensity of party influence varied from one area of the administration to another, depending for example on the attitudes of past and present ministers. Helmut Schmidt was more restrained about promoting party supporters than many in the SPD liked, whereas Horst Ehmke sought a pre-emptive strike against a CDU-dominated bureaucracy.

Meanwhile, during the 1970s the city-state elections in Berlin, Bremen and Hamburg showed SPD state governments that the gradual process of party politicisation of administration could be an electoral liability. Scandals, notably over public contracts, suggested that the entanglement (*Verfilzung*) of public and private interests could be at the expense of administrative values.[10] Moreover, working-class support was in danger of being lost if the SPD was seen as primarily a party of and for the public service. The condition of the acceptability of the *Parteienstaat* was the highest standards of conduct within the state apparatus: and this condition implied some restraint in the exercise of party power and a respect for, and tolerance of, separate institutional values. Quite simply, adherence to the concept of *Parteienstaat* does not mean an unqualified faith in party outlooks. One can, of course, emphasise party. However, *Staat* is the other dimension of the formula and continues to provide a set of standards with reference to which public conduct is evaluated. Those standards are expected to broaden party horizons. Hence the controversy about *Verfilzung* does not simply reflect the re-emergence of traditional *Beamtenstaat* and *Obrigkeitsstaat* ideas. Above all, the issue is about the proper balance between *Partei* and

Staat, between democratic values and sufficient institutional autonomy to ensure a morally reliable and effective discharge of public affairs.[11]

Party interference in the public broadcasting corporations has been another notable example of threat to institutional autonomy and professional values.[12] State parliaments elect the members of the broadcasting councils and, although restricted by law in the number of parliamentarians whom they can elect, have sought to place reliable party representatives on these councils. The supervisory board, which is selected by and responsible to the council, chooses the director-general (*Intendant*) and approves key appointments. Such a structure has facilitated party penetration. Although they are frequently independent-minded, director-generals are often on the defensive against threats of party intervention. A celebrated instance was the attempt of the CSU to achieve a 'seizure of power' in the Bavarian Broadcasting Corporation in 1971–2. At the end of the 1970s the CDU governments of Schleswig-Holstein and Lower Saxony announced that the interstate treaty with Hamburg which governed the operation of *Norddeutscher Rundfunk* would not be renewed. A bitter *Proporz* politics between CDU and SPD had contributed to its inefficiency, whilst the CDU felt irritated by the station's lack of reflection of its electoral strength. ARD, the joint institution which produces the first programme, is a constant target of party pressure as CDU governments and the Bavarian government complain about the dominance of the 'Red' stations of the north.

Parteienstaat came to occupy a leading role in the theoretical frameworks of left-wing SPD intellectuals. However, as the writings of Hesse (a party 'neutral'), Herzog (CDU) and von Mangoldt (CDU) indicate, the notion was not the exclusive prerogative of the SPD.[13] *Parteienstaat* was a legitimating formula. It recognised the degree of politicisation and became increasingly relevant as politicisation became a more overt phenomenon. In addition, it defined the functions of party and helped to shape political perceptions. Party elites spoke the moralistic language and adopted the didactic style of leadership of the state tradition of authority. It was the tradition to which they were accustomed and which they wanted to salvage from the ruins of the Third Reich. The stress of this conception was on relating specific action or proposals to the leading values of the community with whose defence party leaders sought to identify themselves. Political discourse took on a rationalistic quality. Tradition combined with recent experience to encourage a heightened sense of moral and social responsibility and of the need to offer an explicit defence of public authority and its unique and superior nature. Party leadership displayed a concern to structure political activity within the confines of a formula of political rule which had a clear conception of the limits of the acceptable. Hence the transformation of German political

argument brought about by the identification of the ideas of party and state
and by the parties' occupation of the 'commanding heights' of public
authority can be exaggerated. A tradition of thought about the nature of rule
continued to be explored. The major change was in the institutional reference of the idea of the state. This reference shifted from army and bureaucracy to party and in the process made the idea of the state more compatible
with the competitive processes of politicking which are associated with
democracy.

As a politicising formula, however, the implications of the *Parteienstaat*
were ambivalent. On the one hand, *Parteienstaat* recognised that effective
political rule in the name of the public interest depended on adequate
democratic mechanisms of political choice. On the other, assimilation of the
state tradition of thought about rule by party leaderships posed a danger,
which was recognised most strongly by critics in the SPD, that leadership
would take on an excessive degree of autonomy *vis-à-vis* the party membership. The corollary of leadership's emphasis on its moral function as guardian of integration was a didactic style which was not particularly sympathetic to internal party democracy and which might, according to critics of the
Staatsparteien, encourage radicals into extremism as they sought reform
strategies outside the traditional party framework.[14]

If the deeper source of the continuity of thought about public authority was
to be found in legal tradition, the more visible and vivid manifestation of this
continuity was the privileged position which continued to be held by the
public official, especially the *Beamte*. If the public bureaucracy was no
longer the embodiment of the state idea, public servants increased in importance as an occupational group within both parties and parliaments at federal
and state levels. Over 8 per cent of *Beamte* belong to a party, a far higher
proportion than in any other occupational group.[15] The SPD was characterised by a growing underrepresentation of workers and overrepresentation
of *Beamte*, particularly after it joined the Grand Coalition in 1966. In the CDU
Beamte accounted for 9 per cent of total membership in 1955; in 1966 this
figure had risen to 15.8 per cent and exceeded the figure for workers. *Beamte*
were even more strongly represented in party office and elected public office
than amongst the general membership, especially in the CDU (where in 1968
Beamte provided 33.3 per cent of party officeholders). Overrepresentation
of *Beamte* and other public servants reached a critical level in the state
parliaments. In 1978 the public service provided 46.6 per cent of federal and
state parliamentarians and in five of the eleven states over 50 per cent (46.1
per cent in the Bundestag). Whilst overrepresentation of public servants in
the parties and parliaments was increasing, it was not a new phenomenon.
The German tradition of the *Beamte* in politics extended back into the

nineteenth century when it had been encouraged by monarchical governments which sought pliant parliamentary majorities. Officials continued to
enjoy political privileges which included leave of absence during their
electoral campaign, pension whilst on leave to hold a parliamentary mandate
(as a result of a Constitutional Court ruling of 1975 modified in favour of
higher parliamentary allowances) and job security (the right to take up an
equivalent post on relinquishing elected office). It was also likely that an
occupational group with such educational attainments and career outlooks
would develop 'public-regarding' attitudes which would dispose them
towards political involvement. Their policy and organisational skills were in
turn likely to make them attractive to the parties. However, an additional
factor which encouraged their party involvement was the increasing importance of party affiliation for bureaucratic careers.

Two temptations exist: to emphasise the party politicisation of the public
bureaucracy and other institutions as an example of the emergence of the
Parteienstaat; or to stress the role of officials in parties and parliaments as
indicative of the continuity of the *Beamtenstaat* tradition and of an
administrative view of politics. The theory and practice of party in Germany
is characterised by this ambivalence, and there is, and will remain, scope for
contrasting views about the proper terms on which party and state should be
reconciled. Moreover, in a society which has been used to the identification
of state and bureaucracy confusion is bound to exist about the implications of
so profound a transformation of the institutional reference points of the state
idea. What remains fascinating about West German politics is the complex
interpenetration of the parties with other public institutions, coupled with the
way in which contrasting outlooks and loyalties are fused, and find a
coherence in the idea of the state. Whether one seeks to justify or recommend
party politicisation (*Parteienstaat*) or the role of the officials in the parties
(*Beamtenstaat*), the frame of reference of argument or conduct remains a
concept of the state. Such a concept emphasises the distinctive and superior
character of the public power as well as its unity and dedication to the public
interest. Public organisations are not appraised in discrete and pragmatic
terms as in Britain where the idea of a balanced, pluralistic political order
remains strong. They are appraised in terms of a rational and coherent whole
whose activities are depersonalised because they are governed by detailed
rules and procedures. State is a concept which stresses rational organisation
and the importance of depersonalised power, exercised in the name of a
public interest which is more than just a summation of individual interests.
Hence, as the constitution envisaged parties as essential aspects of the
political order, in Leibholz's words as 'crypto state organs', a party law
(eventually enacted in 1967) was required (Article 21.3) to regulate their

organisation and functioning. The tradition of legalism that is associated with the state tradition has come to pervade party as well as administrative life and finds its fullest expression in the conception of the *Rechtsstaat*. Of course this attempt to plot the points of convergence between *Parteienstaat*, *Beamtenstaat* and *Rechtsstaat* is not designed to disguise the tensions between them, most notably in their views about which institution needs to be ascendant if an effective expression is to be given to the values of the state. One has only to think of the tension between the final authority of the Federal Constitutional Court (which can, for example, determine whether a party is constitutional) and party attempts to place their members on the Court and to use appeal to the Court as an instrument of partisan political objectives. It is the mark of a vital tradition of thought about rule that it can contain a lively and continuing debate.

The historical importance of the concept of the *Parteienstaat* lies in its role (alongside *Sozialtstaat*) as a legitimating formula for the increased scope of politicisation that has characterised the Federal Republic. This politicisation has taken two forms. First, there has been a new awareness of the political character of rule, an awareness which has also found its expression in two other conceptions that have replaced that of the legal positivism of the formal *Rechtsstaat*. The material *Rechtsstaat* stresses the overriding importance of certain substantive political principles governing rule in addition to formal rules of procedure governing the exercise of rule; and the concept of the *Sozialstaat* identifies the state as a civic association whose members enjoy an equal status as citizens. *Parteienstaat* refers to the presence of partisans in the key offices of the state apparatus, a presence which is legitimated by the idea that the parties must occupy the commanding heights of public authority if the democratic character of rule is to be safeguarded. A striking characteristic of the theory and practice of West German politics is a willingness to accept that the effective working of the political order depends, at least in part, on party politicisation of the state apparatus. In the realm of political and legal theories there is a greater interest in the accommodation of state and society and a new readiness to accept that parties are institutional reference points of the idea of the state and cannot be ignored in characterisations of the state.

Second, politicisation has found its expression in a new vitality of competitive politicking. Individuals and groups have sought to impress on public policy their specific interests and ideologies by joining political parties in ever greater numbers, by more active participation in party election campaigns and by forming *Bürgerinitiativen* (citizen action groups). The consequence has been a more intense conflict of interests around particular policy areas like education, housing, energy and environment. *Parteienstaat* has emphasised the privileged role which the constitution has accorded to the parties in the political process of articulating and aggregating interests. The parties are not just viewed as one element within a complex process of interest politics. They are seen as the dominant actors in pluralist politics, responsible, according to the party law, for such broad functions as political education and 'influencing political development'. A concern for their institutional capability of discharging their functions within the process of interest politics was apparent in the party law which, amongst other things, recognised and regulated state finance of their electoral activities. The dominant role of party was understood to follow from their function of mediation between state apparatus and society. These two realms were distinct in the nature of the authority which they embodied and in the activities which they undertook. However, they were mutually dependent. The state was to offset the fragmentation of society and ensured social peace and prosperity by providing a moral integration and a harmonisation of particular interests with the general interest. Its provision of this function was, nevertheless, dependent on maintaining consent within society and on society's willingness to contribute resources to the state. The importance of the parties derived from the way in which they stood astride both realms: on the one hand, they ensured the democratic character of the state by occupying its key posts; on the other, they channelled the expression of political interests within a framework of moral principles for which they felt a special responsibility.

Party came to have a Janus-like quality. First, like British parties, German parties were seen as associations of interest and as the vehicles of particular ideologies, however vaguely defined. Second, the parties were also viewed as essential to the proper functioning of the political order. In Britain their function in political rule was a narrow one: to provide both the government of the day (the ideas to inspire government and the personnel to occupy the posts within it) and organised majorities to sustain government. By contrast, German parties have a broader function of political education and guiding political development which involved, as we have seen, occupying more generally the commanding heights of public authority. This broad conception of party was fundamentally a reaction to a German history which had included the *Obrigkeitsstaat* conception of the Second Empire, a conception of a state above and outside party politics, and after 1919 a 'republic without republicans'. Both experiences suggested that the impartiality of those in public office could not be taken for granted. The association of reactionary and anti-democratic sentiments with the *Obrigkeitsstaat* indicated, in Gustav Radbruch's words, that 'impartiality was the living lie of the *Obrigkeitsstaat*'; whilst the flaws in the functioning of the Weimar Republic taught the need to clean out the stables of public office thoroughly if a lasting change in the character of the German political association was to be secured.[16] Accordingly, and unlike in Britain, the concept of an independent neutral sphere within the public order was weakened.

The result of the weakening of the idea of a neutral impartial realm in public affairs was not simply a capitulation to party. Indeed, the party representatives who presided over the birth of the Bonn Republic were well aware of the economic and legal dangers that could arise from competitive politicking. They sought to safeguard financial stability by creating an independent central bank and basic rights by creating an independent constitutional jurisdiction. Careful attempts were made by the parties themselves to check the possible abuse of political power, an abuse from which they had themselves suffered in the recent past, by a complex system of balances: a federal system which was designed to maintain a decentralised political structure, a Constitutional Court whose purpose was to uphold a normative conception of law, and a Federal Bank whose legal duty was to safeguard the currency. Such institutional arrangements served to channel party activity and to counteract party loyalty. However, the corollary of their importance and strength as institutions was party attempts to use them, for instance through their influence on appointments to the Bank and Court. In 1979 three-quarters of the Court were party members. A Mannheim questionnaire (1972) of twenty-seven past and present judges found that twenty-one put party political calculation and personal acquaintance with the members of the appointing bodies ahead of expert qualifications as the major factors in appointments.[17] Over the years few great advocates or legal theorists have been appointed to the Court. In addition to party *Proporz* over appointments, the Court was drawn into party politics by the opposition's ability to use the 'Road to Karlsruhe' as an extra means of stopping, or at least watering down, federal government legislation. Under the new system of judicial review one-third of the Bundestag or a state government (as well as the federal government itself) could invoke the Court's jurisdiction through the abstract review of norms (*abstrakte Normenkontrolle*) if it felt that an issue had not been properly resolved in the legislative process. In other words, the opposition could appeal to the Court as final arbiter of cases which it had lost in the legislative process. The dangers of a party political abuse of the Court and of the Court appearing a partisan body were posed both by party domination of appointments and party use of the procedure for abstract review of norms.

Similarly, the corollary of a strong Bundesrat was party attempts to use it for partisan purposes. The Bundesrat is a federal organ whose members are representatives of the state governments and not, as in a senate system, elected directly by the people. The objective of this construction was to bring to bear on federal legislation and administration the administrative experience and the expertise of the state executives. Accordingly, there was a widespread agreement that 'obstructive' opposition by the Bundesrat would constitute an abuse of its powers. However, state governments are also party political in composition. The opposition can be expected to use it as an instrument of political influence. Election results and developments in the party system at the state level come to have a major and direct political significance for the federal legislative process: for the second chamber has the right of absolute veto over matters affecting the administrative, financial and territorial interests of the states. As most domestic legislation requires its agreement, the possibility of opposed majorities in Bundestag and Bundesrat excites great political interest. Parties are encouraged to focus on federal issues in state elections, to conduct the formation of state governments from the perspective of the distribution of seats in the Bundesrat and to see federal and state politics in terms of an integrated and comprehensive strategy which aims to coordinate decisions of party governments in state capitals with reference to votes in the Bundesrat.

CONCLUSION

The purpose of this chapter has been to establish the nature and relevance of the *Parteienstaat* without suggesting that it is the 'master-concept' of modern German politics. For example, both the Constitutional Court and the Bundesrat have their own institutional identities or self-conceptions which are established with reference to the concepts of the *Rechtsstaat* and the *Bundesstaat*. These concepts encourage them to see themselves as embodying in their different ways the 'universalistic' political conscience of the community. In the case of the Bundesrat there is a consciousness of responsibility for the federal order as a whole and, therefore, a sense of duty to look beyond narrow partisan or parochial interests. Indeed, the ability of the opposition to participate through its state governments, as members of a state organ (the Bundesrat), in federal policy-making has facilitated the attachment of the major parties to the state tradition and encouraged the sense that it is 'their' state. The major parties, whether part of the federal government or not, are drawn into the unity of public powers which is the state. As a consequence encouragement is given to a collegial or collaborative political style in which 'constructive' bargaining in Bundesrat committees and even in Bundestag committees qualifies the role of opposition. If party government emphasises majorities and the search for majorities stimulates a competitive, even acrimonious political style, *Parteienstaat* is associated with a sense of the parties' shared responsibility for the values and norms of the state, of acting for the 'whole'.

The tension between party government and party state is one of the most fascinating in contemporary German politics and suggests how different from those in Britain are the standards with reference to which party conduct is evaluated. Two contrasting dangers are apparent. On the one hand, the resolute search for party majorities, in order to govern on behalf of particular goals and interests, could lead to an abuse of the idea of the *Parteienstaat*. Such an abuse might take the form of political manipulation of public office to secure rewards for supporters at the expense of respect for objective administrative criteria. *Parteienstaat* would become a façade if the parties proved unable or unwilling to maintain a proper balance between their new function as instruments of political rule, the heirs to the state tradition, and their traditional function of politicking in order to promote particular interests. Anxiety about this danger underpinned the debate about *Verfilzung* at the state level in the 1970s. On the other hand, the collaborative ethos of the state tradition could so envelop or infect the major parties that, as under the Grand Coalition, more violent and extra-parliamentary forms of opposition might arise to counteract a political inertia that is held to be the product of party collusion. The first of these two dangers worried especially the Right which saw 'excessive' pressures for democratisation as a threat to public ethics; the latter danger was a source of particular concern to the Left. However, the dominant characteristic of German party style in the 1970s remained a complex co-existence of the 'audience-appeal' style of majoritarian politics with the didacticism of the *Parteienstaat* perspective. A qualified majoritarianism has been accompanied by a constructive opposition role. The government–opposition dimension existed and had important implications for party conduct, as was revealed by the difficult adjustments which the CDU/CSU had to undergo after 1969. Nevertheless, the legislative process continued to exhibit a high degree of party co-operation and mutual forbearance. The language of party politics remained ambivalent. It reflected both the search for majorities to sustain party government and the moralism of those who are conscious of their special and shared responsibility for the maintenance and defence of public authority.

The counterpart to the diversified political structure of the Federal Republic is a competition of political and legal ideas. These ideas in part reflect the diversity within this structure, in part serve as tools of political argument between its component elements and in part are constitutive of its complex reality. A highly differentiated political structure and the extent of theoretical controversy lead the observer to conclude that pluralism is the defining quality of German politics. However, pluralism remains distant from the German conception of public authority which focuses on the problems of the integration of public power and the institutional requirements of that integration. The German conception of public authority has been shaped in a society whose pervasive fear has been that of disintegration. Public order and the common welfare are seen to depend on a unity of public powers. Underlying the theoretical competition between *Parteienstaat*, *Bundesstaat* and *Rechtsstaat* and their different institutional expressions is a common conception of authority which emphasises the state. The theoretical controversies revolve around contrasting characterisations of the nature of the political association which is called the state and different views about what is distinctive about the constitutional form of its authority. The common point of departure is the assumption that the state comprises various organs whose different types need to be identified and their relationships ordered in a rational manner with reference to constitutional provisions.

Whether the underlying purpose is theoretical rigour or self-justification, the mode of argument about institutions is essentially deductive and moralistic. Policy style suggests a respect for objective and rational assessment as the basis for the authoritative determination of the public interest. Hence, in accordance with the state tradition, *Parteienstaat* maintains a faith in the expert, especially the public official, and in arbitration of conflict from above. Its concern is to guarantee the political reliability of the expert and of arbitration. As a concept of rule it emphasises the need for institutions to mediate between the state apparatus and society; that, particularly in a modern complex and interdependent society, it is impossible to separate these two domains. Maintenance of their distinctiveness cannot depend simply on their separation. It requires a mutual understanding and respect in which the state apparatus is made responsive to society (*die Vergesellschaftung des Staates*) and society is educated into the requirements of state (*die Verstaatlichung der Gesellschaft*). The elevated character of party and its sense of mission stems from this moral function of mediation.

Party has come to share with bureaucracy the concept of the state and, moreover, a concept of the state which had been established historically with reference to public-service values. The complex system of interfused party political and administrative styles which has characterised the Federal Republic is one that the American or British observer finds difficult to comprehend. In Britain party and bureaucracy are recognised as separate spheres in terms of career patterns as well as of values and styles of conduct. Parties provide government, whilst an autonomous self-governing administration executes government policy in a neutral manner on the basis of loyalty to the government of the day. American administration was unable to protect its privacy under the shelter of a concept of the Crown. In the United States party patronage pre-dated the emergence of a highly professionalised administration so that there was an absence of well-defined rules to protect administrative ethics against political expediency. The conception of party was formed by a native populism rather than in the context of larger ideas about public authority like Crown-in-Parliament or the state.

By contrast, in Western Germany party emerged as a major focus of loyalty, even within the public bureaucracy, alongside a high degree of continuity in the administrative sphere. Notions of responsibility to the minister and to party had to be compatible with respect for judicial criteria and methods in the application of law, a respect that was ensured by responsibility to the administrative courts, and with the idea, which was enshrined in public service law, of serving the whole people. The political and legal terms of the accommodation of party and bureaucracy were very different from those of Britain and the United States. If party was a greater focus of loyalty for the official than in Britain, it co-existed with a state tradition of authority which emphasised depersonalisation of power through subordination to rules and a unitary conception of the public interest which stressed respect for certain common shared ends or for corporate community ends. Hence party was not simply an element in a pluralistic process of political bargaining and compromise. Party was a central part of the political order and endowed with the superiority, precedence and mission of integration which the state tradition lends to that order.

Contemporary political analysis has focused much of its attention upon how party outlooks, and particularly their willingness to be conciliatory, have been shaped by electoral arrangements and social structure. The electoral system (as in Britain) or the nature of social divisions (as in the French Fourth Republic) may be hostile to inter-party co-operation. There has also been some interest, on the part of theorists of 'consociational' democracy, in the way in which political stability can be achieved in fragmented societies by a strategic response of party leaders who prefer amicable agreement to the hazards of majority party government (for example, during the first decade of the Austrian Second Republic). This chapter has focused, somewhat unfashionably, on a different dimension: on how conceptions of party have been influenced by inherited legal ideas.

The failure to see this connection is perhaps surprising. In the 1970s British party-political style was labelled 'adversary', a term which is supposed to suggest a new development but which in fact suggests an affinity of character between legal and party political argument. British (or, perhaps better, English) law and politics have long presented the spectacle, part theatrical and part sporting, of a clash between personalities who are rated in terms of their rhetorical skills of advocacy. In both cases this debating style has offered a wide range of emotional satisfactions both for players and spectators: emotional satisfaction is an important element in the management of conflict. Above all, modern British party politics reflects the 'sporting' theory of justice which is embedded in, and nourished by, the common-law tradition and parliamentary procedure, both of which have in turn common feudal roots. The norm of party politics has become a contest for government between two rival teams of politicians, 'ins' and 'outs', who present contrasting alternatives. The principal setting for that contest is Parliament which has been the great educator of party political style. Parliament's sporting sense and sense of theatre find their expression in the qualities which are prized in the great party leader: essentially the qualities of the actor–manager and of gamesmanship. These are also the qualities of the great legal advocate. This affinity of law and party politics is deep and strong: for Parliament and the common law were both opponents of monarchs who wished to throw off the shackles of the feudal order in favour of their own centralised power. Indeed, Parliament had originated from the feudal monarch's court where law was declared and administered; and it retained some aspects of a court in the judicial sense a well as acting as a legislature and organ of consultation.

By contrast, post-war German political attitudes have favoured an investigative and collegial style of party politics. Such a style offers a great deal of rational satisfaction; it attempts to clarify not only the particular interests involved in an issue but also those shared or corporate ends which constitute the public interest and form the basis of community. Even before 1918 the SPD had sought to make full use of the Reichstag committees, which emphasised inter-party negotiation, as a method of influencing policy. However, it took much longer to dispel the doubt that party government could transcend mere 'horse-trading' compromises. The condition of a rational political style seemed to be an impartial government above party. Many people during the Weimar Republic welcomed Hindenburg's Presidency as a return to this condition. However, the failure of that Presidency, even when armed with the wide powers of emergency decree, to resist Nazism hastened the demise of the idea of an impartial government. As we have seen, a spirit of *Sachlichkeit* was implicit in the post-war emergence of the idea of party government in a *Parteienstaat*, the central aspect of which was the parties' shared responsibility for the whole. One aspect of this development was that the parties took on board the state tradition of authority with its Roman-law background: its notion of an authoritative decision-maker who was responsible for realising the public good; and its inquisitorial style of argument, according to which the truth is to be discovered by objective investigation rather than by partisan debate. In contrast to the British idea of party government and its associated practice of adversary party politics, *Parteienstaat* offered an inquisitorial style of party politics. The state itself and its offices of public authority did not belong to the parties; and the parties were not the state. They had taken on a special responsiblity for the concept of the state, a concern for ensuring the proper conditions for the authoritative exercise of public authority.

The theory and practice of party government in Germany remains torn between the adversary implications of the search for organised parliamentary majorities to support party governments and the collegial and investigative outlook of *Parteienstaat* which emphasises the wider moral and social responsibility of parties for the effective functioning and democratic character of the state. If the British conception of party has been shaped primarily in the parliamentary arena, the German view of party has been forged in two arenas which have been brought into closer relationship but not fully reconciled: the electoral arena of party 'games' in which the prize has become government; and the moral arena of legal and political conceptions of state in which the prize is the credibility and respectability of party government as a whole and of individual parties in particular. The state tradition has encouraged both high-mindedness and dissimulation in the German parties: on the one hand, a view of politics as a collaborative effort; and on the other, a use of the language of state as an instrument for the satisfaction of one's wants.

Even if their attitude to the language of state is strictly calculative rather than the expression of a normative identification, German party politicians confront a dilemma when faced with the problem of how to address their political messages in order to make a favourable impact. Should they seek partisan advantage in the pursuit and use of public power? Or should they strive for the moral reliability of identification with a public authority devoted to a dispassionate quest for the public interest? If the dilemma is not peculiar to German party politics, the character of that dilemma is distinctively German.

NOTES AND REFERENCES

1. On Crown and state see K. H. F. Dyson, *The State Tradition in Western Europe* (Oxford, 1980).
2. A. H. Birch, *Representative and Responsible Government* (London, 1964).
3. A. Beattie (ed.), *English Party Politics*, vol. 2 (London, 1970).

4. Notably under the influence of G. Leibholz, *Strukturprobleme der modernen Demokratie*, 3rd edn. (Karlsruhe, 1967).
5. On the history of attempts to keep out 'unreliables' up to the so-called *Berufsverbote* of the 1970s see K. H. F. Dyson, 'Anti-Communism in the Federal Republic of Germany: the Case of the Berufsverbot', *Parliamentary Affairs*, 1975, pp. 51–67.
6. H. W. Schmollinger, 'Abhängig Beschäftigte in Parteien der Bundesrepublik: Einflussmöglichkeit von Arbeitern, Angestellten und Beamten', *Zeitschrift für Parlamentsfragen*, vol. V (1974) p. 71. There are three types of public servants: *Arbeiter* (workers), *Angestellte* (employees on a contractual basis) and *Beamte* whose duties and privileges are exceptional and laid down in public-service law (they have, for example, security of tenure and non-contributory pensions). Unlike in Britain public officials of these three types are to be found at all levels of government and in all public law institutions including public enterprise, education and the universities.
7. This figure and those below are taken from B. Steinkemper, *Klassische und politische Bürokraten in der Ministerialverwaltung der Bundesrepublik Deutschland* (Cologne, 1974).
8. 'Political' officials are detailed in public-service law and include state secretaries at federal and state levels and division heads at the federal level. Interestingly, the Steinkemper survey showed that party membership was higher amongst division heads at the state level ('non-political' officials) than amongst division heads at the federal level. Clearly party membership is not simply confined to 'political' officials.
9. For details of what happened in the Bonn bureaucracy with the change of power, especially after 1969, see K. H. F. Dyson, *Party, State and Bureaucracy in Western Germany* (Beverly Hills, 1977) pp. 20–37.
10. For details of the issue of *Verfilzung* see Dyson, *Party, State and Bureauacracy*, pp. 37–43. On the case of West Berlin see J. Raschke, *Innerparteiliche Opposition: Die Linke in der Berliner SPD* (Hamburg, 1974).
11. Critics of the *Parteienstaat* of the Federal Republic like Wilhelm Hennis are concerned that too much emphasis on party and the material preference of party members (for example, through patronage) could unleash a new anti-party outlook. Such a danger could become real if the parties' preoccupation with partisan advantage and interest satisfaction proved greater than their moral concern for, and identification with, the political order. Hennis fears that pressures for 'democratisation' could reduce the likelihood of responsible and balanced party leadership. W. Hennis, *Die Missverstandene Demokratie* (Freiburg, 1973).
12. For a full treatment see A. Williams, *Broadcasting and Democracy in Western Germany* (Bradford, 1976).
13. K. Hesse, *Grundzüge des Verfassungsrechts der Bundesrepublik Deutschland* (Karlsruhe, 1967); R. Herzog, *Allgemeine Staatslehre* (Frankfurt, 1971); H. von Mangoldt, *Das Bonner Grundgesetz* (Berlin, 1953). The SPD intellectuals like Ehmke and von Oertzen were concerned to build social change and politicisation into the theory of the state and found inspiration in the Göttingen seminar of the eminent conservative jurist Rudolf Smend who provided a material analysis of the state. For Ehmke the function of party was to strengthen the 'steering capacity' of the state with respect to the management of social change.

14. For an extreme presentation of this view see W.-D. Narr *et al.*, *SPD-Staatspartei oder Reformpartei* (Munich, 1976). This criticism was more moderately expressed in T. Ellwein, *Das Regierungssystem der Bundesrepublik Deutschland* (Opladen, 1973) p. 74. On the controversy about the imperative mandate in the SPD see Dyson *Party, State and Bureaucracy*, pp. 11–15.
15. These figures and those below are taken from Schmollinger, *op. cit.*
16. G. Radbruch, 'Die politischen Parteien im System des deutschen Verfassungsrechtes', in G. Anschütz and R. Thoma (eds), *Handbuch des deutschen Staatsrechts* (Tübingen, 1930) p. 289.
17. These figures are taken from the article 'Justiz' in *Der Spiegel*, No. 46 (1978) pp. 84–98. The Mannheim questionnaire was undertaken by the Institut für Sozialwissenschaft of Mannheim.

6 Problems of Party Government in West Germany – A British Perspective

WILLIAM E. PATERSON

The theme of party government is one which has attracted continually increasing attention in recent years. The two best known contributions by Richard Rose and Anthony King were focused, as one would expect from their provenance, fairly firmly on Britain and the United States.[1] Kenneth Dyson and Gordon Smith have been notable among British political scientists in their analysis of the role and concept of party government in West Germany.[2] In West Germany itself, the topic in its different facets has attracted the attention of a whole series of distinguished practitioners and analysts. Among the most influential have been Hans Apel, Gerhard Leibholz, Wilhelm Hennis, Gerhard Lehmbruch, Udo Bermbach and Peter Haungs.[3]

West German political scientists have traditionally regarded Britain as the *Musterbeispiel* of successful party government.[4] In this they have reflected a conventional British view which has only recently been challenged. In a revised edition of *The Problem of Party Government*, which came out only two years after initial publication, Richard Rose, responsive to the imperatives of the changing public and elite mood, wrote a new introduction, entitled 'A Crisis in Party Government', followed by a very insecure-looking question mark.[5] This change which reflected deepening public dissatisfaction drew attention to a number of elements which together were said to constitute a crisis in party government. These features included the difficulty governments had in actually governing (the ungovernability thesis), the bypassing of parliament involved in the theory and practice of 'tripartism', the decline in electoral turnout, the steeply declining membership of the Labour Party, the decline in the number of party identifiers,[6] and the fragmentation of the party system as a result of the two elections in 1974. Expectations that this crisis would lead to the demise of the two major parties have proved somewhat premature. Rather, to adapt a simile used by David Calleo in a quite different context, 'Like ageing sopranos they refuse to retire. Their technique remains impressive even if their voices grow feeble and their repertory more restricted'.[7]

In contrast, the system of party government in West Germany, the legitimacy of which had apparently been called into question on both the Left and Right of the political spectrum during the period of the Grand Coalition 1966–69, appeared to enjoy not only the support of the West German population as evidenced in electoral turnout and distribution of party preference, but also attracted plaudits from non-German political scientists.

In an influential paper in 1976, Gordon Smith referred to West Germany having acquired the classic hallmarks of successful parliamentary government.[8] These he took to be: governments consistently based on parliamentary majorities; the availability of alternative governing formations (implying a developed concept of opposition); the origination of public policy from within the party nexus; and the provision of political leadership embedded in the parliamentary process.[9] While Smith's general conclusion may be endorsed, there does seem to be some question as to whether public policy does originate from within the party nexus. One way of trying to look at this question is to apply the criteria that Richard Rose developed to define and test the quality of party government in Britain. This procedure enables the focus to remain on the concept of party government rather than the wider and much more frequently discussed theme of the party state.

Rose posited eight conditions for the existence of party government in Britain:

(1) parties must formulate policy intentions for enactment once in office;
(2) a party's intentions must be supported by statements of 'not unworkable' means to desired ends;
(3) at least one party must exist, and after some form of contest, the party should become the government;
(4) nominees of the party should occupy the most important positions in a regime;
(5) the number of partisans nominated for office should be large enough to permit partisans to become involved in many aspects of government;
(6) partisans given office must have the skills necessary to control large bureaucratic organisations;

(7) partisans given office must give high priority to carrying out party policies;
(8) party policies must be put into practice by the administration of government.

Rose concluded that only one condition – and that the least restrictive – namely the choice of a government after an election contested on party lines, is unequivocally met in Britain.

PARTY GOVERNMENT IN BRITAIN AND WEST GERMANY

The criteria suggested by Richard Rose can be applied to both Britain and Western Germany, and in this section the various conditions will be examined in relation to both countries. The first two criteria can be taken together:

(1) parties must formulate policy intentions for enactment once in office;
(2) a party's intentions must be supported by statements of 'not unworkable' means to desired ends.

In establishing that the first and second conditions are not met in Britain, Rose makes a useful distinction between the legislative and co-operative elements in governmental policy.[10] The legislative element can be stated in a form suitable for an act of parliament, statutory instrument or order in council. In contrast the co-operative elements of governmental policy cannot be realised by legislation alone. The test of policy here is not whether it can be translated into draft form but to what extent it is acceptable to organisations taking decisions independently of parliament. There has been a steady growth of the co-operative element at the expense of the legislative element as the state has extended its responsibilities. This shift has been accompanied by a tendency on the part of political parties to play down detailed policies before taking office.

The other major element identified by Rose is the belief that the governing party is more likely to lose a general election if its achievements are made unattractive than an opposition is likely to win by offering hypothetical benefits. Moreover the preparation of detailed policy statements while out of office can be politically dangerous, in so far as it encourages factional disputes within the opposition ranks, or stimulates a 'scare' campaign by the government of the day.

The legislative/co-operative distinction is as important, perhaps even more so for West Germany, given the prevailing ideology of social partnership. This ideology implies a strong orientation, sometimes called 'concerted pluralism' or 'limited pluralism', to working with and through the most important groups in society.[11] Such an approach militates against too many prior commitments before taking office. However, perhaps the most important factor in the Federal Republic working against the detailed formulation of policy intentions for enactment once in office is the character of the major West German parties as *Volksparteien*.[12] The theory and practice of the catch-all party, with its necessary emphasis on aggregation works strongly against too sharp a set of advance policies.

While the CDU/CSU always proclaimed itself to be a *Volkspartei*, the SPD only changed from a party of 'mass integration' (Neumann) to being a *Volkspartei* under the pressure of the overwhelming success of the CDU/CSU in the first ten years of the Federal Republic. The adaptation of the *Volkspartei* model brought with it a decreased emphasis on the need for the party to articulate detailed alternative policies. The alternative offered lay more in the area of personnel than in the presentation of alternative policies. This change is brought out well in two contrasting statements by Kurt Schumacher and Willy Brandt. Kurt Schumacher (1949): 'The essence of opposition is a permanent attempt to force the government and its parties by concrete proposals tuned to concrete situations to pursue the political line outlined by the opposition.'[13] Willy Brandt (1961): 'In a sound and developing democracy it is the norm rather than the exception that parties put forward similar, even identical demands in a number of fields.'[14]

There has of course been some criticism of the concept of the *Volkspartei* in the SPD. It is generally recognised, however, that the major attempt by the party to come to terms with the criticisms made of the *Volkspartei* in the drafting of the *Orientierungsrahmen für die Jahre 1975–85* produced a programme that was still general rather than detailed, and it was in any case regarded by almost everybody in the party as very unlikely ever to be put into effect.[15]

The close relationship between the political parties and the bureaucracy, a theme which will be taken up in detail later, has meant that administrative expertise carries a great deal of influence in the councils of all the main parties. This influence normally results in the production of policies which are accompanied by statements of 'not unworkable' means to desired ends.[16] The major exception to this general practice lies in the field of foreign affairs where political parties in opposition have produced policies which are valued for mobilisation and integrative purposes but which are often unaccompanied by any clear "workable" means to desired ends.[17]

(3) At least one party must exist and after some form of contest become the government.

This condition is clearly met both in Britain and West Germany, although in the Federal Republic coalition rather than single party government is the rule.

(4) Nominees of the party should occupy the most important positions in a regime.

'Perhaps the best measure to distinguish the relative hold of party elites on a political system as against that of other elites is to ask how far positions of political influence can be obtained through, as compared to outside party channels' (Hans Daalder).[18]

The number of partisan appointments is relatively small in the United Kingdom. There is a conventionally observed distinction between political leadership and administration. Partisan appointments are limited to the ministerial team, with political and administrative careers being sharply demarcated. This convention has been breached in recent years by the increasing appointment of 'irregulars' but they remain essentially marginal figures in Whitehall.

In the Federal Republic the number of ministerial appointments is smaller than in the United Kingdom. The total number of ministers and parliamentary state secretaries is usually about 35–40, less than half the British ministerial team. In contrast to incumbents of ministerial office in former German regimes, they have invariably been partisan appointments. Between 1949 and 1977 only three ministers were appointed who were neither members of parliament nor party members. One of the three was subsequently elected to the Bundestag and the other two had very short periods in office.

An even greater departure from former German theory and practice is represented by the gradual abandonment of the concept of the *Beamte* (public official) as being *überparteilich* (above parties). Bärbel Steinkemper in West Germany and Kenneth Dyson in Britain have drawn attention to the development of a 'party book administration'.[19] Steinkemper showed that by 1972 over half the senior officials (state secretaries, heads and departmental heads of division) at state and federal level were party members.[20] Steinkemper demonstrated further that public officials who were party members reached positions of influence quicker than non-party members.[21] Indeed at the federal level some 15 per cent of political officials in

Steinkemper's sample (30.8 per cent of state secretaries) had actually had a political career.

(5) The number of partisans nominated for office should be large enough to permit partisans to become involved in many aspects of government.

As we have seen in the United Kingdom, the partisan element is constituted by the ministerial team. Ernest Marples, one of the more energetic ministers, calculated that he was not able to devote more than a quarter of a thirteen-hour day to departmental paperwork. According to Rose:

> Ministers are rarely sufficient to form a critical mass within a department for they average three or four per government department. The critical mass consists of the sixty to eighty civil servants on whom they depend to make their directions trickle down through the department.[22]

This fifth condition is clearly met in West Germany. It is not just that public officials, particularly successful ones, often have a partisan affiliation, but that appointments to a huge penumbra of governmental and non-governmental organisations have a partisan colouring.[23]

(6) Partisans given office must have the skills necessary to control large bureaucratic organisations.

Richard Rose demonstrates convincingly that the highly restrictive criteria of eligibility for ministerial office, that is membership and level of performance in the House of Commons, combined with the condition of generalist, non-expert ministers and frequent ministerial reshuffles (only France, Finland, Italy and Belgium have shown a greater rate of turnover in post-war Europe) results in this condition not being fulfilled in the United Kingdom.[24]

In West Germany the rate of ministerial turnover is much lower. There is a tradition of expert ministers with occasional notable exceptions like Gerhard Schroeder and Helmut Schmidt who have held a number of different portfolios. Many of the ministers have themselves been public officials. Of the 18 members of the CSU cabinet in Bavaria in 1978, 14 were former public officials.[25] The political leadership of the bureaucracy is, as we have seen, partisan and is thus in a strong position to control the ministries.

(7) partisans in office must give high priority to carrying out party policies.

The general picture in Britain is that the pressures already outlined normally result in ministers becoming departmental rather than party spokesmen. This condition seems to raise especially interesting considerations in the Federal Republic and it is worth examining the topic from the perspective of factors internal and external to the party.

PARTY PERSPECTIVES

In the long period of Adenauer's ascendancy, the CDU/CSU served mainly as a *'Kanzlerwahlverein'*. It was an instrument of political rule and Adenauer clearly gave priority to governmental rather than to party goals. The party, bereft of organisational resources and mortgaged to the chancellor's electoral appeal, was in a very weak position to impose goals on an unwilling chancellor. It was also clear, given Adenauer's own definition of his chancellor role, that the party was constrained in its relations to other ministers as well.

One of the most important elements in the transformation of the SPD from a working-class movement to *Volkspartei*, which appeared to be a precondition for winning office, has been a marked reduction in authority accorded publicly by party leaders to party goals.[26] In 1960, by which time the SPD had really become a *'Regierungspartei im Wartesaal'*, Willy Brandt said:

> I am perhaps not making a statement that will win easy popularity when I declare that I cannot simply be an instrument for expressing the will of the party, but that after earnest thought and on my own responsibility, I shall have (if elected) to make decisions which are vital to the interests of our nation.[27]

In 1969 Brandt reminded delegates at the party conference that governmental policy would have to be asserted even against party friends, and in 1972 he declared, with even less respect for party shibboleths, that party conference resolutions may have an effect but are in no sense a substitute for governmental policies.[28] This assertion of autonomy and the priority of governmental rather than party considerations has been made even clearer during the chancellorship of Helmut Schmidt.

The close relationship between the political parties and the bureaucracy is a two-way process in which, while the administration is now staffed by party-card holders, especially in senior positions, administrative values are often decisive in party discussion. In all political parties the percentage of public officials in the membership has grown. While public officials constituted 4 per cent of the West German population in 1973, they made up 13 per cent of the membership of the CDU (1976), 12 per cent of the CSU (1976), 14 per cent of the FDP (1977) and 10 per cent of the SPD (1977).[29] This rise in the number of party members who are public officials has been accompanied by an even stronger trend for these same officials to win public office. In 1968 *Beamte* accounted for 9.9 per cent of the membership of the SPD but 19.7 per cent of those elected to public office.[30] In many state parliaments over a half of the parliamentarians are public officials.

In a number of *Länder* characterised by one-party dominance, this intermeshing of party and bureaucracy, usually accompanied by *Ämterhäufung* (accumulation of offices), has reached very high levels. In several SPD-governed *Länder* the suspicion that the party was being pervaded by administrative rather than political values led to a counter-reaction. This response took the form of suggesting various methods – such as the doctrine of the imperative mandate – by which representatives would be bound by the views of the party organs that had originally mandated them.[31] Over a longer period this counter-reaction has failed as the Left in the party has lost ground and the almost universal picture is one of the predominance of administrative/legal values.[32]

At parliamentary level the impact of administrators and administrative values reflecting the change in parliament is very marked, and it is normally combined with penetration by interest groups. Hans Apel, in his account of policy-making in the political parties, has demonstrated the dominance of experts in the formulation of policy.[33] All three parliamentary parties have a series of major and minor policy-making committees. The members of such committees are, or become, experts. These experts are, moreover, often the representatives of interests. Klaus von Beyme, in his article on 'The Changing Relations between Trade Unions and the German Social Democratic Party', cited the example of the Bundestag Committee on Labour and Social Order, 70.3 per cent of whose members belong to trade unions, and the Agricultural Committee of which 77.7 per cent of the membership were farmers.[34]

It has proved extremely difficult to reduce the power of experts and representatives of interest groups and subordinate them to the control of the whole party, since – so the argument runs – if the power of the party expert is reduced, then even more power will be given directly to the interest groups and public officials, unmediated by party considerations. Within the parties, for instance, it is difficult to subordinate the experts on social policy to more stringent controls by the specialists on economic and domestic policy. The imperatives of coalition government mean that it is necessary to come to an agreement with the experts of the coalition partner in secret, and consequently the full parliamentary party only learns what its representatives have decided from the majority report of the relevant Bundestag committee.

We have considered at some length factors internal to the political parties which affect the priority the leadership gives to carrying out party policies. There are, of course, several wider factors which act to reduce the priority given to the implementation of party policies. These can be set out fairly briefly.

West German governments are almost invariably coalition governments, and the priority given to party policies has often to be sacrificed to the exigencies of coalition argument. The formation of governments is normally preceded by the fairly detailed working-out of a coalition agreement and all governmental policies must command the agreement of both coalition partners. The principle of government by parliamentary majority is qualified by the existence of a dual majority at federal level. Since it often happens (as at present) that the opposition party to the federal government is more strongly represented in *Länder* governments, and thus disposes of a majority in the Bundesrat, there is a structural imperative for the government to co-operate with *Länder* elites.

The primacy accorded to party policy is also constrained by the theory and practice of judicial review as operated by the *Bundesverfassungsgericht* (Federal Constitutional Court). The institution of judicial review means that possible objections by the *Bundesverfassungsgericht* have to be taken into account in the preparation of every bill. There has been a tendency recently for the court to expand its role. The danger inherent in this development for party government has been well expressed by Richard Löwenthal:

The attempt to turn the Court into an organ of quasi-everyday revision of legislative decisions, and the recent readiness of the Court to accept this role (and indeed to 'discover' in the constitutional text a basis for detailed legislative precepts in a variety of fields), is bound to lead to a distortion of the division of powers. It is rooted in the assumption that fundamental rights of the citizens are constantly endangered by their elected representatives, and that judges who had been selected indirectly by inter-party compromise represent a 'superior' kind of objectivity compared with representatives of the people elected on the basis of an openly proclaimed political programme. This is bound, first, to discredit the democratic process whose results are subordinated to a 'non-partisan' interpretation of law; then to blur the delicate but vital borderline between the necessary review of democratic decisions under the rule of law and their gradual replacement by the transgressions of a 'rule of the judiciary'; and, finally, to discredit the judges themselves, increasingly tempted into political pronouncements that are beyond their competence.[35]

There are three further factors which serve additionally to constrain the priority given to the carrying out of party policies. The first relates to the politics of status preservation. Klaus von Beyme argues that doctors, farmers and a number of other groups are particularly firmly opposed to a change in their status and income.[36] Given the importance of the co-operative element in governmental policy, the 'politics of status preservation' acts to reduce the margin for party goals over quite a wide area.

Traditionally in West Germany there have been a number of important areas which were deliberately insulated from party politics. In particular the autonomy of the Federal Bank from party politics has been often contrasted favourably with the position of other central banks which are directly subordinate to political control. In recent years the number of partisan appointments on the Council of the Bank has risen sharply.[37] However, these appointments are unlikely to make the Bank much more amenable to party control. Of the twenty members of the Bank's council the nine Bank directors are appointed by the federal government and the eleven presidents of the state banks by the federal government on the recommendation of the Bundesrat. The addition of these eleven presidents means that it is extremely unlikely that one party will completely dominate that Bank's councils. In any case the long terms of appointment and the necessity of winning the confidence of the banking community contribute very greatly to the continued autonomy of the bank from immediate party political priorities.

A final factor that is sometimes used as an explanation in analysing why political leadership in West Germany appears to be able to allow only a low priority to party goals is the concept of liberal corporatism. Gerhard Lehmbruch defines liberal corporatism as:

> an institutionalised pattern of policy formation in which large interest organisations cooperate with each other and with public authorities not only in the articulation (or even intermediation) of interests but in its developed forms in the authoritative allocation of values and implementation of such policies.[38]

Although Austria is normally regarded as the most developed example of liberal corporatism, West Germany is often also pressed into this category. This is usually done by pointing to the *Konzertierte Aktion*, a tripartite system of consultation between the government, trade unions and employers, established in 1967. There are, however, a number of cogent arguments for not placing West Germany in the liberal corporatist category.

Firstly, *Konzertierte Aktion* was always limited in scope being confined almost exclusively to the area of income policy. As a body its deliberations had no binding force, indeed its purpose as conceived by Karl Schiller was not to act as a direct forum for wage-bargaining but for the government with the aid of macroeconomic projections to inform business and labour about the expected consequences of their own policies and about the probable results of the government's own actions.[39] The weaknesses inherent in *Konzertierte Aktion* become apparent in the widespread wildcat strikes of September 1969, since they demonstrated the possibly disruptive consequences of erroneous economic projections and the limits of autonomy of the trade union leadership from their base. The strike by ÖTV in 1974 (the first in the public service) which resulted in a wage award far above the level recommended by the Federal Government and which contributed to Brandt's resignation, seriously undermined *Konzertierte Aktion*. In 1977 the DGB withdrew from *Konzertierte Aktion* as a protest against the decision of the employers to take the codetermination law to the *Bundesverfassungsgericht*.

The rise and fall of *Konzertierte Aktion* points to the difficulty in describing West Germany as liberal corporatist. Whilst interest associations, both business and labour, are relatively highly centralised they are relatively weak in concentration. Thus the DGB has no formal authority and little real influence over the wage policies of its constituent unions. Corporatist steering is thus virtually excluded. Whilst West Germany is not an appropriate example of liberal corporatism, it is still of course true that the large and well-organised interest groups do tend to act as a constraint on the primacy of party goals since they are a crucial part of the environment that any government has to take into account.

(8) Party policies must be put into practice by the administration of government.

In relation to the United Kingdom, Richard Rose concludes that the key variable is the government itself. The Conservative Government of 1970–74 was much more successful than its Labour predecessors in office since they had worked out their legislative policies in detail and they brought into Whitehall a group of special advisers and political secretaries who had been working under the aegis of the Conservative Research Department.[40] Given the constraints already discussed, it is relatively rare for the administration to have specifically party policies to implement. In the sixth Bundestag 93 per cent of bills were passed unanimously.[41] The close identification already mentioned with the political parties does mean a responsive administration which is likely to implement policy.

Rose concludes that the obstacles to party government in Britain are very considerable and that only the third condition, the least restrictive one, is met in Britain. In West Germany the preconditions for party government look more favourable. From our discussion it is clear that conditions 2, 3, 4, 5, 6 and 8 are satisfied in West Germany but that it is extremely doubtful that conditions 1 and 7 are fulfilled. The barriers to party government do not appear to lie as in Britain in the administration, since the administration has been colonised by the political parties. They appear to reside more in the structures of the parties themselves, the key role played by administrators in the political parties and in a range of general systemic factors such as federalism and coalition government.

At this point it is relevant to return to the original question: How far is it true that public policy originates in the party nexus? Policy is clearly made by partisans in West Germany, but is it *party* policy? The picture that emerges from the case studies discussed by Braunthal and Lehmbruch suggests that it is relatively rare for party policy to be adopted as public policy. In Braunthal's account, party was most important during the period of the Grand Coalition.[42] Braunthal argues that the eight points of the coalition agreement between Brandt and Kiesinger were largely realised in the period 1966–69. Yet this conclusion does not represent a very strong argument for the primacy of party goals since 'the points' were bi-partisan and in any case were broad and declaratory. Braunthal further argues that since 1969 very few specifically SPD policies have found their way into the statute books.

In Lehmbruch's account, policy is seen typically to emerge from the interaction between interest groups and the bureaucracy.[43] A good example would be the Cartel Law of 1957 and its amendments in 1965 and 1973. The essential bargaining during the preparation of the Bill took place between the administration and business representatives largely outside the party system. More specifically, it can be argued, Lehmbruch's example shows the difficulty that a political party with a specific policy (in the case of the 1976 Codetermination Law the SPD) has in securing its adoption. In order to ensure the passage of the Bill, major concessions had to be made to the FDP and the form of the law was also severely constrained by the anticipated reaction of the *Bundesverfassungsgericht*.

CONCLUSION

There is no crisis of 'party government' in the Federal Republic in the sense that some commentators have asserted to be true of Britain.[44] There are, however, several problems associated with the practice of party government in its West German form. The problems posed for government are not acute. The degree to which the civil service is no longer 'neutral' makes alternation to that extent more difficult. There were a number of problems in 1969 and it is likely that the accession of a CDU/CSU government, after a long period of SPD/FDP administration, would bring with it personnel problems for the CDU/CSU.

The accommodation between the political parties and the state represented by the adoption of the concept of the *Volkspartei* and the increased participation of *Beamte* in the political parties has resulted in a reduced emphasis of the role of party in an emancipatory and participatory sense. This means that despite the degree to which the West German system meets many more of Rose's conditions than does the British system, the chances of changing the political priorities of the system in a major way through participation in a political party are at least no higher and probably lower than in the United Kingdom. The development potentially delegitimises the representative system for many of the intelligent and critical youth who, disillusioned by the results of participation in established political parties, seek solace in *Bürgerinitiativen* and fringe movements of all kinds.[45] This tendency is particularly disappointing to SPD leaders who, like Brandt, were proud of the extent to which they had been able to integrate an earlier generation of critical youth after the collapse of the APO in 1969.

NOTES

The author would like to thank the Nuffield Foundation for help in connection with research for this article.

1. Richard Rose, *The Problem of Party Government* (London, 1976), Penguin edition. Anthony King, 'Political Parties in Western Democracies', *Polity* (1969), pp. 112–41.
2. Gordon Smith, *Democracy in Western Germany: Parties and Politics in the Federal Republic* (London, 1979). Kenneth Dyson, *Party, State and Bureaucracy in Western Germany* (London, 1977).
3. Gerhard Leibholz, *Strukturprobleme der modernen Demokratie* (Karlsruhe, 1967). Wilhelm Hennis, *Verfassung und Verfassungswirklichkeit. Ein deutsches Problem* (Tübingen, 1968). Gerhard Lehmbruch, 'Liberal Corporatism and Party Government', *Comparative Political Studies* (April 1977)

pp. 91–126. Udo Bermbach, 'Probleme des Parteienstaates: Der Fall Littmann', *Zeitschrift für Parlamentsfragen* (October 1970) pp. 342–63. Peter Haungs, 'Die Bundesrepublik – ein Parteienstaat? Kritische Anmerkungen zu einem wissenschaftlichen Mythos', *Zeitschrift für Parlamentsfragen* No. 4 (December 1973), pp. 505–25.

4. Haungs, *op. cit.*, p. 521.
5. Rose, *op. cit.*, pp. xv–xxxii.
6. I. Crewe, J. Alt and B. Särlvik, 'The Erosion of Partisanship 1964–75' (paper presented to the PSA Conference, Nottingham, 1976).
7. D. Calleo, *The German Problem Reconsidered: Germany and the World Order 1870 to the Present* (Cambridge, 1978) p. 207.
8. Gordon Smith, *'The Party Tradition in Germany and the Contemporary Party State'* (ASGP Conference, Loughborough, 1976).
9. *Ibid.*, p. 2.
10. Rose, *op. cit.*, pp. 372–5.
11. Klaus von Beyme, 'The Politics of Limited Pluralism: The Case of West Germany', *Government and Opposition* (1978) pp. 263–87.
12. Otto Kirchheimer, 'Der Wandel des westeuropäischen Parteiensystems', *Politische Vierteljahresschrift* (1965) pp. 20 ff.
13. Cited by Otto Kirchheimer in R. Dahl, *Political Oppositions in Western Democracies* (Yale, Newhaven, 1966) p. 242.
14. *Ibid.*, pp. 246–7.
15. See John Herz, 'Social Democracy versus Democratic Socialism. An Analysis of SPD Attempts to Develop a Party Doctrine', in Bernard E. Brown (ed.), *Eurocommunism and Eurosocialism* (New York, 1979) pp. 246–83.
16. See Eckhardt Barthel, 'Verwaltung und Partei – wer bestimmt wen?' *Die Neue Gesellschaft*, No. 12 (1978) pp. 998–9.
17. W. E. Paterson, *Political Parties and the Making of Foreign Policy: The Case of the Federal Republic* (PSA Conference, Exeter, April 1980).
18. Hans Daalder, in his article 'Parties, Elites and Developments in Western Europe', in Joseph La Palombara and Myron Weiner (eds), *Political Parties and Political Development* (Princeton, 1969) p. 75.
19. Dyson, *op. cit., passim.* Bärbel Steinkemper, *'Klassische und politische Bürokraten in der Ministerialverwaltung der Bundesrepublik Deutschland'* (Cologne, 1974).
20. Steinkemper, *op. cit.*, p. 47.
21. *Ibid.*, p. 53.
22. Rose, *op. cit.*, p. 394.
23. See especially work by K. H. F. Dyson, also his article, 'The Ambiguous Politics of Western Germany: Politicization in a State Society', *European Journal of Political Research*, No. 7, 1979, pp. 375–96.
24. Rose, *op. cit.*, p. 399.
25. Dyson, *art. cit., European Journal of Political Research*, p. 383.
26. W. E. Paterson, 'The German Social Democratic Party', in Paterson and Thomas (eds), *Social Democratic Parties in Western Europe* (London, 1977).
27. Cited in G. Braunthal, 'The Policy Function of the German Social Democratic Party', *Comparative Politics* (July 1977) p. 142.
28. *Ibid.*, p. 142.
29. Table in Hans Kremendahl, *Vertrauenskrise der Parteien* (Berlin, 1978) p. 59.

30. Dyson, *Party, State . . .*, p. 45.
31. *Ibid.*, pp. 11–15.
32. Barthel, *op. cit.* W. D. Narr, H. Scheer and D. Spöri, *SPD, Staatspartei oder Reformpartei?* (Munich, 1976).
33. Apel, *op. cit.*, p. 339.
34. Klaus von Beyme, 'The Changing Relations between Trade Unions and the German Social Democratic Party', *Government and Opposition* (1978) p. 401.
35. Richard Löwenthal, 'Why German Stability is so Insecure', *Encounter* (December 1978) pp. 31–7.
36. Beyme, *op. cit.*, p. 412.
37. Dyson, *art. cit.*, *European Journal of Political Research* pp. 388–90.
38. Lehmbruch, *op. cit.*, p. 94.
39. Gerhard Lehmbruch, *Social Partnership in West Germany* (ASGP Conference, Liverpool, 1979).
40. Rose, *op. cit.*, pp. 411–12.
41. K. von Beyme, *Das politische System der Bundesrepublik Deutschland* (Munich, 1979) p. 163.
42. Braunthal, *op. cit., passim.*
43. Lehmbruch, *op. cit.*, pp. 117–20.
44. Nevil Johnson, *Die englische Krankheit* (Stuttgart, 1977).
45. For criticism of the political parties, particularly the SPD from this perspective, see especially H. Scheer, *Parteien kontra Bürger? – Die Zukunft der Parteiendemokratie* (Munich, 1979).

7 Institutional Structures and Political Culture

M. RAINER LEPSIUS

Both within and outside Western Germany the apparent stability of her political system is sometimes called into question. The doubts raised refer primarily to whether there is a reliable political culture, a firm value orientation which would safeguard the democratic regime in time of crisis. Has the stability of the political system over the past thirty years only been the result of favourable conditions? Does it rest solely on sustained economic growth, on performance rather than on commitment? Is the Federal Republic only a fair-weather democracy?

Such doubts are substantiated by the sudden breakdown of the Weimar Republic, by the Nazi period, or, in pointing to more recent events, by the operation of the *Radikalenerlass*, the enforced exclusion of Leftists from the civil service and the extension of surveillance in connection with terrorism. The problem of national identity in a divided country is also used to create uncertainty about the reliability of the democratic and Western orientation of the Federal Republic.

Political culture, however, is not only the product of inter-generationally transmitted values, of socialisation into patterned belief systems. Political culture also operates within an institutional structure and develops in accord with experience of such institutions. The structure and performance of political institutions exercise an influence upon the political culture, just as political culture influences the character and functioning of institutions. There is an interdependence between the two: value orientations do not develop in empty space, nor can institutions be sustained without legitimising commitments. We have to assume a circular movement between political culture and political institutions, even if it appears difficult to attribute causal priority to one or the other.

In the case of Western Germany, the inauguration of new political institutions in the formative years between 1946 and 1952 gave the institutions a lead in the development of a new political culture. This is not surprising: the development and socialisation of value orientations take longer than the design and the establishment of institutional structures. On the assumption that for Western Germany the success of the institutional structure has contributed to a specific political culture, the following analysis elaborates some interrelations between political institutions and political culture. This perspective is deliberately one-sided, and it should be clearly understood that the approach does not imply an under-estimation of the importance and the impact of belief systems and internalised value commitments for a political culture. The following comments are deliberately tentative; they aim to develop a general perspective rather than to present a rigorous analysis. For the latter it would be necessary to enter into much greater detail and much more explicitly to attribute implications of the institutional properties for political culture than can possibly be achieved in a preliminary account.

PARTY SYSTEM AND COMPETITIVE CENTRISM

The development of the parties in the Federal Republic led to a three-party system. The major innovation was the creation of the CDU which succeeded in integrating former parties – Catholic, Protestant-conservative, and middle-class parties – into one political organisation. The second important factor was the inability of the Communist Party to establish itself as a substantial part of the political system after 1946. The anti-Communist sentiments in the population, constantly kept alive by the actions of the Russians in their occupation zone and the legal discrimination against Communists in Western Germany, prevented the re-emergence of a Communist vote which, in the Weimar Republic, had averaged 12 per cent at Reichstag elections.

The party system therefore includes neither the authoritarian Right nor a Communist Left in opposition to the democratic parliamentary regime of the Federal Republic. All components of the party system are in principle able to co-operate, whether in opposition or by forming coalitions. The permanent exclusion of a substantive disloyal opposition of the Left or the Right means that there are no restrictions placed on the parties. This fact not only allows the formation of alternating governments without endangering the stability of the political regime, it also forces the parties to aim at winning a majority at elections and that means to enlist the support of voters outside the traditional *milieux* of the respective parties and their mobilising and socialising agencies.

This situation should be underlined in contrast to the position in the Weimar Republic. From 1890 onwards the parties in Germany had been oriented towards mobilising a specific sociocultural *milieu* and defending its boundaries. Such a party system leads to an institutionally induced prolongation of social cleavages and a tendency to dramatise specific values in order to integrate sociocultural *milieux* symbolically.[1] A fragmented party system continuously produces specific political cultures and seeks to distinguish supreme value syndromes. Any form of political action, however, is an attempt to integrate ultimate values into pragmatic decisions. If this task is left to the government, the level of integration is too high to produce a political culture which is prepared to accept pragmatism and the need for compromise between contradictory ultimate values.

Furthermore, if the parties are not in a position to integrate specific sociopolitical values within their own organisations, they will face a need to construct an overriding value syndrome on the basis of which they will be able to compromise whenever they have to form a coalition. This overriding value was German nationalism, a source of legitimation for very divergent political actions. In passing, it may be surmised that the rapid success of the nationalistic propaganda of National Socialism after 1930 was related to the fact that, with the disintegration of the traditional party system and the increasing orientation of the parties towards the particularities of their respective *milieux*, nationalism was set free to become the supreme legitimising value syndrome of the Nazis, with the aid of which they could enlist support from very different social *milieux* with heterogeneous interests.[2]

The overcoming of the traditional sociocultural boundaries between Protestant and Catholic Germany, the labour movement and the bourgeois camp by the CDU and the SPD, the latter through the adoption of the Godesberg Programme in 1959, was the precondition in post-war Germany for the development of a *general* political culture, one penetrating different sociocultural *milieux*.[3] The normative core of this political culture, as expressed by the parties, is related to the Basic Law, and it can be formulated still in very much the same terms. Today, the parties are the main agencies for the integration of divergent values into political action. As this function is no longer left to the government, there is no need for a dramatised ultimate value 'above the parties', namely nationalism. The political process is perceived as a legitimate compromise, not as a clever – however dirty – game of value-unrelated action that is only *ex post facto* legitimised by its success, an attitude formerly enjoying considerable support among the Protestant middle classes. The development of the so-called catch-all parties has contributed to the decline of two properties of the traditional German political culture: nationalism and *Realpolitik* – right or wrong. The parties present themselves as centrist and they act in a centrist manner. The latter feature is induced by the fact that all parties participate in the legislation and administration of the Federal Republic, regardless of whether they win a national majority or not. The need for co-operation between majority and minority parties is institutionalised by the federal structure of the political system. No party can play at an all-out opposition, nor can it practise an exclusion of the opposition. The *Länder*, with different parties forming the individual governments, have a monopoly of administration, and – by means of the Bundesrat – the possibility of participation in federal legislation. Even when the minority in the Bundestag does not control a majority in the Bundesrat, the party that is in a national minority still retains a substantial influence on the political process through its control of a number of *Länder* governments.

Discontent with the catch-all parties is evinced primarily by the well-educated and politically most involved part of the population, that section which is at the same time relatively secure in its economic position and social influence. Intellectuals, particularly students, have been demanding real alternatives between the parties since the 1960s, advocating long-term programmes for the reconstruction of society. However, the issues on which the intellectuals proposed alternatives tended to be selective: educational reform, ecological awareness, equality for women, policies for minorities.[4] These issues do not affect the general institutional structure of the political system, the consensual orientation towards external and internal security, and economic stability. The rapport between dissenting intellectual minorities and the general population is limited; instead, their influence depends upon their cause being adopted by the parties, and the parties have been successful in integrating a substantial section of the dissenting intellectuals. This process of integration does cause stormy debates within the parties, as has been evident for the SPD in recent years. Since the margins of victory are fairly narrow on a federal level, as well as in some *Länder* and local communities, extreme positions taken by a party are liable to result in an immediate loss of general electoral support.[5] Centrism is therefore institutionally induced and sanctioned by electoral results.

The centrist political culture of the parties has been very successfully transmitted to the population at large. At national elections the established parties have been able to enlist the support of 80–90 per cent of the total electorate. If only the turnout is taken into consideration, then between 95 and 99 per cent of the voters are integrated into the three established parties. The level of this aggregation undoubtedly proves the ability of the party system to win legitimacy and to promote a centrist and general political culture in the people.

Yet the parties operate in a highly competitive field. Small changes in voting behaviour define and alter the chances of winning. As a consequence, a strong rhetoric of conflict is maintained between the parties, and that may sometimes produce an impression of a dissent over values. This 'rhetoric of conflict' is conducted by the established elites – precisely those which at the same time are co-operating in the legislation and administration of the Federal Republic. They are interrelated by the procedures of institutionalised conflict resolution and by a general consensus on these procedures. The conflictual atmosphere is integral to competitive centrism and does not lead to a differentiation of the general political culture into contradictory or exclusive sub-cultures.[6] Competition forces the parties towards centrist behaviour and also to the integration of minorities. Both effects have contributed to bridging traditionally different political cultures to form the normative core of a general political culture, and that becomes institutionalised in the party system and structures the actions of the political elites.

FEDERALISM AND CO-OPERATIVE DIFFERENTIATION

The federal structure of the constitution has developed into a general pattern of organisational differentiation for all political institutions. The relative autonomy of the German *Länder* as political entities constitutes the core of the federal structure. According to the Basic Law, the *Länder* are the bearers of administrative authority on which the Federation has to rely – with the major exceptions of the foreign service, the military and the federal police forces. The administrative monopoly of the *Länder* leads to an organisational differentiation in which the intermediate level between the local and national levels has a powerful, ultimate authority. The regional level thus retains a focus of co-ordination, dependence and interest integration within the otherwise highly centralised political–organisational pattern of the Federal Republic.

The second element in German federalism is related to the firm position of the *Länder* in the legislative process, even when – as has been the case in the past decade – the legislation of the Federation has become increasingly decisive. Revenue-sharing on a co-operative basis may have diminished the legislative importance of the *Länder* assemblies, but it has enhanced the control capacity of *Länder* governments and administration, for they can now influence the general political direction through the growing number of planning and coordinating joint bodies, the *Bund–Länder Kommissionen*.[7]

This all leads to a situation in which the differences between regions in economic, cultural and traditional aspects are declining, while the regions as political units retain their competence and power in the political process. They serve as lower-level organisational units for the formation and articulation of interests. This function can be seen most clearly in the case of the Bavarian CSU. The specific role played by the CSU is not so much the result of some special Bavarian regionalism, but rather the opportunity it gives for an independent unit to gain sufficient veto power to influence the policy of the national CDU organisation. In all probability the Federal Republic has less regional inequality than other large West European states, but at the same time its federal structure gives its regional units a greater weight in the decision-making process than is the case for other countries in Western Europe.

The federal principle has become the universal pattern of organisational differentiation. It is not only the existence of the *Länder* – the parties are also organised on a regional basis, and so are the trade unions, the interest groups, and the radio and television networks. The regional differentiation of central institutions is more than an organisational pattern for administrative purposes, it is the basis for the establishment of relatively autonomous units below the national level, which together determine national decisions, counteracting the centres and integrating the peripheries. Symbolically, this structure is well represented by the fact that the Federal Republic has no national centre, no dominating metropolitan area and capital. The allocation of power is dispersed to many cities throughout the country. There is no London or Paris, there is not even a 'double capital', like Rome and Milan, or Madrid and Barcelona. The dispersion of institutional and regional power and influence has a specific effect on the political culture of the country: neither institutionally nor territorially is there a dominating centre, and in consequence there is no antagonism between centre and periphery. The strength of the centre rests upon the co-operation of relatively autonomous regional units: the administration, the parties, the unions and the interest groups.

INDUSTRIAL RELATIONS AND MULTIPLE-INTEREST INTERMEDIATION

One of the basic institutional innovations of the Federal Republic is the system of industrial relations, as it was established in the early 1950s and since further developed.[8] In the present context it is not possible to describe this elaborate system in detail. However, some properties can be specified which may be considered influential for the political culture in respect of the institutionalisation of industrial conflict in the Federal Republic.

Firstly, the high degree of interest aggregation has to be taken into account. Trade union structure is based on the principles of the industrial union and that means that a few unions possess an organisational monopoly in specified occupational fields. With the exception of the clerical workers' union, the *Angestellten Gewerkschaft*, usually there is only one member union of the *Deutscher Gewerkschaftsbund* operating in any one firm. This frees the unions from boundary conflicts and inter-union competition and allows them to concentrate on the interests of all employees in an entire segment of the occupational structure, rather than on the specific interests of particular occupations or local groups. Structurally, the unions are in a position to aggregate employee interests at a high level. This ability is reinforced by the system of collective bargaining with its wage/tariff agreements. The negotiations for the *Tarifvertrag* are conducted by a restricted number of authorised bodies, *tariffähige Verbände*, namely the unions and employers' associations. Collective bargaining takes place at an advanced level of organised interest formation and is focused on the economic situation of an entire sector within a defined region, for which the bargaining agencies have competence to conclude wage and other agreements. The high level of interest aggregation results from the internal structure of the organisation of the unions and employers' associations as well as from the boundaries of jurisdiction of the *Tarifvertrag*. What is often considered as the 'responsible attitude' of the German unions – or from a Marxist perspective, the lack of an aggressive class consciousness of the unions – is due to the fact that the 'action space' of the unions is structured by the role they have to assume in free, collective bargaining, within the *Tarifautonomie*, and the need to act at a level of decision-making where the general economic performance of society has to be taken into consideration.

Secondly, the nature of the *Tarifautonomie* induces a process of self-legitimation in industrial relations by the union and the relevant employers' association. As their agreement is a contract similar to any other contract between private parties, it can come about only with the consent of both parties. There are no provisions for compulsory settlement by the government or the courts to which the unions or the employers' associations could delegate responsibility for a *Tarifvertrag*. They have to assume full responsibility.[9] The content of agreements has to be legitimised by the contracting partners and is sanctioned as any other contract by private law and the courts. The breaking of a contract can be penalised by the award of high damages, so that, as long as they are in force, contracts are very stable. In such a situation, the unions and the employers' associations have to rely upon one another, and each is legitimising the other as the only available partner. The exclusion of state intervention and state responsibility places the unions and employers' associations in an arena of ultimate decision-making competence, mutual acceptance, and public accountability.

Below the level of the *Tarifvertrag*, interest intermediation takes place within firms through the institution of codetermination (*Mitbestimmung*) and on the factory level (*Betriebsverfassung*) through the workers' councils. All three levels are well institutionalised, while two other possible levels are not utilised for interest intermediation, namely the lowest level of the workshop/department and the highest level of the state. The institutionalisation of interest intermediation on the three levels leads to a differentiation of competence and to a high degree of specificity of issues for each arena. At the factory level, the emphasis is placed on the conditions of work and employment, while 'economic' questions are not subject to negotiation. At the company level, the focus is on the general economic performance of the firm, not on the grievances of the employed. The high degree of interest aggregation is thereby supplemented by the separation of specified issues which are negotiated at intermediate levels. Such a system is likely to produce a pragmatic and issue-oriented attitude towards industrial conflict. However, there has to be a flexibility between the levels in order to facilitate the transfer of an issue from one arena to another until it becomes adequately defined and negotiable. This elasticity has to be provided by the unions and employers, reinforcing their instrumental and pragmatic attitudes. What is considered to be the relative stability of German industrial relations is to a large degree defined by the institutionalisation of multiple-interest intermediation mechanisms.

This system employs a variety of organisational principles. At the factory level the *Betriebsrat* in its negotiations with management is restricted to using its legal power of veto in matters of employment. The parity of representation at the level of codetermination calls for a consensual agreement on policy questions affecting the firm. It is only at the level of collective bargaining in relation to the *Tarifvertrag* that conflict resolution can take the form of an open struggle, with the unions having the right to call a strike and the employers' associations able to use the weapon of the lock-out. The ultimate sanctions of power are located at the highest level of interest intermediation and are subject to formalised procedures to ensure an internal legitimation for their application. The unions are required to obtain a positive vote from their members (*Urabstimmung*) before calling a strike. This requirement gives the top management of the organisations (unions and employers) a monopoly in the use of ultimate means, but it binds their competence to the consent of their respective memberships. A comparatively low propensity to strike is the result of the specific institutionalisation of industrial relations. The means of enforcing interest intermediation are heterogeneous, and the possible course of action within each arena of action is related to the methods available. Collective bargaining is structured by the power relations between the unions and employers; codetermination rests on the parity of representation in decision-making; the workers' councils rely upon a legally defined veto power. Differentiation of arenas, definitions of competence, and a heterogeneity of procedures characterise the system of industrial relations which is further structured by an elaborate labour law with the provision of special courts.

Other fields of interest intermediation are not differentially institutionalised to an equal degree. However, the general pattern is one of a high level of interest aggregation on the part of interest groups and, at the same time, a differentiation of arenas. The pattern of multiple-interest intermediation is structured both by the need to win support from the catch-all parties to gain access to legislation and by the differentiation of administrative competence between the federal and *Länder* governments. Besides legislation and administration, the accessibility of the courts opens up the judicial arena as a third mechanism for interest intermediation. All regulations of matters relating to wages are the result of bargaining processes carried on between countervailing groups. High interest aggregation and differentiation of arenas of interest intermediation bring about a situation in which conflicts are likely to become specified and instrumentalised rather than to accumulate and to remain diffuse. Political culture is influenced by the regulatory capacity of the system of conflict resolution and the instrumental skill in making use of its procedures rather than by the dramatisation of values and demonstrations of collective power.

LEGALISM AND NORMATIVE INTEGRATION

The German political style is legalistic and influenced by normative standards as they are defined by the judiciary.[10] This is caused by the high value attributed to the *Rechtsstaat* and by the capacity of the judiciary to control public administration (*Rechtsmittelstaat*) as well as legislation (*Verfassungsgerichtsbarkeit*). The courts of administrative law are in a strong position to inhibit administrative action. Individuals or groups of individuals, in so far as they are adversely affected by administrative actions, can use the courts to overrule the administration. This power is intended to secure the individual rights of the citizen, but it also serves to influence the legislative and administrative authorities to act in a highly legalistic manner so as to avoid judicial intervention. There is a tendency towards a circular stimulation: the more that acts of the administration can be inhibited by judicial action, the more the administration calls for explicit regulations, and the greater will be the number of detailed laws.

The outcome of such a circular process of legalism is apparent in the case of the *Radikalenerlass*. The exclusion of Communists and other radicals from sensitive positions in the public service has been organised in such a way that any person whose application for a public-service appointment has been rejected has to be given the reasons for not being employed. The affected person can turn to the courts of administrative law and have the case re-examined. The courts ask for evidence of the alleged radicalism, and that in turn has to be supplied by the authorities. This procedure leads to the development of a practice of surveillance which now extends beyond a reasonable limit, the more so as an application for *any* position in the public service has to be included on the principle of equal treatment.

There are a number of other examples of the unintended consequences of the *Rechtsmittelstaat*. With the need to limit the access of students to certain disciplines in universities, medicine for example, rulings of the courts have stipulated that before any applicant can be turned down by a university, evidence must be presented that the capacity of that university in a particular field of study is exhausted. To present such evidence, a large number of regulations concerning the teaching load, the number of compulsory courses and the number of students per course were enacted. An enormous bureaucratisation of the universities took place in order to provide the state administration with evidence that could be used in legal proceedings. The tendency for individuals to make use of the courts is facilitated by their high accessibility. The more people are willing to go to court, the more the judiciary becomes involved in the mediation between individual interests and the public administration, and in consequence the more legalistic the administration becomes.

The establishment of a supreme court of constitutional law (*Bundesverfassungsgericht*) was certainly one of the major institutional inventions of the Federal Republic.[11] Its influence upon the political culture of elites and also on the perception of the political process by the general public has been considerable. The strong position of the *Bundesverfassungsgericht* allows it to overrule the legislation of Parliament, and furthermore, as has become evident in recent years, the Court has established criteria which act to pre-define the legislative process. This has led to a tendency to put nearly all major pieces of legislation before the Constitutional Court to be judicially approved, interpreted, partially revised, or annulled. The *Grundlagenvertrag* between the two German states, the legislation on abortion, codetermination, university organisation, political parties, control of television networks and many other issues have been directly or indirectly affected by the rulings of the Constitutional Court. The possibility that the Court may be called upon to rule on any piece of legislation has strengthened an awareness of the need to achieve a formal compatibility of legislation with the principles of the Basic Law as interpreted by the Court. This 'anticipated orientation' towards possible intervention by the Court has dramatised the key role of legal criteria for all legislation. There is a second tendency connected with the impact of constitutional jurisdiction (*Verfassungsgerichtsbarkeit*), namely to shift controversies from the political to the judicial arena and to use rulings of the courts as the criteria for political consensus. The old formula, *Roma locuta causa finita* can be applied: if the Constitutional Court has given its ruling, the issue is closed.

There is a long tradition in German political culture to regard the judicial ethos of *Rechtsstaatlichkeit* as a substitute for democracy. Even today, *Rechtsstaatlichkeit* and the judicial interpretation of the constitution is ultimately placed higher than democratic decisions. The constitution as interpreted by the rulings of the Constitutional Court is the core of the normative integration of German politics. Legal criteria are ultimately the dominant ones for decision-making, as well as for the legitimacy of the content of legislation. Political action is bound by the law, and the constitution provides the normative base on which legislation has to be judged.

CONFLICT RHETORIC AND THE CRITIQUE OF VALUES

This attempt to single out some properties of the institutional structure of the Federal Republic has concentrated on new elements that developed after 1945: the party system, federalism, the system of industrial relations, the supreme court of constitutional law. There are, of course, other elements, but the four mentioned here have had a decisive influence on the political orientation of the elites. German political institutions have a tendency to bring together all political elites into an elaborate mechanism of co-operation in differentiated arenas of political action and to give them a common orientation on the legally sanctioned procedures of interest intermediation. Competitiveness of the pluralistic elites is induced by the struggle for votes or for shares of the national product. The institutional setting encourages an instrumental attitude with a strong consensus on procedures, and it discourages the dramatisation of cleavages and value antagonisms. It is the constitution which provides the framework and the legitimation for the necessary value compromises. It is the competition between the elites which gives rise to the rhetoric of conflict in making use of traditional value cleavages. This conflictual style is particularly employed to mobilise the population before elections, in the course of labour disputes, and on issues of moral conviction. But this mode of conflict only peripherally touches on the institutional setting itself. That setting symbolises the underlying consensus on the basic political order.

A more fundamental critique of the values of the political system of the Federal Republic is voiced by those elites that do not participate in the institutionalised political process. They are primarily intellectuals who are able to homogenise their convictions on ultimate goals and who are not forced to take pragmatic action or to seek compromises. There are three main sources of the radical critique of values, all in a long tradition and in themselves highly respectable and related to the values expressed by the constitution. The first stresses the value of equality and becomes politically relevant in the critique of capitalism. The emergence of neo-Marxism of all kinds has accentuated this fundamental criticism. The second stresses individual freedom and becomes politically relevant in the critique of bureaucratic institutionalism. It has given rise to the *Bürgerinitiativen* and the protest potential against city planning and nuclear power as well as in ecological questions and other civic issues. The third stresses the need for a moral identity and becomes politicised in the critique of the retreat of the state from legally enforcing moral standards and licensing pluralistic values. They argue that there is a tendency for a general decline in morality and evidence of a *Kulturverfall*. There are many shades and combinations of these three sources of the critique of values. Most important has been the old Protestant fundamentalism with its deep suspicion of institutions. From time to time it forms coalitions with old socialist anti-capitalism and pacifism. This pattern has been evident from the early years of the Federal Republic, then focused on the struggle against rearmament, and today in the campaign against nuclear energy.

The radical critique of the values of the political system serves as a counterpart to the institutionalised value compromise of the established elites. It is in this respect more of a corrective than a delegitimation of the political order. At the present time a larger section of young people are retreating from the established order and are searching for alternative cultures. They demonstrate this general 'ideal drift' in the perception and evaluation of political institutions.

The new elements of the political culture of the Federal Republic – the acceptance of institutionalised compromise and legitimised interest intermediation – have continuously to be transmitted to new generations that have not shared the experience of National Socialism and the post-war reconstruction period. Both periods are no longer points of reference to evaluate the present state of society, and they no longer serve to legitimate the political order as was the case for the older generations. The perceived deficiencies of society and the political system are directly related to the institutions of the Federal Republic which for the younger generation therefore appears to look more deficient now than it did formerly for older generations. The standards of evaluation are changing with the change of generations.[12]

Yet as long as the ethic of conviction (*Gesinnungsethik*) of the critical intellectuals remains in an equilibrium with the ethics of responsibility (*Verantwortungsethik*) of the political elites and both control each other, the radical critique of values increases the awareness of the deficiencies of the political and social order and contributes to the innovative capacity. The institutional order places the political elites in a strong position to uphold a political culture that accepts the heteronomy of values in a democratic society, values which rest in the conviction that the procedures of democratic rule are the foundation for the pursuit of individual freedom. The success of the institutional order of the Federal Republic over the past thirty years has by now created a tradition which, short as it is, has provided legitimised standards for a democratic political culture which is increasingly in line with the political culture of the traditional democracies.[13] Present strains within the institutional order and divergencies in value orientations in the Federal Republic resemble those evident in other Western democracies.

NOTES AND REFERENCES

1. Among many other references: M. R. Lepsius, 'Parteiensystem und Sozialstruktur: zum Problem der Demokratisierung der deutschen Gesellschaft', in G. A. Ritter (ed.), *Die deutschen Parteien vor 1918* (Cologne, 1973); and E. Matthias and R. Morsey (ed.), *Das Ende der Parteien 1933* (Düsseldorf, 1960).
2. M. R. Lepsius, *Extremer Nationalismus* (Stuttgart, 1966).
3. For a comprehensive presentation of the German party structure see H. Kaack, *Geschichte und Struktur des deutschen Parteiensystems* (Opladen, 1971); J. Dittberner and R. Ebbighausen (ed.), *Parteiensystem in der Legitimationskrise* (Opladen, 1973); also: G. Pridham, *Christian Democracy in Western Germany* (London, 1977); H. K. Schellenger, *The SPD in Bonn, A Socialist Party Modernises* (The Hague, 1968).
4. Long before the student movement, established intellectuals were calling for a fundamental reform of the educational system, see G. Picht, *Die deutsche*

Bildungskatastrophe (Munich, 1964), and the first major intellectual effort of the SDS, the motor of the early student movement, was concerned with the university reform. This and other reform proposals take the basic qualities of the political system for granted. The position of the established parties was never seriously challenged, neither by the *Gesamtdeutsche Volkspartei* (GVP) nor by the *Nationaldemokratische Partei* (NPD) nor will it be challenged by the new Party, *Die Grünen*.

5. Clearly to be seen in local elections as for the city councils in Munich or Frankfurt, where long-standing SPD majorities were lost after prolonged ideological controversies in the local SPD.

6. In recent years this was attempted with slogans like '*Freiheit oder Sozialismus*' or '*Abbau des Sozialstaates*'. Usually such slogans are shortlived and forgotten immediately after a campaign.

7. Among many books on German federalism see N. Johnson, *Government in the Federal Republic of Germany: The Executive at Work* (Oxford, 1973); F. Scharpf, B. Reisert and F. Schnabel (eds), *Politikverflechtung: Theorie und Empirie des kooperativen Föderalismus in der Bundesrepublik* (Kronberg, 1976).

8. A short overview is provided by W. Kendall, *The Labour Movement in Europe* (London, 1975); see also K. von Beyme, *Gewerkschaften und Arbeitsbeziehungen in kapitalistischen Ländern* (Munich, 1977).

9. For a more detailed analysis see H. Weitbrecht, *Effektivität und Legitimität der Tarifautonomie* (Berlin, 1969).

10. G. Schram, 'Ideology and Politics: The *Rechtsstaat* Idea in West Germany', *Journal of Politics*, 33 (1971). K. Dyson, 'The Ambiguous Politics of Western Germany: Politicization in a "State" Society', *European Journal of Political Research*, 7 (1979).

11. D. P. Kommers, *Judicial Politics in West Germany: A Study of the Federal Constitutional Court* (Beverly Hills–London, 1976).

12. While in the 1950s the entire adult population had been socialised under the impact of the Nazi period and the war, and the Weimar Republic remained a personally experienced reference-point for about two-thirds, in the 1970s this generation was shrinking and today comprises only one-half of the adult population of the Federal Republic.

13. See the data in S. H. Barnes, M. Kaase *et al.*, *Political Action, Mass Participation in Five Western Democracies* (Beverly Hills–London, 1979).

8 The Government/Opposition Dimension and the Development of the Party System in the 1970s:
The Reappearance of Conflictual Politics

GEOFFREY PRIDHAM

THE 'VANISHING' KIRCHHEIMER THESIS

The decade of the 1970s witnessed a qualitative change in the nature and conduct of the Opposition role in the German Federal Republic arising out of the bi-polar development of the party system. This change was inaugurated by the intensification of Government/Opposition conflict after the abrupt ending to the Grand Coalition and the 'change of power' in 1969, and has disproved many of the assumptions or fears of the 1960s about the decline of conflictual politics in West Germany. In particular, Kirchheimer's thesis of the 'vanishing opposition' failed to carry conviction as a full-scale interpretation of party development within a few years of its appearance in the mid-1960s, for while a fair description of immediate or past events it did not take sufficient account of political determinants deriving from the dynamics of the party system, especially the course of individual parties and their interrelationships.[1]

Kirchheimer writing in 1965 highlighted several features of West German politics relevant to the then current performance and perception of the Opposition role – the influence of traditional German concepts about the position of the state as above partisan allegiance and historically conditioned reservations about the possibility of 'loyal opposition', parliamentary institutional requirements favouring bargaining-type politics, the reduction of competitive space through welfare-state management and the uncomfortable presence of the political neighbour, the DDR, as a disincentive to any form of 'principled opposition' within the Federal Republic, at least from the Left – but he over-emphasised the co-operative aspects of the Opposition somewhat to the exclusion of its competitive ones. This was of course a true reflection of the immediate situation as of the mid-1960s in the light of certain historical factors, but Kirchheimer's thesis lacks comprehensiveness as a long-term interpretation of both the overall and further development of the West German party system. The trend of events in the 1970s has therefore countered his hypothesis, but how does this relate to the different trend of the 1960s when measured together within the whole framework of party development since the end of the Second World War? Is it at all possible that the trend of the 1980s might see a reappearance of patterns of behaviour supporting convergence rather than divergence in party interrelationships, or rather not? This study, while focusing on the Government/ Opposition dimension during the course of the 1970s, also seeks to draw some broader conclusions about its importance with respect to the West German party system.

The key to understanding this problem is to view forms of Opposition as relatives rather than as absolutes. For the purposes of this discussion it is necessary to define the terms employed, as sometimes these have been confusingly applied in the literature on the subject. 'Principled opposition' refers generally to that which is against the established political system, or as Kirchheimer writes, it 'indicates the desire for a degree of goal displacement incompatible with the constitutional requirements of a given system'. This may operate both through parliament (as shown by the Weimar experience) or outside it in the form of extraparliamentary movements or parties of fundamental protest. The Federal Republic has experienced little such 'principled opposition', for in so far as this is identified conventionally with the extreme Right and extreme Left the former has suffered from the negative memory of the Third Reich and the latter from the impact of the Cold War and the security threat from the Eastern bloc. Less conventional or partial forms of 'principled opposition' did, however, emerge at the start and finish of the third decade of the Federal Republic – the New Left student radical protest of 1968 (known as the APO or Extra-Parliamentary Opposition) which was anti-authoritarian in outlook and involved an attempt to re-ideologise German politics, and the environmentally conscious ecologists who appeared in the late 1970s and, drawing on popular discontent with the established parties, called into question official assumptions about the need for economic growth. This study concentrates on the nature of Opposition in the parliamentary arena because that was the dominant focal point for party competition, and only includes mention of extra-parliamentary features where these have conditioned the behaviour of the dominant parties. Thus, the SPD managed successfully to absorb after 1969 much of the activist body of the APO so far as it remained in politics, while in the early 1970s the new CDU/CSU Opposition attracted the greater part of voting support for the neo-Nazi NPD which had enjoyed a temporary rise during 1966–68. Both developments reinforced the bi-polar trend and in effect encouraged inter-party conflictual behaviour. The ecologist challenge is more diffuse in ideological terms, and consequently complicates possible responses by the main parties.

When looking at 'loyal' or system-supporting Opposition in West Germany, which is the subject of this discussion, the most valid analytical distinction is between 'competitive' and 'co-operative' Opposition. However, two qualifying points must be made which underline in political practice their relative application. Firstly, while the distinction between competitive and co-operative Opposition is a qualitative one there may at the same time be difference of degrees within each form. Competitive Opposition can range from the intransigent (sometimes mistakenly called 'principled') to the moderate, and it can also be differential, arising more in some policy areas than others. Co-operative Opposition may derive either from political factors such as party strategy which may change (such as the SPD's post-Godesberg line of the 1960s aimed at governmental participation), or from institutional requirements (notably the exigencies of the West German federal system). It usually takes the form of *de facto* or informal co-operation in legislative work, accompained in its purest kind by the absence of regular or systematic criticism in public of Government policies, although it may acquire more formal tones especially if the Opposition party in question follows this course with a reasonable prospect of this leading to an eventual coalition with the force(s) in Government. It is a question of preferring effective 'influence' over 'distant control'.

Secondly, despite the qualitative distinction between competitive and co-operative Opposition it is feasible that in practice a party performing the role of Opposition may follow elements of both. There has never in the history of the Federal Republic been an absolute one or the other, although the SPD in the 1960s came closest to the latter. On the other hand, the high-points of competitive Opposition occurred in the first and sixth legislatures (1949–53 and 1969–72), both predominantly over major areas of foreign policy – Adenauer's *Westpolitik* and Brandt's *Ostpolitik*. These were two cases of intransigent Opposition in response to new policy initiatives coloured by frustration at the failure to achieve, or loss of, national office. Yet each case of polarisation over major policies coexisted with a high level of effective co-operation over areas of domestic policy, especially when secondary or minor questions, which of course comprise much of the bulk of the legislative work, were under debate: the SPD voted for 84 per cent of all bills during 1949–53 (and for 58 per cent of high-political matters), while during 1969–72 the CDU/CSU supported 93 per cent of all bills (voting against or abstaining on such major measures as the Moscow and Warsaw treaties of 1970 and the budgets of 1970 and 1971).[2] The period of the seventh and eighth legislatures (1972–80) did not, however, witness a return to deliberate co-operative Opposition as in the first half of the 1960s leading to the formation of the Grand Coalition, and if historically this period has most in common with that of the middle and late 1950s this analogy lacks the essential ingredient of any comparable move by the CDU/CSU Opposition towards its own version of a 'Godesberg'.

The decade of the 1970s has seen, despite the CDU/CSU's traumatic electoral defeat of 1972, a certain persistence of competitive, at times even intransigent, politics in the form of a sharpened bi-polarity alongside the continous co-operative element. This combination of both competitive and co-operative forms of Opposition may create special problems for the party in question in maintaining and projecting its public profile, especially as competitive politics always attracts more attention. There is the further subjective factor that in times of high political tension or crisis the inclination of West German party leaders from both sides to use doomsday language about each other leads to the above-mentioned distinctions being exaggerated, notably in the confusion of polemical exchanges or intransigent behaviour with 'principled Opposition'. For instance, this occurred over Brandt's much-remembered assertion in the autumn of 1969 that the formation of his Government represented 'the beginning of democracy', and in the emotive debates over anti-terrorist legislation during the later 1970s. In other words, no one period of Opposition in the Federal Republic should be viewed too one-dimensionally.

With this need for relative distinctions between forms of Opposition in mind, the method followed here is to consider both comparatively and uniquely West German characteristics of this dimension, for the former, while usually omitted in a discussion of the case of the Federal Republic, provides a useful objective context for assessing the peculiarities of the West German Opposition and factors which have conditioned its operation. This study will then look directly at the oppositional behaviour and strategy of the CDU/CSU during the third decade of the Federal Republic before concluding whether and how there has been any major transformation of the Opposition role. In doing so, it is emphasised once again that historical and socio-economic factors are by no means the exclusive determinants of this role, which may also be much subject to intrinsic developments in the party system, notably party interrelationships and strategies which may of course affect the balance between competitive and co-operative elements in the conduct of Opposition. This hardly needs stating in view of the dominant and central part played by parties in the functioning of the West German political system.

THE GOVERNMENT/OPPOSITION DIMENSION: A COMPARATIVE PERSPECTIVE

The value of adopting a comparative angle on the West German Opposition is to relate developments in this one case to general trends in comparable political systems elsewhere, especially in Western Europe, and thereby ask whether problems of Opposition politics seemingly peculiar to West Germany might be explained more fully in this broader context. Thus, the difficulty of accepting the concept of a 'loyal opposition', which in West Germany has arisen for historical and situational reasons (especially relating to the DDR), has also been encountered since the Second World War in Italy and France, because of the existence of strong Communist parties in Opposition, where the 'Euro-communist' trend in the 1970s at least in the former case has complicated, more than erased, this problem. In both cases certainly, memories of political instability earlier this century have also counteracted ready acceptance of the Opposition role as *per se* an essential feature of parliamentary work and a justification for alternation in power.

A more general feature, which occasioned much concern among political observers in the 1960s, was the apparent decline of the Opposition role in liberal democracies with the preference by parties performing it for 'the techniques of consensus rather than those of straight competition'.[3] This critique, which even surfaced in Britain where the Opposition role enjoyed a relatively long history of legitimacy, pinpointed in particular as a major causal factor the expansion of government and hence 'administrative' politics with the effects this had on limiting the scope for competitive Opposition. Kirchheimer's interpretation was a reflection of the same general thinking, but it is important to stress that this was by no means unique to the Federal Republic.

In the 1970s, this concern about declining Oppositions generally lessened, above all because the turn of international economic developments, with high inflation, the world energy crisis and the slowing of economic growth, has made somewhat redundant former assumptions about bountiful government and has tended to sharpen sociopolitical conflict domestically with repercussions on competitive party politics. Among the major West European states, this has occurred in Britain and France, not to mention West Germany, although in Italy the trend has been the opposite, primarily as a consequence of the 'historic compromise' strategy of the PCI. Unlike Italy, the political variables in the Federal Republic reactivated rather than de-emphasised polarisation, even though the 'bite' of the new economic situation was felt less painfully there than in many other countries because of the maintenance of economic stability. These variables, which came more to the fore after the first alternation in government in the history of the Federal Republic in 1969, included a stimulated party-political mobilisation after that event and some return to fundamentalist political debate, the changing East–West environment, a more critical political consciousness at a popular level involving a rejection of 'pragmatism' and a greater concern over social questions. Thus, bi-polarity which had been developing in the party system during the 1960s became reinforced by the polarisation which followed in the 1970s. As the former factor is crucial to an understanding of the Opposition role in the 1970s, it is worthwhile to look briefly at the background of this bi-polar development.

Party development in West Germany may be conveniently divided into three unmistakable periods with respect to the Government/Opposition dimension: the decade of the 1950s with CDU/CSU dominance in Government, where smaller centre–Right parties, notably the FDP, acted as coalitional satellites; the decade of the 1960s as a period of transition, which saw the decline of CDU/CSU dominance and the gradual move of the SPD towards governmental participation; and the decade of the 1970s of the Left–Liberal coalitions without equivalent SPD dominance. The third decade was important as a new phase in West German party development because by then there had developed a more equal balance of strength between the two main parties, indicated by the fact that each overtook the other in electoral strength in turn in 1972 and 1976. In fact, the gap between them had continuously narrowed since the ascendancy of Adenauer, as shown in Table 8.1. The 1976 result did appear to reverse the trend somewhat, but it was counterbalanced by the FDP's supporting role for the SPD. This greater symmetry in the West German party system was an outcome not least of the development of 'catch-all' parties or *Volksparteien* both on the Right, with the CDU/CSU in the 1950s, and the Left, with the SPD in the 1960s – Godesberg revisionism undoubtedly paid electoral dividends in the latter case – and was reflected in the increasing combined vote for the two parties during the whole post-war period: from 60.2 per cent in 1949 and 74.0 per cent in 1953 to 90.7 per cent in 1972, 91.2 per cent in 1976 and 87.4 per cent in 1980.

TABLE 8.1   *Declining difference in electoral strength between CDU/CSU and SPD, 1953–80*

Bundestag election	Percentage gap
1953	16.4
1957	18.4
1961	9.2
1965	8.3
1969	3.4
1972	1.1
1976	6.0
1980	1.6

Except for 1972, the CDU/CSU was always the stronger of the two parties.

This bi-polar development, matched by a growing uniformity of the party-political scene in the various *Länder* over the same time, has not, however, created a straightforward two-party system, even though the combined vote of the two main parties in West Germany has been greater than that of their equivalents in Britain as of the 1970s. The decisive difference between the two countries is the parliamentary strength and governmental role of the third party, for while the FDP shares with the British Liberals certain common characteristics – a distinctly smaller electorate than that of the two main parties and one which is relatively unstable, lacking a hard core of voters, as well as problems of maintaining a clear identity in the centre – it does contrast with the British party in its long record of national government (21½ years up to the end of the 1970s, in other words longer than either the CDU/CSU or SPD) and its potential balancing role between the other two parties since the existence of only three *Fraktionen* in the Bundestag from 1961. Following its earlier experience in Government with the Christian Democrats under Adenauer and Erhard, the FDP coalesced with the SPD in the 1970s to an extent that it assumed many of the features of a bloc-party. This centre–Left position of the FDP therefore supported rather than detracted from the bi-polar development, although it naturally remained concerned that this should not magnify its problems of individual profile. On the Opposition side, relations between the CDU and CSU became less unified over the decade with the latter's increasing insistence on autonomy and acquired some elements of a bloc between two forces within the bi-polar context.

Is it possible to say that West German party development has with regard to the Government/Opposition dimension produced a qualified alternating system – 'qualified' because of the aforementioned inter-party relationships? In other words, the Federal Republic, similar now to Britain in some respects, lacks the ready alternation in power between the main parties. Such alternation is after all the exception rather than the rule in post-war Western Europe, bearing in mind the absence of such an event in the first 20 years or more of the French Fifth Republic, the uninterrupted period of Christian Democratic rule in Italy ever since the War and the impression made by the Social Democrats' loss of power in Sweden in 1976 after 44 years in office. In other smaller states, there has been more fluctuation between governmental and oppositional positions, as in the Benelux countries, though here the clear divide between both sides has been lacking notably with Holland's traditional 'politics of accommodation'. None of them has approached a polarised Government/Opposition dimension, except possibly Austria since the end of her long-term Grand Coalition in the mid-1960s.

West Germany emerges as one of the main examples of a clear-cut Government/Opposition divide in Western Europe in the 1970s, but the absence of easy alternation in power is a salient feature of the West German bi-polar system. The one case of alternation that has occurred, in 1969, involved a long and laborious process over a decade with the SPD's implementation of a basic policy change and 'probationary' spell in Government under the Grand Coalition, and was only ultimately possible because of its alliance with the FDP which itself had to undergo a partial programmatic change. This inflexibility of the Government/Opposition dimension in the Federal Republic exists because it does not possess the essential prerequisites for a ready alternating system and only acquired one of them in the 1970s. There are three such prerequisites as seen comparatively.

Firstly, there must be a form of electoral system which facilitates interchange in national office between major parties. The classic example is of course the British constituency-based majority system which 'exaggerates' electoral strength in terms of parliamentary representation, whereas the West German form of modified proportional representation only allows a straightforward alternation between main parties (without the intermediary of a coalitional relationship) when the Opposition challenger succeeds in obtaining upwards of nearly 50 per cent of the popular vote (depending on the size of the small parties excluded from Bundestag representation because of the 5 per cent rule) for an absolute majority of seats. This was only obtained once in the first 30 years of the Federal Republic with the CDU/CSU's 50.2 per cent in 1957, although it came close to it again in 1976 with 48.6 per cent.

Secondly, there must be a reasonable parity of electoral strength between the two major parties, although the strength of one may be 'topped up' by a stable coalitional alliance, as with the SPD in 1976. According to Kaltefleiter, the difference between Government and Opposition parties for making alternation feasible should be, judging by the experience of modern industrialised societies, no more than 5 per cent, combined with the existence of a potential body of floating voters.[4] Voter movements outside the 5 per cent range are not to be expected save in exceptional times of crisis. The adverse economic trends from the early mid-1970s did have some effect on electoral behaviour in the series of *Land* elections during 1974–76, producing several sharp reverses for the SPD (in three cases well outside the 5 per cent range), coupled with various political determinants such as Brandt's loss of authority and, more generally, the normal swing against the party in Government. Electorally motivated polarisation arose therefore in the 1970s because by this time there was sufficient parity between the main parties (with the SPD relying on its alliance with the FDP) to promote competition, unlike say in the 1950s, as shown by Table 8.1.

Thirdly, an alternating system is not finally possible without political attitudes, broadly speaking, accepting its value. Positive acceptance is naturally more likely with the successful practice of such a system, so that the absence of any such occurrence before 1969 tended to produce fundamentalist rather than functional perceptions of this possibility – the preferred term *Machtwechsel* instead of *Regierungswechsel* suggested this attitudinal difference. However, the actual change from the Grand Coalition to the Left–Liberal coalition in 1969 featured, despite accompanying polemics, some evidence of a rational acceptance that as such it would benefit the health of the political system, a view even held among some Opposition sympathisers.[5] In the rather highly politicised atmosphere of West Germany in the 1970s such acceptance of alternation was of course associated with party-political allegiances, but expectations arising out of the reappearance of polarisation are such that alternation has become regarded as a realistic if not acceptable possibility, at least compared with earlier decades. There are nevertheless other problems of legitimacy attached to the Opposition role, but these are more suitably discussed in the next section.

SPECIAL FEATURES OF THE WEST GERMAN OPPOSITION ROLE

Reference to the comparative perspective shows that several problems of the Opposition role evident in the West German case have been also visible in other West European parliamentary democracies, such as a Government party's advantages of authority and prestige as well as its quasi-monopoly of news creation and superior resources of policy information, an Opposition's difficulties of maintaining a credible profile in view of this imbalance, and of course the impact of the international and economic environment in a stated period of time which, common to such countries, may affect governmental performance. For instance, high-political foreign issues both allow the party in office a clearer and sometimes freer scope for establishing policy initiatives and accordingly restrict the chance for an Opposition to act more than in the domestic field because of the less open nature of diplomacy and the possible requirements of national solidarity; whereas economic trends, particularly when adverse, may enlarge the scope for competition between both sides. If there are differences in these respects between the Federal Republic and these other parliamentary democracies, they may at least in part be attributed to a common habit in German politics at both elite and popular levels of 'worrying' about the implications of political behaviour.

This leads us to a consideration of those particular aspects of the West German political system which bear on the Government/Opposition dimension and distinguish it from other countries, and thereby expose the limitations of any tendency among Anglo-American political scientists to measure the Federal Republic consciously or unconsciously against a Westminster-style model of parliamentary politics. These unique characteristics of the West German Government/Opposition dimension may be categorised as attitudinal and institutional.

The question of attitudinal factors reintroduces the problem of traditional political concepts and historically conditioned responses to the party-political game. It became almost a convention in looking at the first two decades of the Federal Republic to dwell on the continuity with the pre-Nazi past as inhibiting an easy acceptance of party-political conflict as legitimate. This problem naturally received nourishment from the negative memories of the Weimar experience, where polarisation had become more and more 'principled'. Thus, Joachim Raschke writing in 1968 on the role of the Bundestag in the West German parliamentary system noted in referrring back to the Hohenzollern monarchy that 'the Opposition always found it difficult in Germany'.[6] In the early 1970s in a general survey of West German politics, Kurt Sontheimer elaborated on this mentality:

Comprehension of the Opposition's role is not sufficiently developed in the German public and not even in Parliament itself; Germans appear to have little sense of the critical function of a parliamentary party which continually accompanies the Government programme and its execution with its criticism or alternative suggestions; a Government, many think, must be allowed to do as it likes; it does not do to be continually finding fault with it.[7]

Michael Hereth devoted a study published in 1969 specifically to this theme, and explained the 'odium' of the Opposition role essentially as deriving from a persistence of traditional concepts, notably the emphasis on administrative values and on the authority of the state as features of *obrigkeitsstaatliches Denken*.[8] Similarly, Rudolf Wildenmann has commented on the strong 'governmental' orientation of the majority of the West German population, and Dieter Grosser on the undervaluation of parliamentary Opposition by voters, journalists and academics in the Federal Republic.[9]

These traditional attitudes were not discouraged from official quarters or by governmental experience during the first decade and more of the new post-war West German republic. Even though Adenauer characterised the Opposition as 'a necessity for the state', his own conduct as Chancellor served to undercut the legitimacy of the Opposition role – and indeed he had good party-political reasons for doing so – not only in his famous remark that the election of the SPD to national office would entail 'the ruin of Germany' but on many occasions in parliamentary debate.[10] It could also be said that the SPD contributed to this lack of Opposition legitimacy at the time by its strategic change from the late 1950s, or as Kirchheimer puts it succinctly: 'The SPD consciously strove to eliminate parliamentary Opposition as a desirable pattern for the conduct of political business.'[11] Hereth himself saw the SPD's formation of a government with its old political enemy the CDU/CSU in the Grand Coalition (1966–69) as 'the acquiesence of the Social Democrats in the German past' and as their 'flight into the institutionalised togetherness of a common government'.[12] However, the very fact that the continuing devaluation of the Opposition role received such critical attention among political commentators in the latter half of the 1960s was itself a salutory indication of a potential or possible change in attitudes, which might distinguish the Federal Republic from its Weimar predecessor. This critical discussion did of course largely precede the first change of power in 1969. It might also be added that, paradoxically, the strong governmental vocation of the three main parties had already underlined a significant departure from Weimar parliamentary life.

The distinct executive-orientation of the post-war West German political system has been further evident in various institutional respects. Most visibly, this has been seen in the strong importance accredited to the figure of the Chancellor in governmental performance and the parliamentary mechanisms supporting his tenure of office. This feature has had its public counterpart in the plebiscitary function expected of the Chancellor in elections, which certainly denotes a different and more personalised perception of the executive role compared with Britain. Mention should also be made again here of the West German electoral system, which may work to the advantage of the main governing party once it has achieved national office.

There is, however, one basic feature of the West German political sytem, again marking it off from the British case as well as from other examples in Western Europe, which modifies this national executive-orientation in relation to the Government/Opposition dimension and indeed limits the accretion of administrative and political power at the centre – that is, the federal structure of the state. This both promotes policy convergence between the parties on the basis of the principle of co-operative federalism, and provides an executive outlet for the Opposition party as some 'compensation' for its exclusion from national political office though not as an equivalent political 'prize'. In the former respect, much depends on the party-political balance in the Bundesrat and the extent to which *Land* governments choose to act together in a partisan manner as distinct from a straightforward defence of regional interests. In the latter respect there have been many more instances of an alternation in power regionally than nationally, a tendency encouraged by the fact that Opposition parties have usually mobilised their voters more effectively in *Land* elections than those in power in Bonn and taken advantage of anti-Government swings.[13] Alternation between the two main parties took place in North-Rhine Westphalia in 1956, 1958 and 1966; Bavaria in 1954 and 1957; Hamburg in 1953 and 1957; Schleswig-Holstein in 1950; Lower Saxony in 1955, 1959 and 1976; and West Berlin twice in the mid-1950s, with coalitional relationships significantly playing a crucial part in these instances. In several cases, though, alternation involved little more than a short break in the continuous hold on a *Land* government by one main party, as in Bavaria, Hamburg and West Berlin. Only in Bremen, Hesse, the Rhineland-Palatinate and Baden-Württemberg has such alternation not taken place, although grand coalitions have featured in some of these *Länder*. The growing uniformity of the West German party system regionally to accord with the three-party constellation at the national level and the emergence there too of bi-polarity has meant that from the early 1970s 'nationalising' influences have more than before affected both the operation of co-operative federalism and partisan perceptions of *Land* politics.

The key question which therefore requires an answer a decade after the formation of the Left–Liberal coalition is whether the change of power in 1969 and the performance in Opposition by the CDU/CSU during the course of the 1970s have in any way modified the traditional interpretation of this role. The Christian Democrats did provide numerically the strongest Opposition in the history of the Federal Republic, lending the role greater representational and political weight, while as such the Opposition was less diffuse than it had been on earlier occasions. (The CDU/CSU Opposition provided 48.8 per cent of the Bundestag seats in 1969, 45.4 per cent in 1972, 49.0 per cent in 1976 and 45.5 per cent in 1980 compared with the SPD Opposition's 38.1 per cent of the seats in 1961 and 40.7 per cent in 1965. In 1949 the combined Opposition had provided 48.3 per cent of the seats, but this consisted of mixed and disparate parties like the KPD and several small centre–Right parties like the Bavarian Party, the Centre Party and the *Wirtschaftliche Aufbau-Vereinigung* (WAV) apart from the SPD, which by itself accounted for 32.6 per cent of the seats. In 1953 the Opposition provided 31.4 per cent of the seats (the SPD 31.0 per cent), while in 1957 the SPD held 34.0 per cent of the seats and together with the FDP 42.3 per cent in the combined Opposition. These figures are to the nearest decimal point.) This question may be considered in both functional and attitudinal terms. Both aspects are linked in that oppositional performance might itself help to condition wider responses to the concept and practice of parliamentary Opposition.

THE CDU/CSU'S OPPOSITION BEHAVIOUR AND STRATEGY, 1969–80

The Opposition role as interpreted and pursued in the 1970s should be judged with two features in mind – the importance of enhanced bi-polarity, and the nature of the CDU/CSU as a political party. The superior strength itself of the new Opposition from 1969, compared with any previous Opposition, combined with the sudden break with the official harmony represented by the Grand Coalition as the outcome of party-political convergence over the decade of the 1960s, undoubtedly brought the growing bi-polar situation between the two party blocs more into play. This created the structural condition for a new phase of competitive politics, as evident in the use made of the Bundestag as a public forum for criticising the Government by the CDU/CSU and its electorally-motivated behaviour in the belief that (unlike the SPD in the 1950s) it was realistic to aim at winning an absolute majority. Relations between the two main parties, following their not entirely happy co-operation in Government, became polarised during the decade such that any return to a Grand Coalition became out of the question and was never seriously voiced. The CDU/CSU was itself very conscious of adopting a stronger oppositional line from that in preceding legislatures. In fact

Kurt-Georg Kiesinger, who remained as CDU chairman after his loss of the Chancellorship in 1969, deliberately referred in his party's early days of Opposition to Schumacher's concept of an active presentation of alternative policy proposals in this role.[14]

Yet any strict comparison with the SPD Opposition during the first Bundestag of 1949–53 cannot be taken too far. While the bi-polar Government/Opposition divide now promoted competitive politics, various characteristics of the CDU/CSU as a different kind of party from the SPD also conditioned its performance of the Opposition role. Despite the shock of the loss of power, the CDU/CSU had a more self-confident view of itself as a rightful governing party springing from the central part it had played in the early history of the Federal Republic and especially in the reconstruction period of the 1950s. Hence, the apt comment of Bruno Heck, the CDU general-secretary, that the CDU/CSU acted in Opposition like a 'government without ministries'. Partly because of this self-image, as well as the fact that its own electoral strength did not require a rapproachement with the SPD in Government, the CDU/CSU was not forced to consider adopting its own 'Godesberg' of strategic policy convergence. Programmatic revision therefore did not arise, all the more because the CDU/CSU was distinctly less programmatically conscious than the SPD, although the CDU especially found it necessary in Opposition to try to fill its programmatic lacunae following 20 years' continuous 'pragmatic' experience in Government. The series of programmatic principles and positions formulated by the CDU – the revised Berlin programme of 1971, the theses of the Hamburg congress 1973, the Mannheim Declaration of 1975 and the Basic Policy Programme (*Grundsatzprogramm*) of 1978 – did not involve a programmatic détente with the SPD, but rather an attempt to emphasise its self-identity in contradistinction to the Government.

The significance of the *Machtwechsel* of 1969 was undoubtedly perceived at the time and was indeed encompassed by fundamentalist assertions which were not merely occasioned by its lack of precedent. These were particularly evident on the CDU/CSU side where its automatic claim to a governing role seemed affronted, seeing that it emerged as the strongest single *Fraktion* in the Bundestag while the 'change in power' departed from the convention that the largest party should hold the Chancellorship. In the subsequent weeks and months accusations that the 'coalition of losers' (Barzel) amounted to 'the great betrayal', a 'putsch against the voters', a matter of 'existential importance' and a 'fundamental reorientation' of German politics led to a dramatic sharpening of the political atmosphere in the Bundestag. Few Opposition politicians at this time took a more philosophical view of the event. Only Bruno Heck, speaking at the CDU congress in November 1969, chose in reference to parliamentary experience in liberal democracies to underline the functional implications of the *Machtwechsel* by reminding his party that, 'The Government creates the facts and largely determines the themes' and that, 'Opposition parties are as a rule compelled to adapt in the long-term to the Government parties' decisions over great policy matters'.[15]

This lesson from other parliamentary states did not, however, cut much ice with the CDU/CSU in its oppositional behaviour, for its reaction to the *Machtwechsel* was not solely a polemical expression of its frustration at exclusion from national office but also drew on beliefs pervading the Opposition ranks that questioned the legitimacy of Government policies. These surfaced at various points during the CDU/CSU's Opposition in the 1970s notably over *Ostpolitik*, and were reflected in such statements as by Karl Carstens, CDU/CSU *Fraktion* chairman, in 1974 that his party was the 'only political force' opposing subversion of the 'democratic order based on freedom' and that the Government had an underdeveloped sense of 'constitutional loyalty'.[16] On another occasion, during the debate in the Bundestag on anti-terrorist laws in autumn 1977, the 'change of power' of 1969 was raised again as an issue in an emotive exchange between Dregger and Wehner. Alfred Dregger, presenting CDU/CSU criticisms of the draft legislation, argued provocatively that a clear-cut distinction must be drawn between supporters of the democratic constitution and 'extremists' of all kinds, including left-wing Socialists in the SPD, and in this connection attacked the latter party for encouraging the polarisation arising from the *Machtwechsel*.[17]

There were several signs during the 1970s of a repetition of negative attitudes towards the Opposition role, springing from both sides of the political divide. This tendency was noticeable of course in the CDU/CSU's reluctance to embrace fully its Opposition status as already indicated, not only in the first period after the 1969 election when it based its approach on the assumption of a possible early return to power because of the Government's small and unstable majority, but again in the mid-1970s when its impressive performance in *Land* elections revived the same hope. Equally, the SPD now in Government appeared to practise some of Adenauer's habits from the 1950s of undercutting the legitimacy of the party in Opposition. Willy Brandt was prominent in doing so both during and after his Chancellorship, calling into question the CDU/CSU's democratic credentials and in one instance accusing it of being a 'security risk for the Federal Republic in foreign as in domestic policy, economic as well as social'.[18] Such fundamentalist criticisms of the Opposition received an emphatic airing during the CDU/CSU's constitutionally based attempt to remove Brandt and his Government from office by the constructive vote of no confidence in April 1972 (the first use of this provision in Article 67 of the Basic Law). This initiative following the collapse of the Government's majority produced high political tension in Bonn, spontaneous demonstrations by SPD/FDP supporters, the threat of political strikes by the trade unions in the event of the election of Barzel as Chancellor, and the CDU/CSU being branded as a *Kanzlersturz-Partei*. Later in the 1970s, the Opposition's use of its majority in the Bundesrat caused regular fusillades from the Government side about 'obstruction' in the upper chamber and the pejorative term *Neinsager*, which had been widely employed in the early 1970s in reference to the CDU/CSU's Opposition to *Ostpolitik*, was now heard again.

Far from this active use by the CDU/CSU of its strong representative weight being considered a normal element of parliamentary life and political conflict, it was interpreted frequently in the light of traditional ideas that the Opposition role had to be justified in a 'constructive' way. In this respect, there was no real change in relations between Government and Opposition parties during the 1970s. At the very end of the decade the prospects for a lessening of mutual antagonism hardly seemed bright with the CDU/CSU's nomination of Strauss as Chancellor candidate for the 1980 Bundestag election. This produced a pungent attack reminiscent of the 1950s by Brandt on Strauss, whose victory would mean 'fear in Germany, fear for Germany and fear of Germany' and a return to Weimar conditions. In short, such fundamentalist polemics were a feature of competitive politics in the 1970s and tended to distinguish the West German from the British case.

They did not however, unlike the 1950s, lead to any conversion of the Opposition to accepting that the SPD in Government was calling the political tune and laying the policy groundwork for the country's future course, because of the more even balance between the two sides of the Government/Opposition divide. There was no apparent likelihood of an 'SPD State', replacing the 'CDU State' of the previous decades,[19] with which the Opposition would have to come to terms. Moreover, as a key factor when assessing the maintenance of bi polarity between Government and Opposition during the 1970s, the regular series of *Land* elections in eleven states each time – as during 1970–72, 1974–76 and 1978–80 – guaranteed that party behaviour would remain almost permanently electorally oriented (certainly more so than in the UK). In this situation, where the Opposition fluctuated menacingly around or just below the 50 per cent level as a trend, competitive politics which was at the basis of these polemical relations had a certain self-generating effect.

At a more objective level, on the other hand, there were different ways in which the Opposition after 1969 acquired greater credibility and legitimacy.

Firstly, various institutional and procedural changes were implemented to strengthen the role of the Opposition as a minority force and controlling agent in parliamentary work, beginning with the 'small parliamentary reform' of 1969. This had in fact been agreed on by the major parties towards the end of the Grand Coalition, when it was expected that one of them would assume the position of Opposition,[20] and promoted Opposition procedural responses to Government actions and new rights of initiative in plenary sessions as well as some greater facility in the use of parliamentary committees' controlling functions.[21] The question of the constitutional power of the parliamentary Opposition did not cease there, for a standing conference of the chairmen of the three parties' *Fraktionen* began to meet from 1973 to investigate further ways of countering the procedural imbalance favouring the Government as against Parliament. On the basis of the first discussions, some changes were carried into effect in several *Land* parliaments as well as additional prospective reforms being considered for the functioning of the Bundestag.[22]

Secondly, taking advantage of these institutional reforms the new CDU/CSU Opposition very soon made its presence felt in parliamentary work. Against the background of a polarised atmosphere, plenary debates became livelier and this tendency was promoted by the greater cohesion of the Government *Fraktionen*, compared with earlier legislative periods, and their reluctance to seek consensus with the Opposition even in committees,[23] as well as Barzel's skilled leadership in channelling the parliamentary energies of the CDU/CSU. The procedural reforms were noticeably applied in the newly established practice after 1969 for Opposition leaders to speak immediately after Government ministers, thus encouraging a sense of adversary politics, a habit favoured in particular by Strauss and also by Barzel in his search for personal confrontation with Chancellor Brandt in plenaries. In so doing, Barzel set a precedent for a stronger concept of 'Opposition leader' which his successors Carstens and Kohl were required to follow. It is significant that criticisms from within the *Fraktion* of the latter two's leadership performance focused on this aspect, such as the recurrent view that Carstens was 'administering' the Opposition more than directing it politically, and the persistent discontent with Kohl's performance after 1976 as he failed to satisfy demands for dynamic leadership even though he was severely handicapped by the weaker solidarity between the CDU and CSU. Kohl's unimpressive record as Opposition leader in the Bundestag contributed to his declining popularity which in turn affected party morale broadly.[24] In short, it became more firmly established that the Opposition image was determined in the first instance by activity in the plenaries, an assumption readily accepted by the mass media.

Thirdly, the new political weight of the Opposition as shown by its superior representative strength and cohesion compared with the 1950s and 1960s had important political consequences. These focused on the Bundesrat where for the first time an Opposition party enjoyed a majority over the Government (of one until 1976, when it increased to eleven because of the change in power in Lower Saxony). The result was the unprecedented situation where bi-polarity introduced a stronger element of partisan tension within the federal structure and one which furthermore attracted public attention.[25] Although the clear divide between Government and Opposition forces did not fully emerge until 1972, because of overlapping coalitions between the federal level and the *Länder*, there were early signs that the CDU/CSU was considering stricter coordination in Bundesrat work of the *Land* governments that it led to combat the Government, an inclination reinforced by the fact that most prominent leaders of the party were minister-presidents. The elevation of its control over the Bundesrat majority to a key feature of the CDU/CSU Opposition's political line was underlined by Kiesinger: 'The CDU is the Opposition, it is the Opposition in the Bundestag and it is the Opposition in the Bundesrat – that is, the Federal–political Opposition; and it is the task of the Opposition to cause difficulties for the Government until such time as it falls.'[26] One CSU leader went further in stressing a co-legislative role, for according to him the Government could '... assume that the Union (CDU/CSU) will make responsible use of its majority in the Bundesrat; this is shown for example by the legislative initiatives of the Bundesrat which are accepted by the Bundestag'.[27]

This problem of divergent majorities between the two parliamentary chambers naturally raised the question of how the CDU/CSU has married or formed a balance between the co-operative and competitive aspects of its Opposition role. While public debate and political attention has been drawn more towards the latter aspect, especially as it has tended to arise most over major issues, a considerable degree of legislative work has been carried out on the basis of bi-partisan accord. Polarisation does not after all, it must be emphasised, have to embrace the full spate of affairs which pass through the Parliament, simply because many mundane matters are not controversial. Apart from such non-controversial areas, the distinguishing point is whether co-operative politics is motivated by a strategic convergence between parties (as in the 1960s, but not in the 1970s), an electoral concern to demonstrate a 'responsible' image for the Opposition party (an assumption which reflected remaining traditional concepts) or a more active desire to assert its own stamp on policy-making in contrast to the Government. The third alternative was that which most characterised the first Opposition period of 1969–72, when the CDU/CSU initiated 122 of the 171 bills which originated on the floor of the Bundestag, an approach which aimed at maintaining the party's credibility as the 'rightful' governing force. It did not, however, pay the expected political dividends, so that after the 1972 election there was more emphasis on the second alternative even though polarised conflict continued over certain foreign and sociopolitical (e.g. abortion, education) issues. In the Bundesrat itself the heightened partisan divisions during the course of the 1970s illustrated not only the impact of polarisation but also the problems of intermixing co-operative and competitive aspects deriving from imcompatibility between bipolar party tendencies and the coordinative requirements of the federal structure. As a consequence, the national CDU/CSU leadership was not always successful in arranging a unified position among party representatives in the Bundesrat, and there were even occasions when the CDU/CSU *Land* governments supported Bills opposed by the CDU/CSU Opposition in the Bundestag.[28]

The difficulties encountered by the CDU/CSU during the 1970s in combining competitive and co-operative roles in the context of bi-polarity leads directly to the final question of the party's strategy, which means the approach adopted by the Opposition for promoting its return to Government. This emerges from the preceding discussion because the two strategic alternatives facing the CDU/CSU related explicitly to the contrast between competitive and co-operative Opposition. The exigencies of the three-party constellation and the electoral system demanded that, on the level of principle, the choice was between aiming for an absolute majority and hence mobilising all available forces to oppose the Government parties or attempting to win over the FDP to a future coalition, in which case more emphasis needed to be placed on areas of harmony rather than discord.[29] However, the pursuit of these strategies in practice encountered both the problem of everyday politics of adjusting short-term developments to such a long-term approach and the inflexibility of the West German party system with its absence of a ready alternation in power.

The first problem arose within the CDU/CSU over the perception of its political position, for in practice the line pursued by its leadership was often marked by hesitation and division over the two alternatives and some degree of following both at the same time. In this respect there was some variation between its three Opposition periods during the 1970s. In 1969–72 the CDU/CSU lived in the permanent expectation of an early or immediate return to power in the event of the Brandt Government's collapse. However, when its longer-term role in Opposition was confirmed by its traumatic electoral defeat in 1972, the CDU in particular turned its attention to the intermediate task of re-establishing party credibility through organisational reform and an attempt at programmatic revival (what CDU General-Secretary Biedenkopf called a 'thematic offensive'), an approach which attracted new groups of voters in 1976 – a remarkable achievement considering the CDU/CSU did this from a position of Opposition and even though Kohl's personal appeal, although then achieving credibility, could hardly be described as charismatic. The fact, nevertheless, that the CDU/CSU did not actually win the 1976 election in the sense of achieving power, which, reflecting the bi-polar perspective of party positions, reduced the psychological impact of Kohl's considerable electoral achievement and rapidly brought into the open basic divisions within the Opposition over the alternative strategies. The eruption of discord between the CDU and CSU leaderships, exacerbated by the prospect of a third period in Opposition, highlighted these divisions because they became personalised through Kohl's known preference for an alliance with the FDP and Strauss's more aggressive line of aiming for an absolute majority and to this end launching his brainchild of a national CSU. The problem was that the intra-CDU/CSU truce after the temporary rupture of the two parties during the Kreuth crisis in 1976 only served to postpone the taking of a conscious decision to opt for one strategy or the other, which although perhaps allowing for some flexibility in everyday politics contributed to confusion among party ranks. As time proceeded, the evident lack of response by the FDP to Kohl's veiled overtures erased the one option and in turn further helped to undermine his authority as Opposition leader. On the eve of the 1980 election therefore the aim of an absolute majority had, by default, become the only strategy for the CDU/CSU.

The lack of the coalition alternative for the CDU/CSU during the 1970s underlined how much the bi-polar development had reinforced the rigid constraints on an alternation in power, for in theory at least the 'capturing' of the FDP offers the easier means for the transference of power between the two main parties. This situation arises partly from the West German practice where inter-party alliances mean formal coalitions, unlike say in Italy where a variety of informal and sometimes fluid arrangements between parties may take place. This procedure requires that the preparatory stages before a full coalition may be embraced are elaborate, with the need for some programmatic rapprochement on the part of *both* parties concerned and for announcing coalitional preferences before an election compaign. The process is inevitably somewhat long-term, all the more so at the national level, since the parties in question wish to avoid any loss of public credibility that might come from too sudden a switch in coalition partners. This latter problem applied particularly in the case of the FDP, because any such move had to carry the sufficient consent or understanding of both its members and voters so that the political inclinations of its leaders (and some during this period were suspected of harbouring a preference for the CDU/CSU) are not the exclusive determinant of its own strategic course. The strategic dilemma for the FDP was a major one, since at the same time as supporting a coalitional relationship it had to maintain an independent profile as a party. In an era of bi-polarity, when press comment concentrated emphatically on the relations of the FDP with the other parties rather than on any other of its aspects, this task imposed heavy demands on its leadership.

CONCLUSION

In conclusion, Government and Opposition roles have become more sharply defined during the course of the 1970s as a consequence of the long-term bi-polar development in the party system and more immediately of the 'change of power' of 1969 and the realistic prospect that this could happen again in the near future. In this situation, polarisation has had to some extent a self-generating effect among party elites for its existence may depend not merely on differences of policy content between the main parties, but also on rivalry for national office where there is sufficient balance between them to make the outcome of elections reasonably uncertain, which was not the case in the 1950s. Equally, bi-polarity, lending as it does more distinct contours to party-political positions, has facilitated the political orientation of voters. This change in the Government/Opposition dimension has been a qualitative one, and since it has already lasted more than a decade it amounts to a new phase in West German party development. The Grand Coalition seems in retrospect an exceptional interlude in coalitional relationships, all the more so as time proceeds, now that the SPD has succeeded in establishing its own credibility as a governing force as well as the CDU/CSU.

The continuation or confirmation of this bi-polar competition between the West German parties is of course open to further developments during the 1980s. The return of the CDU/CSU to office would give renewed impetus to the alternation of power and possibly to increased polarisation. However, there is also room for uncertainty. For instance, if the SPD were freed from the constraints of government policy-making, the party in Opposition could become less cohesive, with possible pressures challenging the 'pragmatic' values of Godesberg-style reformism, and this development would make the SPD's relationship with the FDP less harmonious. If the CDU/CSU were to be faced with a prolonged period in Opposition, a final rupture between the CDU and CSU could be provoked. A further pessimistic outcome would involve some fragmentation in the established party system arising, say, as a consequence of a final CDU/CSU split or through the anchoring of the ecologists in the party system. All such possible scenarios involve some structural modification in the party system, which cannot be entirely ignored simply because of the effects of the 5 per cent clause restricting parliamentary representation. Nevertheless, such has been the strength of the trend towards bi-polarity and conflictual politics that this itself should not be underestimated as a major influence on party development in Western Germany.

Finally, what influence has bi-polarity and the sharper Government/ Opposition dimension had on the role of Opposition itself? As elsewhere, Opposition politicians often tend to regard their role as one of political impotence, and the desire for national office is strong in West Germany. Nevertheless, in some respects this role has acquired a greater legitimacy despite the occasionally bitter polemics, while the Opposition's more evident effectiveness has been harmed more by the CDU/CSU's internal leadership disputes than by external factors. Certainly, the existence of a weighty Opposition has helped to strengthen Government solidarity in the bi-polar context. Traditional German concepts restricting the scope for partisan approaches to policy-making in the state still remain, but there have been some signs of their erosion. This is due partly to the greater international and domestic confidence in the Federal Republic as a political system, which has emerged in the 1970s and which *Ostpolitik* and West Germany's much-lauded economic performance helped to promote, so that the reduced fear of 'principled Opposition' within the system has accordingly made legitimate opposition more acceptable. Also, the more critical public awareness of social and political issues since the late 1960s together with the rise in political participation outside elections, without this being associated with anti-system mobilisation, has induced a less instinctive antipathy to the question of political conflict. In so far as the main parties have responded to or reflected these deeper forms of change, they have channelled them through the parliamentary arena. In this sense, the 'remaking' of the German political culture has had some by-effects on the Government/Opposition dimension, but it should not be forgotten that the West German case in this respect has its own unique features as much as other West European examples. The overall result has been a more competitive political situation in the Federal Republic than at any time before the 1970s. Even taking into account factors of uncertainty in the future, there is a probability of this continuing in the 1980s for while conflictual politics had only reappeared from 1969 it was made possible by the bi-polar trend which had been developing for nearly a decade before that.

152 *Party Government and Political Culture in Western Germany*

NOTES AND REFERENCES

The author wishes to acknowledge Pippa Pridham's contribution in the form of perceptive comments on and corrections to the original draft version.

1. Otto Kirchheimer, 'Germany: The Vanishing Opposition', in Robert A. Dahl (ed.), *Political Oppositions in Western Democracies* (New Haven and London, 1966) pp. 237–59.
  2. The figures are taken from Joachim Raschke, *Der Bundestag im parlamentarischen Regierungssystem* (Berlin, 1968) p. 36; and Hans-Joachim Veen, *Opposition im Bundestag: ihre Funktionen, institutionellen Handlungsbedingungen und das Verhalten der CDU/CSU-Fraktion in der 6. Wahlperiode 1969–1972* (Bonn, 1976) pp. 191–2.
  3. See G. Ionescu and I. de Madariaga, *Opposition: Past and Present of a Political Institution* (Harmondsworth, 1968) pp. 74–6.
  4. W. Kaltefleiter, 'Oppositionsstrategie im parlamentarischen System', *Aus Politik und Zeitgeschichte*, 4 August 1973, pp. 3 ff.
  5. Lewis Edinger, 'Political change in Germany: The Federal Republic after the 1969 Election', *Comparative Politics*, July 1970, pp. 552, 567.
  6. Raschke, *op. cit.*, p. 34.
  7. Kurt Sontheimer, *The Government and Politics of West Germany* (London, 1972) p. 130.
  8. Michael Hereth, *Die parlamentarische Opposition in der Bundesrepublik Deutschland* (Munich, 1969) pp. 17–18, 154–5.
  9. Rudolf Wildenmann, 'CDU/CSU: Regierungspartei von morgen – oder was sonst?', in R. Löwenthal and H-P. Schwarz (eds), *Die zweite Republik: 25 Jahre Bundesrepublik Deutschland – eine Bilanz* (Stuttgart, 1974) p. 361; Dieter Grosser, 'Die Sehnsucht nach Harmonie: historische und verfassungsstrukturelle Vorbelastungen der Opposition in Deutschland', in Heinrich Oberreuter (ed.), *Parlamentarische Opposition: Ein internationaler Vergleich* (Hamburg, 1975) p. 206.
 10. See Hereth, *op. cit.*, pp. 129–30 for examples.
 11. Kirchheimer, *op. cit.*, p. 243.
 12. Hereth, *op. cit.*, p. 156.
 13. The SPD Opposition achieved this in *Land* elections during the first decade and a half of the Federal Republic; see R. J. C. Preece, *'Land' Elections in the German Federal Republic* (London, 1968) pp. 20–1. The CDU/CSU Opposition has benefited from the same tendency during the 1970s.
 14. Veen, *op. cit.*, pp. 196–7.
 15. CDU, *17. Bundesparteitag der CDU, November 1969* (1969), p. 36.
 16. *Deutschland Union-Dienst*, 2 January 1974.
 17. *Die Anti-Terror-Debatten im Parlament: Protokolle 1974–1978* (Reinbek bei Hamburg, 1978) pp. 345–57.
 18. *Rheinischer Merkur*, 21 November 1975.
 19. On the thesis of the 'CDU State', see G. Schäfer and C. Nedelmann, *Der CDU-Staat: Analysen zur Verfassungswirklichkeit der Bundesrepublik* (Munich, 1967) which discussed the imprint of the party on the West German political system.
 20. Veen, *op. cit.*, p. 13.

21. For details of these parliamentary reforms, see *ibid.*, pp. 120–5.
22. See J. Echternach, 'Stärkung der Oppositionsrechte – Zum Stand der Verhandlungen zwischen CDU/CSU, SPD und FDP', *Zeitschrift für Parlamentsfragen*, no. 1 (1975) pp. 3–9.
23. Veen, *op. cit.*, pp. 77–8, 81–2.
24. See *Der Spiegel*, 2 April 1979, pp. 90–2 for poll on CDU/CSU voters.
25. See Gerhard Lehmbruch, 'Party and Federation in Germany: A Developmental Dilemma', in *Government and Opposition*, Spring 1978, pp. 151–77 for a discussion of the incompatibility between the bi-polar party system and the federal structure.
26. P. Schindler, 'Missbrauch des Bundesrates? Dokumentation einer aktuellen Auseinandersetzung', *Zeitschrift für Parlamentsfragen*, no. 2 (1974) p. 159.
27. *Ibid.*, p. 160.
28. Peter Pulzer, 'Responsible Party Government and Stable Coalition: The Case of the German Federal Republic', *Political Studies*, June 1978, pp. 202–3.
29. This choice was recognised within the CDU/CSU itself as immediately after the failure to achieve power in the 1976 Election, see article on Opposition strategic thinking in *Die Zeit*, 8 October 1976.

9 Parties and the Conditions of Political Leadership

NEVIL JOHNSON

Political parties in the Federal Republic have over the years gained a remarkably high degree of public recognition as the organisations on which the effective operation of the political system depends. In sharp contrast with the position in earlier periods of modern German history, it is now more or less a truism that the parties have become established and accepted. This undoubtedly goes for the four major parties represented in the Bundestag and most provincial parliaments. But it applies in some important senses even to minor parties, some of them transitory and all of them struggling to survive: for example, they can gain a measure of public financial aid provided they attract the support of 0.5 per cent of the total vote.[1] Indeed it is only on the fringes of political activity where it becomes hard to distinguish between parties, political clubs and conspiratorial groups that public recognition fades away.

There are two sides to this establishment and acceptance of the parties. On the one hand it reflects actual patterns of behaviour and action: how the voters have declared their preferences, how the politically active have organised themselves, what politicians have achieved and the impact of all this on the shaping of opinion and the sustaining of habits and loyalties. On the other hand it expresses too the impact of normative commitments, some of the most important of which are enshrined in the constitution and have been reinforced by practice and interpretation during the past thirty years. The Basic Law quite deliberately legitimised parties in Article 21. This was done by recognising their role in 'the formation of the political will of the people' and by imposing on parties an obligation to conform in respect of their internal arrangements and goals with democratic principles. Parties which do not in this sense accept their constitutional obligations stemming from the Basic Law are liable to be judged unconstitutional and as a result may be dissolved.[2] The decisive terms of Article 21 have, however, proved to be the foundation for a much wider constitutionalisation of the parties, that is to say for their formal recognition within the institutions of the Federal Republic. Parliamentary institutions provide a clear example of this process at work: within the procedural framework of the Bundestag the parties – or the *Fraktionen* as they are called in that context – are recognised as key components.[3]

LEADERSHIP AND *WILLENSBILDUNG*

This short chapter is, however, concerned with only one aspect of the public recognition of parties and one which, moreover, arises indirectly from the interdependence of the two principal commitments regarding parties contained in the Basic Law itself. The main questions to be raised here concern what is known in German as the *Willensbildung* inside parties and the implications which changes in the conditions under which this takes place may have for political leadership in the Federal Republic. *Willensbildung* denotes the formation of opinion, or as some might prefer to put it, the shaping of a will, a term which evokes ever so faintly Rousseau or Hegel. As already mentioned, Article 21 (a) of the Basic Law refers to the parties sharing 'in the formation of the political will of the people'. Here the reference is to the world outside the parties, to the electorate which has political choices to make. But the immediately following condition relating to the need for the internal structures of parties and their aims to respect democratic principles entails that there must be an analogous process of *Willensbildung* inside the parties and that, in principle at least, the legitimacy of a party's claim to contribute to the wider popular *Willensbildung* depends upon the extent to which the parallel process internal to the parties also conforms to democratic standards. The Party Law of 1967 represents the official confirmation of the intentions of Article 21 of the Basic Law. Here an attempt is made to provide regulatory conditions both for the discharge by the parties of their primary public function – the formation of the political will of the people – and for the maintenance within them of procedures conducive to the formation of their own policies in a democratic way.[4]

How the formation of opinion inside a political party and the establishment of policies or programmes take place depends extensively on how the party is organised, what rights its members have, how the representative principle is applied, how actively people are involved in party activity at different levels of the organisation and so on. These remarks do not, however, focus on the impact on the internal *Willensbildung* of structural conditions inside the parties. The concern is rather with the significance of changes in recent years in the kind of people involved in the intra-party formation of opinion, in their educational backgrounds and in their range of interests and approach to party work. It will be argued that changes are taking place which encourage an intensification of the process of opinion formation in relation to policies inside the parties and an enlarged role for intellectuals in this process. Over the longer term this is likely to have important consequences for leadership, that is to say both for the conditions of party leadership as well as for the type of potential leaders emerging. At the same time it must be stressed that shifts of this kind in the character of the party *Willensbildung* can exert an influence only gradually and unevenly. Prevailing styles of leadership still clearly reflect the pragmatic orientation of political activity in the Federal Republic and acceptance of the need to allow leaders substantial discretion in their handling of issues and problems that arise. What is under discussion here is not major changes in the terms of leadership that have already taken place, but rather tendencies within the parties which may erode the foundations for what have become familiar and widely accepted styles of leadership. Such leadership has been pragmatic, flexible in its response to demands voiced within the political system and, at its best, decisive and public-spirited.

This style of leadership has been closely related to some of the basic conditions of post-war German political development. It is a familiar fact that the stability and success of the principal German parties owe much to their character as popular or people's parties. In other words they are not sectarian in outlook and support, they rest neither on appeals to beliefs rigidly held by particular groups, nor to the interest of specific sectors of society. They are open and seemingly undogmatic, committed to the mobilisation of the widest support possible and to governing in the interests of the whole population.[5] That this pattern of development was established is attributable to several factors: to widespread agreement in the post-war period on the practical objectives of economic reconstruction, to the revulsion against ideological politics, to the style of leadership and success of Adenauer and to the structure and outlook of the Christian Democratic movement which dominated the first two decades of the Federal Republic's existence. Together these factors compelled the other parties to conform or to disappear, and the result was a vast simplification of political alignments, the emergence of a party system best characterised as a two-bloc alignment, but qualified in operation by the residues of federalism, proportionality and coalition.

It is in this context that the prevailing style of leadership has to be set, a style shaped decisively by those who have held the highest office in the Federal Government.[6] Adenauer established the decisive example from the start, offering a style of leadership which rested on pragmatism in the choice of policies, a direct appeal to the electorate at large, and on assertion of the prerogatives of the political office which he held for fourteen years. Whilst by no means indifferent to the importance of party as a means of mobilising support, he had no hesitation in relegating to a secondary position the claims to a major role in policy-making of the rather tenuous Christian Democratic Union party organisation which stood behind him. All his successors tried to lead in a similar way just as most of the unsuccessful contenders for high office also gave promise of sticking to the same ideal. His immediate successor, Erhard, lacked the practical politician's skill to lead in this way and fell victim to the dissatisfaction of the parties, including in the first place his own, the CDU and its sister party the CSU (Christian Social Union). Kiesinger had to act under the special constraints of a Grand Coalition between 1966 and 1969 which severely limited the leadership he could offer, but during his time in office (and for a very short while afterwards in opposition) it was clear that he professed fidelity to what we can call the Adenauer model. Brandt, like Erhard, believed that vision was more impor- tant than tactical skill and when the vision ceased to sustain concrete achievements, he gave way in 1974 to the present Chancellor who, more than any other, conforms to the model handed down by Adenauer. Set against this view of leadership one of Brandt's principal weaknesses was to listen rather too much to the Social Democratic Party and to take his cue too often from arguments proceeding within it. In contrast Helmut Schmidt often conveys the impression of listening to the party only as much as is necessary and of responding to the demands expressed inside it only to the extent that to do so will not endanger the policies and leadership on which his own position – and that of the party – depend.

All this is to argue that the dominant idea of leadership is marked by a strong conception of the discretion that a leader can and should claim. Leaders are not to be seen enveloped in the grey folds of collective decision-making, their image is not that of party bureaucrats, they are not even regarded in the first place as brokers and negotiators, no matter how much brokerage they may in reality have to undertake.

THE PARTIES IN STATE AND SOCIETY

It is in the light of this experience that what can now be regarded as the dominance and pervasiveness of party is somewhat puzzling. It might have been expected that parties, and especially the two major parties, would have become organisations held together chiefly for the purpose of fighting elections and putting forward candidates for office. Instead, whilst they certainly perform these functions, they have in addition consolidated their hold on many sectors of public life and established a kind of hegemony in society as the organisations through which political opinion is formed and from which political direction and leadership have to come. To a remarkable extent the independent, the constructive nonconformist, the eccentric have all vanished from public life. From social and economic organisations outside the public sphere (and therefore at least in part outside the far-reaching influence of party) there are but few creative impulses to the shaping of public opinion on issues of importance. Despite the respect paid to 'experts' and to learning, the individual scholar and thinker now makes only a modest impact on how problems are defined and how they might be tackled: the German professor as an individual likely to enjoy both social prestige and sapiential authority belongs more to the past than to the present. Nor has the Federal Republic much familiarity with the kind of opinion-forming which is facilitated through the royal commission type of inquiry in Britain, a device which despite the motives of prevarication and even evasion of responsibility by governments associated with it, nevertheless does testify to a belief that not all wisdom is party wisdom.

The consolidation of the dominant position of the parties in political life and in many other areas of organised social activity has been assisted, of course, by such measures as the establishment of a public financing system to support their electoral activities and indirectly the maintenance of effective organisations for exerting an influence on public opinion. True to the predilections noted long ago by Michels, German parties have been keenly aware of the advantages conferred by careful and extensive organisation for the purpose both of engaging their own active supporters and of building up support in society. Careers can be (and are) made in and through party organisations and parties have succeeded in penetrating many areas of public service and of activity outside the conventional limits of government. The penetration of the public sector by party is assisted by the relatively flexible and generous conditions governing participation in politics by officials of different kinds. Officials can be active inside a party and stand for election on its behalf without sacrificing their professional status and prospects.

The parties owe their success, however, to their own efforts as well. During the past decade the main German parties can pride themselves on having maintained a relatively high level of public interest and involvement in their work. Membership has not fallen; on the contrary it has tended to rise so that the principal parties – SPD, CDU, CSU and FDP – have together not far short of two million members. State financial support has been invaluable but it has not entirely supplanted a substantial flow of income from members, supporters and party profit-making undertakings. If we look at the infrastructure of party organisation, both at a national level and below, it shows no serious signs of decay or neglect, and the manner in which election campaigns are conducted testifies to the vigour and determination of those involved to achieve the maximum impact on the voters. Yet alongside so much which underlines the preoccupation of the parties with political persuasion in the market-places and with establishing the claims of their leaders to be qualified for high office, there have been changes in the pattern of active membership inside the parties, in the kind of activity actually carried out through the party organisations, and in the conception that many have of the purpose or role of a political party. Inevitably these changes have an impact on current leadership and they may well have an even greater influence on the kind of leadership that can be provided in the future.

The points so far made suggest the existence of a somewhat paradoxical situation. The parties have conformed to the model of non-ideological competition for voter support: their appeal has been wide and their readiness to bargain and compromise high. Leadership has been in differing degrees pragmatic and directive, sensitive to the need to maintain a public reputation for competence and flexibility. Yet at the same time the parties have steadily consolidated their own structures of party life and activity, extending their penetration at all levels of the political system and in many other sectors of society outside the conventional sphere of politics as well. This is a matter of considerable importance and reveals a difference between the Federal Republic and many other democratic societies. Party penetrates widely and deeply in West Germany and party commitment or sympathy is generally accepted as the most significant single differentiating characteristic in very many sectors of public life. In contrast, parties have in many countries – in Britain, in France, in the USA for example – a much narrower and more specific role. They are in the first place the means of organising political choice and they do this periodically when elections take place. This process involves primarily the choice of persons: programmes, policies and ideology influence the choice, but the context out of which these matters take shape and become objects of public discussion is far less monopolised by parties than is usually the case in the Federal Republic. In other words, parties are held to have a fairly specialised political function, discharged in a social environment which they can hardly claim to dominate even if they wished to.

In this regard the position is different in the Federal Republic. There parties have become pervasive, seeing themselves as 'bearers of the state' (*Staatsträger*) in virtue of their mission to express the political will of the people. To a remarkable extent parties which still recognise their origins as organised social forces, voluntary associations of citizens, aspire to absorb and direct social life in the name of the political role which they fulfil. As a result the traditional dichotomy between state and society so often drawn in German political thinking can be given a new interpretation and significance: it can be held that society is directed not by the autonomous state expressive of public interest values, but by those forces within it which have successfully established a claim to embody the state in virtue of their ability to express the political will of the majority.

The grounds for making such a claim do, however, remain ambiguous. To some extent the parties are simply engaged in legitimising the strategies they pursue to maximise support amongst those groups in the electorate on which each of them chiefly relies. There would still be genuine hesitation in advancing in an open way what might be described as a hegemonic claim, and in any event it is hard for competing parties collectively to do this. Nevertheless many of the political practices in the Federal Republic seem to imply something like such a claim on behalf of the established parties as a whole. The fact, for example, that so much legislation[7] is finally approved unanimously and after a procedure dominated by opportunities to formulate distinctive party views on every aspect of legislation, underlines the dominance of the parties as the sources of authoritative decisions.

THE CHANGING CHARACTER OF PARTY MEMBERSHIP

The contention now to be advanced is that the evolution in the role of the parties just sketched out, and some of the circumstances accompanying it, threaten the continuance of the kind of strong political leadership which on the whole has been regarded as desirable in the Federal Republic. What has happened is that in virtue of the constitutional role assigned to them parties have been constrained to think more and more in terms of their contribution to shaping political opinion. As the logic of the responsibility conferred on them for the *Willensbildung* in society was pursued, more attention began to be paid to the processes of opinion and policy formation within the parties. This received a special impetus in the late sixties as a result of the intensification of arguments about democratisation. Such arguments could quite properly be applied to the internal life of parties and to the conditions under which their *Willensbildung* took place. Gradually the concern with defining policy positions within the parties became a dominant feature in the work of many active party members. That the results rarely had a direct and speedy impact on the policy decisions of those in office has not so far been regarded as all that serious, no doubt in part because there has continued to be a lively awareness in all parties of the need to maintain popular support amongst an electorate largely disposed to trust the competence of those in office rather than to respond enthusiastically to the ideas and schemes of assiduous and dedicated party members.

The increased emphasis on the formation of opinion inside the parties reflects, however, far more than the impact of democratisation theories on them. Nor is it simply a response to the need to have a party position on a wide range of policy matters on account of the extended interests now acquired by the parties. A major factor influencing the attention given to the intra-party *Willensbildung* has been a steady change in the outlook and qualities of many of the party activists. The proportion of intellectuals or of people with an academic education active in all the parties has been steadily rising for over a decade. To an increasing extent the parties risk becoming at the level of active participation unrepresentative of the population at large and of their own supporters as well.

There are serious difficulties in the way of providing a reliable quantitative assessment of the proportion of active members in all the main parties who can reasonably be classified as intellectuals in virtue of their educational background and attainments. A fairly reliable indicator of their presence is, however, provided by such evidence as is available on the educational and professional background of elected representatives of the parties in the Bundestag and in provincial parliaments. In the Bundestag the proportion of members from some part of the public service sector reached about 40 per cent in 1972 and remained at that level in 1976. Just over 30 per cent were classified as former officials (*Beamte*), about 5 per cent as employees in public service (*Angestellte*) and amongst the category of current and former members of the Government there are enough former public servants to bring the total to around 40 per cent. A further 5.4 per cent were in 1976 classified as former employees of the parties which means that they too can be regarded as more or less within the sphere of public employment. These figures[8] reveal a continuing upward trend from the early years of the Federal Republic, though it needs to be remembered that even in 1957 the proportion of ex-officials and employees in the Bundestag fell little short of 30 per cent.

In the *Landtage* the trends are similar. There it was always likely that officials would be heavily represented, chiefly on account of the presence of so many members holding office in local government. Some steps have been taken in several *Länder* during the seventies to tighten up the rules on incompatibilities with the aim of reducing the local government element, but this has to some extent been offset by the growing strength of the teaching professions as sources of recruits to the provincial parliaments. Thus in Bavaria, for example, by 1976 the proportion of *Landtag* members from public service exceeded a half, about a third of whom could be classified as teachers. And this dominance of public service recruits was particularly marked in the SPD which has lost practically all its representatives drawn from industry and the trade unions. Looked at globally about 46 per cent of the people sitting in all the *Land* parliaments in 1975 can be classed as belonging to the public service group (632 out of 1378) and within this group again something like a third are teachers.[9]

Turning briefly to educational background, it needs first to be noted that most of the officials and employees come from the higher level of the public service. Therefore, they are bound to have a university qualification. In the Bundestag the proportion of members reported as having an academic education has risen from about 45 per cent in 1949 to 70 per cent in 1976. In both the CDU/CSU and FDP the proportion is now round about 80 per cent, in the SPD something like 55 per cent (compared with 29 per cent in 1949 and 38 per cent in 1965).

It is, of course, true that these trends simply reflect in some measure the expansion of higher education and training: they are to be expected. Equally they reflect the importance of formal qualifications in the organisation of German society, a point in respect of which the Federal Republic still differs markedly from Britain. Yet at the same time there can be little doubt that the predominant position of people with a higher education and from public service employment does express the preferences of many of those now active in the parties. The selection of candidates is inevitably biased in the direction of those with the kind of qualifications and skills possessed by the active party members who have a voice in the nomination process at different levels of the party organisations.

The influx of highly educated and articulate party members tends to produce in the lower reaches of the party organisations at least a rather different view of the purposes served by a party than any that has so far been dominant. For such members parties quickly take on the character of organisations dedicated to the production of programmes: the *Willens-bildung* is seen as being directed to the formulation of policy opinions and commitments. Additionally there is often strong support for the view that parties need to be able to offer a coherent diagnosis of the problems in society. Each sectoral diagnosis ought then to be related to the wider theoretical analysis of social and economic relationships. So there develops a commitment to thoroughgoing programmatic thinking founded on rational argument and analysis within the parties. Not surprisingly such a view is likely to be associated with a rather critical approach to many traditional party activities. Electoral campaigning begins to appear to many as a slightly regrettable diversion from the main task of forming opinion on policies inside the party on the basis of rational argument and analysis. A pragmatic and short-term approach to problem-solving is widely viewed as a hindrance to the emergence of comprehensive schemes of beneficent public action.

These attitudes have major implications for leadership. They point towards a depreciation of its significance. For if politics really is an activity to be guided by rational analysis and a proper theoretical understanding of what is to be done, then it is possible to conclude that leadership is potentially redundant. Decisions will, ideally, be informed by the light of reason, leaders will recognise the party as an organisation for the diffusion of a rational appreciation of policy objectives, and leadership will accept a role much closer to that of executant of party programmes. How the people outside the parties, a missing element in these equations, are to be persuaded to accept the programmatic thinking of the parties is a matter generally left unexplored by those who advocate and practise this view of the purpose of party.

The plea for democratisation so often voiced in recent years undoubtedly helps to explain why the ideal of the party as a source of policy programmes has gained a foothold in all parties and in particular has made considerable advances in the SPD. This is not the place to consider the various interpretations and applications of such an emotive and imprecise term as democratisation. What is important is to recognise that democratisation has usually implied the desirability of and the need for more active participation in whatever kind of body is being 'democratised'. The emphasis has been on involving people in the process of opinion-forming and decision-taking on the grounds that only when such conditions are satisfied is it possible to say that people are really taking decisions themselves and thus realising a particular concept of democracy. Inside political parties the theory of democratisation has been assumed by many to mean the encouragement of members to make a contribution to discussion, to take part in argument about policies and objectives, to identify themselves with the internal life of the party. The trouble with this theory when applied to parties is that it assumes that all or a majority of party members want to be active and, moreover, active in the sense of involving themselves regularly in policy arguments. Should this condition not be met – and there are many grounds for believing that most members of most parties have many things to do in life more important than having a voice in internal party argument – the plea for democratisation is liable to have exactly the opposite effect from that proposed by its exponents. Instead of widening participation it may narrow it by seeking to impose on the majority of party members a particular idea of what participation calls for and to what it should be directed.

THE ROLE OF THE INTELLECTUALS

As to the rise of the intellectual in German parties, or more accurately, his return to prominence, it is clear that in some degree an increase in the proportion of party members and more especially, of party activists and candidates for office with an academic education was inevitable. As already noted this is in part a natural consequence of the expansion of higher education which began in the early sixties and has continued ever since. But it is striking that there are several countries in which the proportion of people receiving college and university education is equal to or higher than in the Federal Republic, but in which there has not been such a reinforcement of the role of intellectuals in the parties: the USA and Japan are obvious examples. The peculiarity of the German experience over the past ten years or so is that activity inside the parties, attitudes towards the purposes served by active involvement in them, and the character of the representatives put forward by them have come to mirror in such a marked way the qualities possessed by an intellectual group with academic training amongst the membership of the parties. This trend has been powerful and even dramatic in the SPD; it has been strong too in the FDP; and numerous signs of its presence can be found in the CDU and CSU. Needless to say, nearly all minor parties, and notably the new phenomenon of the *Grüne Liste* (the ecology movement or party), are even more decisively shaped by the academic class – or caste – than are the established parties.

Reference has already been made to the fact that, when considering the role of intellectuals in parties, it is important to remember that it is not just a question of the kind of education such people have had and how it influences their behaviour. We are also concerned with professional groups, with people who have taken up careers underlining their membership of a broad intellectual class. The obvious example is teaching, a profession covering a very wide spectrum of institutions from the primary school to the advanced research institute. The public administration sector in the Federal Republic provides many opportunities for activities offering scope for the application of knowledge and skills gained in the course of an academic education. And, of course, there is now a growing field of publicity, communication and journalism in which the intellectual can find plenty of scope for his talents. It is predominantly from such professional fields that the intellectuals inside the parties now come, from professions concerned with some form of communication rather than with much more practical forms of activity. It is a further consequence of this situation that a high proportion of the recent intellectual intake into the parties has been educated in some branch of the social sciences or law. The latter subject was, of course, always a foundation for a career in public life and its importance has been enhanced by the important role of legal interpretation in the political and social life of the Federal Republic. A significant change that has taken place over the past twenty years is, however, that the social sciences have begun to weaken the monopoly so long held by law.

Much could be said about the character and problems of the social sciences; but in the present context only one point needs to be made, and that is that there is a reasonably high probability that many social scientists will accept in one way or another the validity of some kind of social engineering. Social science rests on the belief that there can be systematic knowledge of social phenomena. Many are inclined to believe that it must follow from this that there is at least a prospect of showing that systematic social knowledge can be used for the solution of problems in society, that is to say for some measure of social engineering. There might be no serious difficulty if the claims of social science and those made on behalf of social engineering went no further than this modest and sceptical formulation of the argument. There is, however, a large and varied ideological component in modern social science and this has in turn been mirrored in schemes for more or less comprehensive social engineering which have gained support, particularly in the SPD. In short, the visionary social scientist easily becomes a visionary social engineer. And, of course, social engineers in this loose sense are likely to have a high propensity to join parties, since parties are seen as the instruments for achieving whatever schemes of social engineering they espouse. Thus it is not surprising that the intellectual intake into the parties during recent years is marked by a strong injection of people who are not only social scientists by education, but who for that reason incline towards a social engineering view of politics and political action. Again, because the ideological component in such a view tends to be reformist and progressive, it is the SPD which has been most affected by this trend.

Reference has now been made to some of the principal factors producing a change in the prevailing view of the ends to which party activity is directed: the call for wider involvement and more intra-party argument; the increase in intellectual membership and especially of people with a social science background; the fascination exerted by notions of social planning or control; the advantages enjoyed by activists inside a party who can rapidly acquire a professional mastery of how to operate within the ogranisation. People inside the parties who do not share these interests then tend to be repelled from active party work, whilst many also feel powerfully the attraction of activities of a completely non-political kind. As the activism of the intellectual grows, so his influence on personnel decisions within the party grows: candidates to delegate conferences and candidates for election tend more and more to reflect the preference of intellectuals for people like themselves. Nor are there many countervailing institutional obstacles in the Federal Republic to the tendency. The internal party organisation is essentially hierarchical from the bottom up, and the principle of delegation upwards on which it rests facilitates the progress of those who have the time and the inclination (as well as the ability) to concentrate on establishing a point of view and a following within the party hierarchy. In fact a successful party career demands specialisation in the methods of manipulating the party organisation and finding a way through it. Moreover, there are few significant popular pressures from constituencies. The constituency (certainly for federal and *Land* elections) is less important than the different levels of party organisation, the use of a list alongside constituencies means that most candidates in constituencies are sure to be elected anyway, and the constituency party organisation tends to see itself rather as at or near the bottom of the party structure than as a kind of autonomous unit in the party as is still often true in Britain. Thus the party activist of an intellectual cast of mind finds few obstacles in the party structures themselves to his progress. He owes nearly everything to the party and activity within it, and is usually insulated against exposure to the objections of the plain man outside the circle of professional party workers.[10]

The developments just outlined have had their biggest effect on the SPD. In several parts of the country – in West Berlin, in Munich, in Frankfurt and Hessen-Süd, in Bremen, for example, the party has been extensively colonised by intellectuals and those with an academic background. *Pari passu* there has been a marked decline in the involvement in party life of members without these educational advantages, notably those who in the past came into the party via the trade union movement. But the problem for the SPD is not simply how to retain trade union and working-class active support: it is also how to retain the support of other professional groups whose members engage in practical and productive activities and without whose support it is harder to sustain the claim to be a party of the people, representative of all sections of the people.

The impact of the intellectual has been felt in the Free Democratic Party too. For the past decade the FDP has suffered from uncertainty about the identity of the electorate to which it wished to appeal. The party sought to shift its voting base from the higher levels of the professions and the public service and business to a much more heterogeneous middle-class clientele, many of whom were believed to hold progressive and reforming opinions. Thus, the FDP has deliberately appealed to a section of society which consists nowadays predominantly of academically trained people. Moreover, in its search for a new electorate the party has chosen to appeal to those to whom a touch of nonconformity and even of protest is attractive. After all, the FDP is itself a continuing protest against the threat of the complete dominance of the two major parties. The internal evolution of the FDP has for more than a decade mirrored the shift in its appeal and in the kind of support it has received from the electorate. It too has had to put up with the sometimes embarrassing behaviour of its Young Democrats organisation which, like the Young Socialists, functions as a kind of Kindergarten for aspirants to a political career in and through the party. And the youth organisations, like the parent parties, have become targets for intellectuals, sometimes in their case the eternal student. At the national level the character of the FDP representation has changed – away from business and commerce, over to the intellectual and public service professions. This in turn mirrors what has been going on inside the party organisation.

The CDU and its ambitious ally the CSU appear so far to be least affected by the rise of the intellectuals. There is, however, no reason to believe that the CDU has been exempt from the general trend under discussion. In the first place, during the years in opposition its organisation has been energetically built up in order to make good the influence lost after 1969 when no longer in control of the Federal Government. This has brought about a professionalisation of the party which has largely closed the gap in terms of the sociology of organisations between itself and the SPD. It has, of course, provided many more opportunities for careers to be made through the party organisation. Second, the party has actively extended its membership and this has inevitably brought into it many people with academic experience similar to that of those going into the other parties too. The qualities of many of those aged about 40–45 who are reaching positions of leadership in the party reflect these changes. Third, the party has in opposition had to think carefully about its programme and its broad approach to the problems faced by the Federal Republic. As a party determined to maintain its claim to be returned to power it had to appear to have policies representing a coherent alternative to those of the SPD and FDP. There is room for doubt whether this has been achieved. The results of this preoccupation with the party's orientation and policies have been blurred by arguments about personalities and who should lead the party (or rather the two parties) as well as by the opportunism in respect of strategy and tactics to which a party in opposition easily falls prey. But that does not alter the fact that the CDU and CSU have had to engage in an internal policy discussion to an extent not known since the early days of the Federal Republic when the Christian Democratic movement was just taking shape. Such circumstances have clearly offered scope to those in the party who have a taste for argument and analysis on account of the benefits of an academic training which they enjoy.

There are no doubt ideological reasons why the impact of intellectuals has, however, so far been less in the CDU and CSU than in the other parties. The doctrinal bias of these parties is still against abstraction and general theorising in politics, suspicious of ambitious schemes of social engineering, and favourable to the interests and opinions of 'the ordinary man' in his various guises. Thus the chances are that it is the more sceptical kind of intellectual who has given support to the CDU/CSU and he (or she) is by definition unlikely to attach such high priority to programmatic argument. Equally important has been the fact that the Christian Democratic parties embrace relatively heterogeneous social and economic interests, the spokesmen for which see politics very much in terms of bargaining and the adjustment of competing claims. This makes for a party environment which has remained resistant to the opinions and preferences of those who by training and outlook would like to see a more coherent attempt to re-define party principles and the relationship of policies to them. Nevertheless, the parties of the right cannot remain immune to the general tendencies at work in German political life. More and more active CDU members come from the service sector of employment, have an academic training and see their career prospects as being closely linked with their party work. In parallel the proportion of representatives from the independent professions and small business has declined. Additionally the two major blocs increasingly compete for the same social groups: there is now little difference in social terms between those supporting the SPD and those supporting the CDU/CSU.[11]

The developments outlined point to the emergence of a somewhat new kind of political class and to a change in the character of the parties themselves. The political class referred to is by no means a narrowly circumscribed elite, nor can it be described as exclusive. Its distinguishing characteristics are academic education, professional activity mainly in the public sector and in the parties themselves, and a readiness to see political work as a job for the professional. Professionalism in this sense puts emphasis on knowing how to operate within a party and on advocacy in that framework. This dimension is added to the more traditional sense of professionalism as indicative of specialised knowledge and experience relevant to particular sectors of social activity and public policy-making. By training and experience many of the members of these new party elites are inclined to believe that political activity needs to be shaped by a coherent view of what is to be achieved and how. Politics is about improving society according to a plan rather than about responding expediently to demands, satisfying claims, warding off dangers. It is this outlook which supports the claim at all levels of the parties for more effort to be devoted to the elaboration of programmes and analysis of the social context in which they would have to be applied. As to the impact of these developments on the parties, they tend more and more to become introverted organisations under such conditions. Their public role in the political system remains and they are subject still to all the pressures involved in competitive electoral politics. Nevertheless, for many of the activists what really matters is what goes on inside their party. They become impatient of the negotiation and bargaining which inevitably accompany the exercise of political responsibility; they think less and less of the representative function of parties on behalf of the electorate, especially in relation to voicing the worries and needs of those outside the parties themselves; their eyes are fixed on a curious combination of future policy visions and personal career prospects held out by active work in and through the party.

LEADERSHIP AND THE PARTIES

We can now return to the question of leadership in parties which have moved or are moving in the directions suggested. In principle it might be expected that leadership of the familiar kind would become more difficult; indeed that this might already have happened. The changes in the attitudes of party members and in the balance between different kinds of member which have been outlined suggest an increasingly critical approach to leadership and a growing reluctance to allow leaders wide discretion in office. Such changes would in theory count against pragmatic politics and point towards an effort to tie leaders more closely to something like a mandate, conferred not so much by the people as by the party membership through its determination of party aims and programmes.

Now we know that no such dramatic change has yet taken place. Party leaders depend on party and must devote considerable effort to maintaining support for the positions they take up, whether in government or in opposition. But party leaders are not tied by detailed and specific manifesto promises in the British manner, and in office they can often show convincingly that they have sufficient room for manoeuvre to take decisions such as they hold to be required by the circumstances rather than of the kind suggested by party programmes or resolutions. No leader has demonstrated this more plainly than Chancellor Schmidt who has taken little trouble to conceal his disagreement with several features of majority opinion inside the SPD. Instead he has often preferred to stick to his own policies, confident that he can carry the electorate with him and outflank such opposition as there may be in his own party. On the other hand this approach of Chancellor Schmidt has not always worked successfully. This is illustrated by the growing difficulty he has encountered in going ahead with nuclear energy development in the face of hostility inside the SPD, and that despite a broad measure of trade union support for such a programme. Certainly the Chancellor has stuck to his own judgment of what is needed in the nuclear field, but the pace at which nuclear generation of electricity can be pushed forward has been slowed down and this owes much to the need to acknowledge the demands of critics within the party.

There are certain conditions which still tend to protect political leaders against the full impact of more argumentative and theorising party supporters. The dynamics of the electoral process in a situation in which there is essentially a two-party competition for the highest offices are important; there is the continuing influence of expectations amongst the public about political leadership and its style which are inherited from the earlier years of the Federal Republic's history; there is the fact that most senior politicians have been moulded by the experience of reasonably firm leadership, not tied too closely to party policy commitments. These factors continue to sustain a style of leadership invested with wide discretion: a large part of the electorate expects German political leaders to be able to take decisions and to ensure that their parties back them up.

Yet this picture fits uncomfortably with the growing emphasis on the *Willensbildung* inside parties and with the attitude towards this very process of determining opinions which has developed as a consequence of the increase in the involvement of intellectuals in the parties. This is particularly the case for the SPD, since it is here that the programmatic tradition is strongest and it is into the SPD that the cadres of academically trained activists have flowed in greatest number. Here it is possible to detect most clearly the beginnings of what may become an acute and debilitating problem for the German parties as a whole. For what is happening is that the foundation and support in the parties for those leadership methods and style that have developed in the political system of the Federal Republic over the past thirty years are gradually slipping away. Here no reference is intended to political radicalism or any 'long march through the institutions'. It is rather that the parties show signs of becoming less concerned with appealing to a broad band of public opinion and with acting as brokers and mediators between interests than with their own programmes and internal arguments. This tendency is accompanied by a retreat into an increasingly theoretical view of politics. At the same time the tight and enclosed character of party organisation encourages amongst their most active adherents the belief that a career can and should be made entirely within the party rather than by acting in a public world on behalf of the party.

These developments have had little direct impact on leadership so far because the parties and the Federal Republic itself can still live on the capital of the recent past. The challenge and the problem lie in the future: how will leadership fare when the candidates for office themselves are overwhelmingly products of the changes in party membership and in the dominant styles of party activity which have been outlined here? Then there will be a situation in which those who aspire to lead will mainly be drawn from those who have helped to establish the idea that what matters is intra-party argument and the process of opinion formation inside the party. Most probably they will be people who see politics as an activity concerned with translating a theory into action, of finding the one right solution to a problem. Yet their claim to lead may well be subverted by their own commitment to the pre-eminence of the process of *Willensbildung* itself: they will have no reasoned ground for asserting that the vocation of politics in a democracy requires of a politician the readiness to assume public responsibility for his own decisions.

The prospect of a development in the direction just indicated can hardly be discounted if we look beyond the present leadership of the German parties. In the SPD it is hard to discern who might at national level prolong the style of leadership provided by Chancellor Schmidt. In the *Länder* there are already examples of a new generation of SPD leaders, some of whom reveal a lack of political skill and a weakness in relation to the party they lead which augurs ill for a capacity to define issues which worry the electorate and to mobilise public support. Similar tendencies can be seen at work in the FDP, no doubt accentuated by the chances of rapid advancement open in a small party to the articulate and ambitious young party activist. In the CDU and CSU, too, the post-war generation of leaders is giving way to a type of politician marked very heavily by his achievements inside the party organisation. Yet in the CDU/CSU it is possible that the years in opposition since 1969 at the national level may still prove a blessing in disguise by ensuring that at least some of the contenders for high office have, through experience in *Land* Governments, acquired a capacity for asserting themselves in relation to the demands coming forward from within the party.

Events and personalities may still reverse the tendencies discussed here. Moreover, the pattern of development is by no means uniform and consistent: there are at all levels of the German political system people who would take with more than a pinch of salt the elevation of programme and policy formulation inside the parties to the status of the most important function discharged by them.[12] And inevitably there are the pressures of day-to-day problem-solving which tell against attaching too much importance to the resolutions and programmes of the dedicated party activists. Indeed, there is a sense in which the intellectual in politics is condemned to undermine the very claims he makes for a perfect *Willensbildung*. For the preoccupation with argument, analysis and programmes deflects attention from the here and now and from close concern with many of the decisions which those in office must inescapably take as a matter of routine. Thus to some extent those with the responsibilities of leadership are freed from day-to-day political pressure by the very fact that so many of those who might be concerned with calling them to account have their attention focused on broader and longer-term issues.

Nevertheless, if the German parties are to maintain that capacity for realistic and effective leadership which on the whole they have so far been able to provide, there is a need to look critically at what is going on within their own organisations. Apart from looking more sceptically at the claims of intellectuals in politics, they may need to question whether it is desirable that the conventions and rules of the political system should offer to career politicians working through a party rather more security of tenure than is good for them. It is important, too, to remember that the politician in a democratic system has in the final analysis only one resource at his disposal: his capacity to communicate, to persuade, to convince. But to communicate he must speak a language which people understand, he must be able to express issues in terms which make some impact on the imagination of ordinary voters, and he must respond to perceived problems. Nothing brings out more vividly the limitations of many contemporary intellectuals in politics than their attachment to jargon, to the specialised languages of the particular disciplines in which they have been trained. That the growth of the social sciences has contributed to the obfuscation of the language of politics in the Federal Republic as elsewhere hardly needs to be stated; but political leadership, if it is to be effective, cannot survive on such an arid diet. Not the least of the challenges facing the parties and their leaders is to find a language which will enable them to maintain their ties with the people.

NOTES AND REFERENCES

1. The Law on Parties 1967, as amended in 1969 after an adverse ruling of the Federal Constitutional Court, provides for such financial support.
2. These provisions have been used successfully on only two occasions when the Sozialistische Reichspartei and the German Communist Party (KPD) were declared unconstitutional and dissolved in 1952 and 1956 respectively. It is probable that very special conditions would now have to be met before any attempt would be made to invoke Article 21 of the Basic Law against an extremist political party. It acts as a kind of background injunction or threat rather than as a source of direct constraint on parties which pursue aims in conflict with the prevailing constitutional consensus.

3. The *Geschäftsordnung* of the Bundestag explicitly provides for the recognition of parliamentary parties or *Fraktionen* in Section IV. In many situations procedures can be brought into play only if supported by a number of Members equivalent to the minimum required to constitute a *Fraktion*, i.e. 5 per cent of the total membership. Such conditions are in reality designed for parties rather than groups of individual members.

4. Part II of the Law on Parties 1967 deals with internal order or organisation. The term *Willensbildung* occurs several times in this statute, e.g. in Section 15.

5. Despite the fact that it has lost support during the past twenty years and is now a relatively small party, the Free Democratic Party is in some respects a 'people's party' just like its rivals: it simply has less success in securing the people's support.

6. The remarks above refer to holders of the Chancellorship; but the experience of the *Länder* provides many examples of a similar approach to leadership and of politicians who established remarkable ascendancy over their parties.

7. In the 7th Bundestag 1972–76 it appears that 72.9 per cent of all draft laws going through to final approval were passed unanimously by the Bundestag: 87.6 per cent can be regarded as 'passed non-controversially'. See *30 Jahre Deutscher Bundestag* (Bonn, 1979), p. 273.

8. Nearly all the statistics quoted here are derived from tables in *30 Jahre Deutscher Bundestag*.

9. See A. Hess, 'Verbeamtung der Parlamente in Bund und Ländern', *Zeitschrift für Parlamentsfragen*, 6 Jg (1975) Heft 1, pp. 34–42.

10. These developments confirm to a remarkable extent Max Weber's view that the professionalisation of politics as a career, the transition from the dominance of 'notables' to that of professionals, represents the emergence of ruling elites who live off politics rather than for politics. The distinction has to be treated with caution, both in its historical application and in relation to the present. But its analytic value remains substantial.

11. See P. Gluckowski and H. J. Veen, 'Nivellierungstendenzen in den Wähler und Mitgliederschaften von CDU/CSU und SPD 1959–79', *Zeitschrift für Parlamentsfragen*, 10 Jg (1979) Heft 3, pp. 312–31. The analysis of these authors suggests that the only marked differences now are that rather more trade unionists vote SPD than CDU/CSU, and rather more small businessmen and independent professional people vote CDU/CSU than SPD.

12. The record of Herr Börner, Minister-President of Hesse since his departure from Bonn in 1976, may be regarded as an illustration of the impact which an experienced and pragmatic party leader may still have even on a party heavily influenced by the trends discussed in this chapter.

10 The German Electorate: Old Cleavages and New Political Conflicts

FRANZ URBAN PAPPI and MICHAEL TERWEY

INTRODUCTION

In recent interpretations of the attitudes and value orientations of the West German electorate the diagnosis of a value change and concomitant 'new politics' are overwhelming. The social science profession has expended some effort in investigating value changes and – as we sometimes read – the breakdown of the bourgeois value syndrome with its stress on occupational achievement and the family as one of the most important institutions of society (Döbert and Nunner-Winkler, 1973; Kmieciak, 1976; Klages and Kmieciak, 1979). The consequences of this value change for voting behaviour were already outlined some years ago by Inglehart (1971, 1977) and today are discussed under the heading 'new politics' (cf. Miller and Levitin, 1976; Hildebrandt and Dalton, 1977). The general assumption of Inglehart is that the long period of relative affluence after the Second World War has nurtured post-materialist values, especially among the younger generation, whereas the traditional class conflict in politics was based on a materialist or acquisitive orientation on both sides of the conflict line: the privileged versus the underprivileged. A decline of the traditional class cleavage is therefore predicted.

This finding is contrary to some orthodox Marxists' reasoning about class conflicts in late capitalist societies. In the sixties East German sociologists argued for a wide definition of the working class, including not only manual workers in the productive sector, but all wage and salary earners (cf. Steiner, 1967), and West German Marxists followed this direction to a certain extent (cf. Tjaden-Steinhauer and Tjaden, 1973). In this respect one can even detect similarities between the German Social Democrats and the Communists, quite apart from all their ideological differences. The SPD claims to be the party of all employees and calls for a 'Europa der Arbeitnehmer' (platform for the first direct election of the European parliament). This is a slightly modified expression of the wide rather than the narrow concept of the proletariat. A general proletarianisation would imply a decline of the impact of traditional middle-class values on politics and a growing importance of class. The Social Democrats should be the party to win the main advantage from this homogenisation of all employees. As the Christian Democrats are seen as representatives of the bourgeoisie and of the religious cleavage, their decline in the long run is predicted – the long run always being the hope of revisionists.

THREE INDICATORS OF THE CLEAVAGE STRUCTURE

Before we continue with these loose predictions of changes in the cleavage structure of the German electorate, it is necessary to define 'cleavages'. Not every change in voting behaviour has the consequence that the cleavage system changes too. We are mainly interested in social cleavages which we define as enduring coalitions between certain population groups and political parties (cf. Stinchcombe, 1975). Prototypes of such coalitions are the alliance of the working class with the SPD and the coalition between Catholics and the CDU. At the mass level, a first indicator of such a coalition is the difference in party preference between members and non-members of the population group in question. Our first task is to investigate whether these indicators of social cleavages remained stable or have changed over the past thirty years.

A change concerning this first indicator of the two main cleavages means, of course, that the cleavage system, too, is no longer the same; but the stability of this indicator is not sufficient to prove the stability of the cleavages. It is possible that a population group is still in coalition with the same party but that the rationale of the alliance is different. Unlikely as this may be, we have nevertheless to take it into account. Thus our second indicator will be a measure of the meaning or main motivation of the average group member for a vote in favour of the group's party. Our second task will be to modify the basic model and use value orientations as intervening variables between social structural determinants and party preference. We are arguing that the membership in a population group will lead to a specific attitude profile, either through socialisation or through common stimuli of interest articulation, and that these political attitudes will have a decisive influence on voting. If we can prove that the long-term attitudinal component of the vote remained more or less the same, we can speak of a stable cleavage system. Short-term influences or cleavage-neutral attitude changes are then supposed to be general influences on the electorate which are independent of the group structure of the population.

A third indicator of the cleavage structure has to be defined with respect to parties. If the average voter of a certain population group is equally motivated to vote for the same party every four years this behaviour makes sense only if the party itself has a certain ideological continuity. We shall assume this continuity, at least for the SPD and the CDU/CSU.

It is important to stress here that the election results for the different parties are not used as indicators of the cleavage structure. A decline of a party can be fully compatible with a stable cleavage structure, even if it is independent of short-term influences. It might happen, for instance, that a population group becomes smaller and that a simple demographic theory of change can explain the decline completely. The problem, of course, is whether there are thresholds beyond which there is no longer a social basis for certain policy alternatives; and as parties are corporate actors they will never follow social structural changes without trying to escape from such disadvantageous situations.

PREDICTIONS AND ASSUMPTIONS

Our main thesis is that the cleavage structure of the German polity has remained rather stable over the past thirty years. The interesting problem then is what we can say about future developments. Extrapolating to future developments will only be possible when we understand the mechanisms which produced the stability in the past.

One explanation of the stability of modern party systems was given by Lipset and Rokkan some years ago. They argued that the modern parties are mass organisations which narrowed the support market (1967, p. 51) and left:

> very little leeway for a decisive breakthrough of new party alternatives. It is not an accident that situations of this type generate a great deal of frustration, alienation and protestation within the organisationally least committed sections of the community, the young, and, quite particularly, the students. (1967, p. 54).

In the meantime we have learned that not all West European party systems show the same stability and that the less stable systems, such as in Denmark, were not necessarily the ones with the most forceful student movements. Instead of investigating the organisational basis we shall ask whether the old cleavage system is held in existence by mechanisms at the level of the social and value structure of the electorate, mechanisms which are either independent from short-term political influences or which gradually integrate new political conflicts into the old system.

We started with the two simple predictions of a decline of the class cleavage on the one side and of the religious cleavage on the other side. With our definition of social celavages in mind we are now able to argue both for the stability of the old cleavage system *and* new political conflicts. If the issue-public concerned with the post-materialist issues of 'new politics' is mainly the younger generation, quite irrespective of its social origin or its present social structural position, then this new conflict line may only be superimposed on the traditional cleavages which will stay more or less intact. The situation will be different when a post-materialist orientation is nurtured by certain social structural positions and not by others. The main problem here is how location in the social structure is properly conceptualised as there are internal structural divisions which cannot be characterised as status or class differences. In contrast to the vertical gradation of occupational status or prestige the concept of *situs* has been developed to denote horizontally distinct spheres of function. In contrast to class-location, *situs* is not defined by basic positions in the general process of production and commodity-realisation (property or authority), but by sectoral differences between occupation groups. Therefore economic sectors may be used as an approximating operationalisation to grasp this dimension of social organisation. We shall test the hypothesis that *situs* differences become an important determinant of political attitudes, in addition to class differences. As the economic interests of the employed population are heavily dependent on the industrial sector, this relationship should have political consequences. Especially in the public sector incomes are relatively secure; we thus anticipate that this sector will be one of the social niches of the post-materialists.

A second reason for our attention to *situs* or the economic sector is that this variable plays an important role for the narrow concept of the proletariat. If a surplus is produced only in the primary and secondary sectors of the economy, and if the exploitation of wage labour is capitalistically organised in the secondary sector, then the workers of this sector should be the vanguard of the revolution. Put into more sociological jargon we should anticipate that political attitudes which are expressions of the old class cleavage have their stronghold among manual workers in industry.

Whether one is an adherent of the narrow or wide definition of the proletariat one has to explain why class conflict has been rather subdued in Western Germany since the Second World War. Some sociologists look for an explanation at the organisational level and mention the institutionalisation of collective bargaining mechanisms (cf. Dahrendorf, 1959; Lepsius, 1979). In the recent discussion of the concept of liberal corporatism some of these older arguments of an institutionalised class conflict are generalised to a broader theory of interest mediation (Schmitter, 1977; Lehmbruch, 1977). This new system is characterised by an elitist bias and the elites of large organisations such as unions may have problems in ensuring the loyalty of their followers.

Neo-Marxists have pointed at social structural forces which help the elites in manipulating the public towards a more passive mass loyalty instead of a true legitimacy (Habermas, 1973; Offe, 1972; Narr and Offe, 1975). At the same time it provides an explanation of why there is no open class conflict in late capitalist societies. Such social structural forces at the mass level are status inconsistencies, cross pressures, heterogeneous influences during work and leisure time, and so on. The most important argument is that the old vertical class structure is being undermined by a new system of horizontal disparities between different domains or functionally specified subsystems of society. In late capitalist societies the life chances of aggregates of individuals are no longer exclusively determined by their market capacity but, to an increasing degree, by politically and institutionally regulated collective goods in areas such as education, housing, and health care. Whether one is dependent on these forms of regulation or not is not just a consequence of one's location in the class structure, but of other positions, such as position in life-cycle. In so far as the same individual can belong, in temporal sequence, to privileged and underprivileged domains, the old cleavage between population groups becomes an internal cleavage between different positions pertaining to the same individual.

For our analysis in the last section of this chapter we shall draw two conclusions from these arguments. We first have to make sure that position in the social structure is conceptualised not only as class position but as position in a broader sense – we have already mentioned *situs* differences and we shall make additional distinctions among the unemployed adult population. Furthermore, we have to pay attention to attitudes of loyalty or political alienation in addition to value orientations which form the link between old social cleavages and party preference. Politically alienated groups and the coalitions of the old cleavage system may be at odds with each other.

THE PARTY PREFERENCE OF POPULATION GROUPS SINCE THE 1950s

The first indicator of social cleavages are differences in voting behaviour between population groups. Theoretically it is difficult to explain which population groups will form the basis of political cleavages. Latent and manifest interest, the capability to build up new organisations, the options of the party elites are all factors which have to be taken into account. For our purposes it is sufficient to start with a simple enumeration of the traditional coalitions of German politics: the coalition of the working class with the SPD and of the Catholics with the CDU. This exposition raises enough problems to be resolved.

The main problem is the asymmetry of this cleavage system. Provided one of two major religious groups is in coalition with one of the two major parties, does this have consequences for the other religious group? This may not be the case, especially because the original conflict, the *Kulturkampf* of the 1870s, was a conflict between the Catholic Church and the state and not primarily one between the two religions. Moreover the party of the religious dimension, the CDU/CSU, is no longer a Catholic party like the *Zentrum*, but was founded after the Second World War as a non-secular party for both Catholics and Protestants. Compared with the Weimar Republic, one would expect that the religious cleavage in the old sense should have disappeared and have been replaced by a religious–secular dimension.

In contrast to the religious cleavage, the class cleavage should have more the character of a zero-sum game between the population groups in question. But even here the situation is less straightforward than the term 'class conflict' may suggest. In the words of Lipset and Rokkan, this cleavage was originally based on 'a conflict between owners and employers on one side and tenants, labourers, and workers on the other' (1967, p. 14). Thus we have to conclude that this was never exclusively a conflict between employees and their employers, and today even less so than at the zenith of the Industrial Revolution. The percentage of the labour force employed by individual employers, rather than by companies, becomes smaller and smaller, with the consequence that the classical bourgeoisie becomes numerically a *quantité négligeable* within the electorate. It is only the petite bourgeoisie or, more generally, the self-employed who fight a surrogate battle on election days for the bourgeoisie.

Following Alford (1963), many researchers have calculated indices of class vote as the percentage difference in vote for leftist parties between manual workers and the middle class. This operationalisation of the class cleavage is a surrogate measure of a surrogate conflict. We prefer to keep the self-employed separate from the white-collar employees and shall investigate the party preferences of the manual workers, the white-collar employees, and the self-employed. We have to exclude farmers from our analysis because they do not have the same economic interests as the rest of the self-employed and there were too few cases to include them in the analysis as a separate category.

Before we discuss stability and change in relation to our first cleavage indicator, it seems worthwhile to look at the outcome of the federal elections since 1949. In Table 10.1, the valid votes in the second ballot (*Zweitstimme*) are differentiated into two groups: first the valid votes for the three parties, the only ones represented in the Bundestag since 1961, are used as the basis for calculating percentages – we are speaking here of the three-party vote – and then the votes for other parties are given as a percentage of all valid votes.

TABLE 10.1 *Election results (percentages) for Western Germany (not including West Berlin): valid votes, since 1953 in list vote (Zweitstimmen)*

	1949	1953	1957	1961	1965	1969	1972	1976
SPD*	40.4	34.5	35.4	38.4	40.8	45.2	46.2	43.0
CDU/CSU*	42.9	54.1	56.0	48.0	49.4	48.8	45.3	49.0
FDP*	16.5	11.4	8.6	13.6	9.9	6.1	8.5	8.0
	100	100	100	100	100	100	100	100
Others	27.8	16.5	10.3	5.7	3.6	5.5	0.9	0.9

* Percentages adjusted for Others.
SOURCE: Percentages calculated from Table 4.2 in Statistisches Bundesamt, 1979, p. 83.

From 1953 to 1972 there is one overall trend which all commentators of German politics up to 1972 have had to interpret: the steady increase in SPD support. The steadiness of this increase seemed to point to social structural causes, and both a growing secularisation (cf. Feist and Liepelt, 1977) and a political reorientation of the growing new middle class (cf. Pappi, 1973) were mentioned as such causes. But the election results of 1976 showed social structural and political determinants to be at odds with each other. Judged only by the election results, one could argue that the German three-party system had reached its equilibrium in the mid-sixties, around which the particular election results are oscillating, the CDU/CSU being the strongest party, but the combined votes of SPD and FDP always being a little ahead.

What we may at least learn from Table 10.1, is that on the surface there is a very stable party system. We should thus not anticipate the emergence of dramatic changes in the more subtle cleavage indicators. But not all population groups have enduring coalitions with political parties, so that there may be enough leeway for new political alliances, even if they are more short-lived than the old ones.

Thus far we have only mentioned coalitions of population groups either with the SPD or the CDU/CSU. Before the First World War, both the workers' movement and political Catholicism were outsiders at the national power centre, but they were firmly organised, not only as political movements but as population groups, with voluntary associations, and regional and local strongholds. At the level of the electorate the bourgeois core of the German empire, the Protestant middle and upper classes, were much less organised as a population group of their own – there was no need for separate organisations because they were the 'nation'. We can see the FDP as the only pure successor in this respect, representing the liberal wing of the old core system. Even if no mass organisations support the FDP more or less exclusively, at the level of the electorate this party should have a stronger anti-Catholic bias than the SPD and a stronger middle-class bias than the CDU/CSU.

Instead of using percentage differences as indices of the class vote and the religious vote we can present the β-effects of Goodman's log-linear model as our cleavage indicators in Table 10.2. With this model we attain two advantages. Firstly, we are able to test whether religion and class are additive components of the vote or whether an interaction term is necessary. And secondly, we can compute the effects on both the log-odds SPD/CDU and CDU/FDP within the same model.

The first important result of Table 10.2 is the rather steady effect of religion on party preference. Catholics have had a much stronger tendency to vote for the CDU than for the SPD or the FDP in all election years since the fifties. We can see no trend in these figures and reject the hypothesis of a declining importance of the religious cleavage, at least with regard to this first cleavage indicator. The continuity of this cleavage is the more astonishing, when we remember the political rationale of the founders of the CDU. They wanted to bridge the gap between religiously conservative Protestants and Catholics. It could be, however, that they were more successful than these figures show. Given the fact that Catholics are more religiously oriented than Protestants, there is the possibility that the CDU has the same following among the religious traditionalists of both churches. But even this hypothesis can be rejected (see for the most recent data Berger *et al.*, 1977). We thus have to conclude that the religious cleavage in its traditional form still plays an important role in German politics.

With regard to occupation, manual workers and the self-employed are as

TABLE 10.2 *Religion and occupation as predictors of party preference in election years since 1953 (loglinear β-effects) post-election surveys since 1961*

Predictors and their categories:
A: Catholics vs. Protestants
B: Occupation: (m) manual employees vs. (n) non-manual employees vs. (s) self-employed (non-farm)

Contrasts	μ	A	B_m	B_n	B_s	x^2	p
			β-Effects			Likelihood ratio x^2 for additive model	
1953							
SPD/CDU	−0.61	−0.55	0.97	−0.07	−0.90	2.50	>0.5
CDU/FDP	1.46	0.66	0.63	−0.14	−0.50		
1961							
SPD/CDU	−0.58	−0.58	0.99	−0.07	−0.92	1.11	>0.5
CDU/FDP	1.38	0.48	0.69	−0.25	−0.44		
1965							
SPD/CDU	−0.52	−0.60	0.74	−0.05	−0.69	1.28	>0.5
CDU/FDP	1.89	0.55	0.82	−0.08	−0.74		
1969							
SPD/CDU	−0.32	−0.42	0.79	0.31	−1.10	0.95	>0.5
CDU/FDP	2.72	1.00	0.89	−0.58	−0.32		
1972							
SPD/CDU	0.11	−0.50	0.84	0.29	−1.14	10.44	0.03
CDU/FDP	1.24	0.55	0.19	−0.53	0.34		
1976							
SPD/CDU	−0.24	−0.59	0.74	0.07	−0.80	5.33	0.26
CDU/FDP	1.39	0.63	0.38	−0.05	−0.34		

SOURCE: β-effects calculated by ECTA from Table 44–11 in Ballerstedt and Glatzer, 1979, p. 451.

NOTE: A simple example may help the reader not acquainted with Goodman's log-linear model approach to understand the meaning of these β-effects (cf. Goodman et al., 1978). In our 1976 sample 158 Catholic respondents preferred the CDU and 92 of them the SPD. That is, 63 per cent of the Catholics were in favour of the CDU, whereas only 34 per cent of the Protestants (111 respondents) intended to vote for the CDU and 66 per cent (215 respondents) for the SPD. In other words, the odds were 1.72 to 1 for the CDU among Catholics and 0.52 to 1 among Protestants. These two odds are to be transformed in such a way that a mean odd (irrespective of religion) and an effect of being Catholic or Protestant can be recognised. The best way to do this is to use the log odds (natural logs) instead of the odds – because in this case a linear model results instead of a multiplicative model – and compute the mean: (ln(1.72) + ln(0.52)) : 2 = −0.06. The β-effect for being Catholic is then: ln(1.72) − (−0.06) = 0.60, which corresponds to the percentage difference of 29. To analyse relationships between more than two variables in this way, we used stable in their party preference as the religious groups. This is at least a valid generalisation for the two-party vote for either SPD or CDU. Only the new middle class of white-collar employees is much less stable in its two-party vote. Till the mid-sixties this group was a little more in favour of the CDU than the SPD. After the Grand Coalition it took a large jump towards the SPD, but this party was not able to hold this group to form a new steady coalition. Contrary to many interpretations, we reject the hypothesis of a declining class cleavage. Our interpretation does not contradict the data of other researchers, but only their interpretation. Since we conceptualise the class cleavage as the contrast in party preference between manual workers and the self-employed, we stress the stable coalitions of the German party system. Dichotomising social class into the two population groups of working and middle class gives the impression of a declining class vote because the new middle class of the late sixties and early seventies gave up its middle position between manual workers and the self-employed and voted more in accord with the first group. But from Table 10.2 alone we cannot detect the political meaning of these changes.

Comparing the SPD/CDU contrast with the CDU/FDP contrast, we see more changes in the social structural determinants of the vote with regard to the small liberal party. Besides the religious effect the most stable influence is the anti-working-class bias of the FDP. In all elections since the fifties manual workers were more in favour of the CDU than of the FDP. In 1972 this was less the case than in other elections, but we suppose that the effort of the party elites of SPD and FDP was well spent in convincing some SPD-voters to vote for the liberal party in the list vote (*Leihstimmen*) in order to keep the FDP well above the 5 per cent threshold (*Sperrklausel*).

Even if our parameters are computed for contrasts between two parties the voters move within a three-party system. Thus in 1969 and 1972 the new middle class did not only move towards the SPD, but the FDP as well. We interpret this shift as a support movement for the social–liberal government and not as a conversion of the white-collar employees to traditional class politics.

The critical question for our topic is whether voter movements will change the old cleavage system or not. Within the framework of the old cleavage

Goodman's ECTA programme (Everyman's Contingency Table Analysis). This programme gives us the possibility to fit an adequate model to the data. A good model would be one with a rather small number of β-effects which succeeds in estimating the influence of particular variables controlling for the others. The advantages of log-linear models in multivariate analysis can of course not be demonstrated completely by our simple example. One of them is for instance orthogonality, another that log-linear β-effects may be interpreted in some way similarly to standardised regression coefficients.

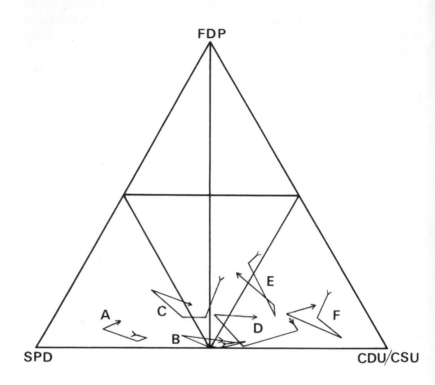

FIGURE 10.1 *The three-party vote of different population groups in federal elections since 1961*

A: Protestant working class
B: Catholic working class
C: Protestant new middle class
D: Catholic new middle class
E: Protestant old middle class (self-employed)
F: Catholic old middle class (self-employed)

SOURCE: cf. Table 10.2.

system we have differentiated six population groups. In Figure 10.1 we present the same data as in Table 10.2 for the federal elections since 1961, but in a different format. We computed the three-party vote in percentages and have drawn these results into a standardised triangle where each vertex corresponds to 100 per cent for the respective party (cf. Miller, 1977, p. 115). The movement of each population group within the party system is then shown as a combination of four vectors starting in 1961 and ending in 1976.

A stable cleavage system would not be a system without change, but a system with parallel movements. When the movements are not parallel, two systematic changes may have occurred:

(1) some groups approach each other – then the respective cleavage becomes less important;
(2) some groups end up more distant from each other than at the beginning – then the respective cleavage is of increasing importance.

Irregular deviations from parallel movements without a clear trend over a series of elections do not indicate a systematic change.

With these guidelines for an interpretation of Figure 10.1, we stress the stability of the old cleavage system. The population groups stay at their respective areas within the triangle and many of their movements are parallel. The new middle class of both denominations is more open to political cues than the working class, they have travelled a longer distance but end up almost full circle as the other groups, too. The self-employed show some deviation from the wage- and salary-earners – especially in 1969, when they move into the direction of the CDU in contrast to the other four groups – but this brings neither Protestant and Catholic self-employed closer to each other, nor both, in the long run, further away from the other four groups. Judged by the evidence of our first cleavage indicator we are justified in entertaining the stability hypothesis a little longer.

VALUE ORIENTATIONS AND VOTING BEHAVIOUR

As outlined earlier, our second cleavage indicator is a measure of the political meaning of a population group's average vote. We do not believe in the stability of a coalition between a population group and a party after it has lost political content, only via traditional group pressures.

With regard to political meaning, it seems to be more difficult to explain the stability of religious cleavage than class conflict, especially if we consider the massive secularisation of the past 20 years. A closer look at this development may reveal characteristics of the dynamics of stability.

For the cleavage itself, the massive secularisation is irrelevant because only the percentage difference in the vote is important, not the overall level of party preference. So we have to show first that religious issues continually played a role in German politics, and secondly that Catholics always stayed ahead of Protestants in their more traditional orientation. Issues with religious overtones have been the school issue, abortion laws, divorce laws, etc. It was the prerogative of the present coalition of SPD and FDP to stress these issues even more than former governments led by the CDU because many of the promised reforms were concerned with this issue area.

With regard to the second criterion, it is difficult to prove the more conservative orientation of Catholics over time because survey data are not available for all relevant value orientations and political attitudes. But the evidence we obtained shows a quite constant gap beween Catholics and Protestants in their religious traditionalism (cf. Pappi, 1977).

Even if these pieces of evidence are enough to explain the continuity of the religious cleavage, we are still curious as to why the CDU as the religious party did not lose more votes, especially since the overwhelming majority of the electorate shows a massive trend towards becoming increasingly liberal in these matters. The solution of this paradox lies in the fact that the positions of the parties did not remain stable in an absolute sense as with positions on a cardinal scale. The Christian Democrats of today are less conservative than the CDU of the fifties but they are still to the right of the SPD and FDP. Provided we accept the attitude towards the divorce law as an example, it can be shown that the people with a neutral position who are satisfied with the *status quo* were more in favour of the CDU in 1976 than in 1953 (cf. Pappi, 1977, p. 222). The CDU of the later period was more acceptable for less conservative voters than the CDU of the early sixties.

As the attitude towards the divorce law comprehends a part of the political meaning of the religious cleavage, we shall use the attitudes towards the unions as a proxy measure of the content of traditional class politics. We may then ask whether the political meaning of the political reorientation of the salaried employees in the late sixties and early seventies was an expression of traditional class politics. As this population group moved into the direction of both the Social Democrats and the Liberals, we suppose that the class hypothesis will fail. Our hypothesis is that this population group moved away from the CDU on the religious dimension. Although the Christian Democrats became more liberal in religious matters, this was insufficient for the new middle class which became the forerunner in the general secularisation. Their options were for the social–liberal government and its reform programme.

To test these rival hypotheses we shall use the following design: we first see which attitude has changed more over time, the attitude towards divorce or towards unions, and whether the change caused a homogenisation of manual and white-collar workers or not. Secondly, we test whether the predictive power of these two attitudes for party preference remained stable or not. Stability in this respect would be a second argument for a stable cleavage system, evaluated this time from the perspective of the political meaning of the old cleavages. If we are able to accept this stability of predictors in the past, we may argue in the third place that the political reorientation of the new middle class can best be explained by that specific attitude variable which has changed most in this population group.

The results of this analysis are presented in Table 10.3. In panel 1 the most impressive result is the massive change in the indicator of the religious dimension, whereas the attitudes toward the unions did not change much. As we can see from the sign of the interaction effect, the two occupation groups indeed came a little closer to each other with regard to their 'class conscious-

TABLE 10.3 *Political attitudes and party preference of manual workers and white-collar employees in 1953 and 1976*

Variables:
  A Time: 1976 vs. 1953.
  B Occupation: manual workers vs. white-collar employees.
  C Attitude towards divorce law: liberal vs. conservative.
  D Attitude towards unions: positive vs. negative.
  E Party preference: SPD vs. CDU.

1. β-Effects of A and B on C resp. D

| | Prediction of | |
Variable	C	D
μ	0.01	0.46
A	0.71	0.09
B	0.08	0.18
$A \times B$	−0.07	−0.11

2. β-Effect of C and D on E among occupational groups in 1953 and 1976

	μ	C	D	$C \times D$
(a) Manual workers in 1953	0.73	0.19	0.38	0
(b) Manual workers in 1976	0.10	0.53	0.52	0.01
(c) White-collar employees in 1953	−0.48	0.38	0.69	0.17
(d) White-collar employees in 1976	−0.48	0.43	0.74	0.21

SOURCE: 1953 Reigrotzki-Study; 1976: ZUMA-Bus (cf. Pappi, 1977).

ness', whereas they drifted apart on the religious dimension. The manual workers were always more conservative in their attitude towards divorce than the new middle class, but this gap was larger in 1976 than in 1953. From panel 2 we see that the predictive power of the attitudes for the two-party vote remained rather stable, at least for the new middle class. We thus conclude that our hypothesis is corroborated and reject the class hypothesis.

Before we consider the consequences of this interpretation for the cleavage system, we have to take into account a change among the manual workers. For them a liberal attitude towards divorce had a more positive effect in favour of the SPD in 1976 than in 1953. Today, workers are more comparable to the new middle class in this respect than in the fifties. We interpret this change as being caused by a strain towards symmetry, guaranteeing that different motives of preferences for the same party do not contradict one other.

Generally, we conclude that the old cleavage system remained stable even with regard to the stronger, second criterion. Our interpretation of the partial reorientation of the new middle class is more parsimonious than the far-reaching assumption of a 'new politics' dimension. The value change, which without doubt was taking place over the past two decades, fitted the already existing religious dimension of German politics. The old party system was a perfect mechanism for transforming the demands of the increasing segments of secular voters. If this dimension becomes less salient a development favouring the Christian Democrats may possibly result.

NEW CONFLICTS FROM 'NEW' POPULATION GROUPS?

We have defined social cleavages as enduring coalitions of certain population groups with a particular political party. The delineation of population groups is therefore a very critical aspect of every analysis of social cleavages. Until now this crucial problem was solved pragmatically. We have chosen those groups which have coalitions with the major parties and have added the respective outgroups; but it might be that our diagnosis of a stable cleavage system, correct as it is at first sight, misses the inner dynamic of interest mediation because we overlook coalitions or affinities of new population groups with political parties.

We use the term 'new' here in the sense of new groups for the cleavage system. The new development is not necessarily the group itself but its political consciousness. An example would be the group of house-owners who became more dependent on state intervention in Denmark and therefore more conscious of their common interests as a group (cf. Esping-Andersen,

1978). Groups with rapid rates of growth or decline are, of course, especially prone to be dissatisfied with the traditional fault lines of political discussion.

As outlined in the introduction, we shall supplement our analysis of the old cleavage system with an investigation of the relationships between *situs* and some horizontal disparities on the one side and political attitudes and party preferences on the other. Since the traditional class cleavage is still in existence, we have to control its influence. Our approach is therefore to compare class differences of political attitudes and party preferences across industrial sectors and horizontal disparities. Whenever social classes behave alike, irrespective of *situs*, then the vitality of the traditional class cleavage is proven. Whenever class differences within a *situs* are irrelevant a new coalition is in *statu nascendi*. This will be an analysis of probable changes in class politics, whereas we omit the religious cleavage in this section.

Our class variable hitherto has been a very crude measure. We used the occupation of the head of the household as an indicator of class position. This procedure can be justified for an analysis of traditional class politics, but not for the formation of new kinds of political consciousness which are less manifest and more linked to the peculiar economic situation of the individual. For all people in the labour force we should now take their own occupation as an indicator of class position.

A second problem of our class variable is the heterogeneity of the new middle class. We shall now split this category into routine non-manual work and a managerial class. Even this new variable is not yet an ideal solution because we cannot distinguish between line and staff functions of managers, in the strict sense, and professional work. As salaried professionals are relatively autonomous in their work and often have some subordinates they are included in the group of 'managers' and not in the group of routine white-collar workers. To treat them as a separate category was not possible because we do not have information on their position within an organisation.

The categorisation of industrial sectors is straightforward. We treat the public sector separately and omit the primary sector because there most people are self-employed farmers who anyway form a separate category as well as other self-employed, irrespective of the economic sector in which they have their business. Only the employees are differentiated according to industrial sectors.

From those in the labour force, we distinguish students, housewives, and retired people. The class position of the retired is indicated by their former occupation and housewives are classified according to the occupation of their husbands.

The first politically relevant attitude variable appearing in Table 10.4 concerns traditional class politics: whether in the occurrence of strikes one's

TABLE 10.4. *Location in social structure, political orientations, and party preferences of the West German electorate.*

Location in social structure (n; % male)	Identify with working class (%)	Unions on strike	Percentage agree with Egalitarian old-age pensions	New politics [a]	Unsatisfied with political system (%)	Party preference SPD (%)	CDU (%)	FDP (%)
1 LABOUR FORCE								
1.1 Self-Employed								
1.1.1 Farmers (41; 83%)	28	35	86	7	13	5	85	10
1.1.2 Others (158; 69%)	8	22	76	16	12	22	63	15
1.2 Employees								
1.2.1 Secondary sector								
1.2.1.1 Manual (353; 78%)	77	85	87	11	9	56	39	6
1.2.1.2 Non-manual (122; 59%)	19	84	78	18	7	38	46	16
1.2.1.3 Managerial (90; 90%)	20	72	61	23	2	46	44	10
1.2.2 Tertiary sector								
1.2.2.1 Manual (97; 69%)	69	88	83	13	11	49	39	12
1.2.2.2 Non-manual (230; 47%)	27	72	82	14	7	44	45	11
1.2.2.3 Managerial (86; 81%)	9	65	75	21	6	38	40	22
1.2.3 Public service								
1.2.3.1 Manual (50; 66%)	71	92	84	15	4	58	31	11
1.2.3.2 Non-manual (195; 64%)	15	81	78	19	8	39	45	17
1.2.3.3 Managerial (140; 72%)	6	77	78	37	8	46	40	13
1.2.4 Sector n.a.								
1.2.4.1 Manual (73; 82%)	78	90	90	11	6	69	23	8
1.2.4.2 Non-manual (75; 41%)	18	78	87	17	6	47	39	14
1.2.4.3 Managerial (50; 84%)	13	62	73	25	8	59	35	5
1.2.5 Sector and Occupation n.a. (70; 47%)	22	67	80	21	7	41	47	12
1.2.6 Apprentices								
1.2.6.1 Manual (11; 73%)	55	90	91	45	18	50	50	0

1.2.6.2 Non-manual (20; 40%)	0	75	78	67	5	57	43	0
2 NOT IN LABOUR FORCE								
2.1 Students (267; 58%)	13	76	81	49	15	56	29	15
2.2 Retired								
2.2.1 Former self-employed								
2.2.1.1 Farmers (31; 39%)	52	33	86	0	10	15	77	8
2.2.1.2 Others (70; 44%)	21	29	82	5	20	26	65	9
2.2.2 Former employees								
2.2.2.1 Manual (430; 46%)	74	85	86	6	13	55	42	3
2.2.2.2 Non-manual (259; 43%)	25	77	79	7	9	35	57	8
2.2.2.3 Managerial (131; 63%)	8	43	63	12	10	20	66	15
2.3 Housewives								
2.3.1 of farmers (11; 0%)	18	43	89	9	10	0	100	0
2.3.2 of other self-employed (56; 0%)	8	23	78	14	13	18	67	16
2.3.3 of manual workers (368; 0%)	70	35	87	5	10	56	38	6
2.3.4 of non-manual workers (196; 0%)	20	72	88	6	9	45	45	10
2.3.5 of managers (27; 0%)	5	63	75	15	7	31	54	15
3 NOT CLASSIFIED (141; 19%)	39	78	90	18	16	34	55	11

[a] People who rank 'Protecting freedom of speech' and 'Giving people more say in political decisions' higher than 'Maintaining order in the nation' and 'Fighting rising prices' (cf. Inglehart, 1971, p. 994).

SOURCE: Frequencies and percentages calculated by using two cumulated samples drawn from the West German electorate (including West Berlin) in 1976 and 1977 by ZUMA (Zentrum für Umfragen, Methoden und Analysen, Mannheim): ZUMA-Bus 76 ($n = 2036$), ZUMA-Bus 77 ($n = 2002$).

sympathy is in general with the unions or the employers (Centers, 1949). Here the largest difference can be observed between the self-employed and the employees. Within the latter group the manual workers are always more in favour of the unions than are the non-manual or the managerial group, but it is astonishing that the widest gap between workers and managers is not in the core economic sector, that is the secondary sector, but among the retired.

In another respect, the retired and the employees in the secondary sector are more alike. The managers in both categories are much less in favour of more egalitarian old-age pensions than the workers. The managers would, of course, be the losers. The managerial group in public service and in the tertiary sector generally is much more in favour of an egalitarian policy and stands in striking contrast to retired managers and managers in industry.

Before we speculate on these results we should pay some attention to subjective class identification. The percentage of managers in industry who identify themselves with the working class is rather high, 20 per cent instead of the low 6 per cent of the managerial group in public service. The managerial group in industry mainly comprises employees from middle management who were often upwardly mobile within the same organisation. In public service the higher positions are almost exclusively filled from outside, by people with university degrees. The social distance between the three groups will therefore be smaller in industry than in public service. In addition, hierarchies are less steep in German industry than for instance in France (Maurice *et al.*, 1979).

Speculating now about the contrast of class politics in the secondary sector and in public service, we suppose that there is a more clear-cut, interest-specific differentiation in industry than in the public sector. As there are good chances for upward mobility, the more common class background of managers and workers in industry does not have the consequence of a united front of all employees against their employers. In the public sector the upper and lower echelons are less alike socially but sometimes more similar in their political orientation. It is especially the 'managerial group' which behaves in a manner contrary to its supposed traditional interest position. If there is a trend away from the old class cleavage, we have to concentrate on this group and its varied components of higher civil servants in the administration and professionals, such as teachers, without a strict management position.

It is this group among the employed which is most in favour of the new politics dimension. Only students and apprentices are more inclined to prefer these issues. The upper civil service may well function as a social structural niche for post-materialists guaranteeing that this orientation of the younger generation does not get lost by being evenly spread over all sectors of the labour force. It may become a new basis for an enduring coalition with a political party but it has not yet become an important one, as we can see from present party preferences.

The data on political alienation show for the first time that horizontal disparities have an impact. People in the labour force are more satisfied with the present political system of the Federal Republic than students, the retired or housewives. Among people in the labour force the self-employed are the least satisfied. An additional corroboration of our interpretation of the difference between the secondary and the public sector can be seen in the evidence of managers in industry being the least politically alienated group, whereas the comparable group in public service is slightly more alienated than the workers in this sector.

What we can learn from Table 10.4 is that there are tendencies for new cleavages but nothing more. The party preference of the different groups follows a very conventional pattern. Quite irrespective of *situs*, manual workers prefer the Social Democrats most, whereas among the non-manual and managerial groups there is a more even distribution between the two major parties.

CONCLUSION

The German polity is characterised by very stable social cleavages. With regard to the core of the population groups we may speak of a politicised social structure. The very phenomenon of the group-anchored character of voting behaviour is an important cause of the continuity of the cleavage system. Thus people have clear criteria as to which parties they should vote for, without feeling the necessity of following all the details of day-to-day politics.

But the conformity to political group norms is not a sufficient explanation for the continuity of the old cleavage system. As Catholics are more in favour of the Christian Democrats than Non-Catholics, and as workers are more in favour of the Social Democrats than middle-class voters, this behaviour must have a special political meaning beyond the mechanism of group processes, otherwise the socialisation of new members of these population groups into the respective political subcultures would cause enormous difficulties, and that is especially the case in a period of increasing individualisation and a decreasing importance of social *milieux*.

The core population groups of the traditional cleavage system are not only voting differently from their respective outgroups, but their party preferences still have the same political meaning as at the beginning of the coalition with a political party. In addition, we could show that even population groups without enduring political coalitions, like the new middle class, have developed motivations to vote for the SPD or FDP which fit into the old cleavage system. Even if wage- and salary-earners today are rather more homogeneous in their class attitudes than some thirty years ago, we found more evidence for another explanation of the increase in Left voting among white-collar workers. They voted for the social–liberal government in the early seventies because of the affinity of their progressive orientation in religious matters to the programme of inner reforms. The massive secularisation of the past fifteen years has been mainly a middle-class phenomenon, but within this stratum different economic interests were unimportant in this process.

Since the mid-seventies many secular–religious issues have been settled. This is why the broad middle-class coalition in favour of SPD and FDP lost followers. Contrary to some adherents of the new politics interpretation (cf. Hildebrandt and Dalton, 1977), we should like to distinguish between a general trend towards secularisation and a post-materialist approach to politics with its stress on democratic and egalitarian values. Next to the students the upper civil service is a stronghold of post-materialism.

It is sometimes argued that the Social Democrats are already the party of the public sector. The best evidence for this argument is the membership figures, especially in those states with SPD governments (Feist *et al.*, 1977). But at the mass level the situation is different. We were able to identify only trends towards new coalitions, but no definite new alliances.

The formation of a new cleavage depends not only on social structural antecedents but on political conflicts and the options chosen by the political elite. Of danger for the existing cleavage system would be an open conflict between the industrial sector and the professional or managerial group of the public sector. The environmental and atomic energy question might be a candidate for such a conflict; but the environmentalist movement must first find or found a party with which an enduring coalition can be formed. Given the overall stability of the traditional cleavage system, and given the coalition of the unions (not opposed to atomic energy) with the Social Democrats, and given the affinity of the Christian Democrats and Liberals to the business community, the prospects of a new political coalition are not very promising.

REFERENCES

R. R. Alford, *Party and Society: The Anglo-American Democracies* (Chicago: Rand McNally, 1963).

E. Ballerstedt and W. Glatzer, *Soziologischer Almanach: Handbuch gesellschaftlicher Daten und Indikatoren* (Frankfurt a.M./New York: Campus, 1979).

M. Berger *et al.*, 'Bundestagswahl 1976: Politik und Sozialstruktur', *Zeitschrift für Parlamentsfragen*, H. 2 (1977) pp. 197–231.

R. Centers, *The Psychology of Social Classes* (Princeton: University Press, 1949).

R. Dahrendorf, *Class and Class Conflict in Industrial Society* (Stanford: University Press, 1959).

R. Döbert and G. Nunner-Winkler, 'Konflikt und Rückzugspotentiale in spätkapitalistischen Gesellschaften', *Zeitschrift für Soziologie*, 2 (1973) pp. 301–25.

G. Esping-Andersen, 'Social Class, Social Democracy, and the State', *Comparative Politics* (1978) pp. 42–58.

U. Feist and K. Liepelt, 'Machtwechsel in Raten', in C. Böhret et al. (eds), *Wahlforschung: Sonden im politischen Markt*, 2nd edn. (Opladen: Westdeutscher Verlag, 1977) pp. 26–56.

U. Feist *et. al.*, 'Strukturelle Angleichung und ideologische Polarisierung', *Politische Vierteljahresschrift*, 18 (1977) pp. 230–56.

L. A. Goodman *et al.*, *Analysing Qualitative/Categorical Data: Log-Linear Models and Latent-Structure Analysis* (Cambridge, Mass.: Abt Books, 1978).

J. Habermas, *Legitimationsprobleme im Spätkapitalismus* (Frankfurt a.M.: Suhrkamp, 1973).

K. Hildebrandt and R. J. Dalton, 'Die neue Politik', *Politische Vierteljahrsschrift*, 18 (1977) pp. 230–56.

R. Inglehart, 'The Silent Revolution in Europe: Intergenerational Change in Post-industrial Societies', *American Political Science Review*, 65 (1971) pp. 991–1017.

R. Inglehart, *The Silent Revolution: Changing Values and Political Styles Among Western Publics* (Princeton: University Press, 1977).

H. Klages and P. Kmieciak (eds), *Wertwandel und gesellschaftlicher Wandel* (Frankfurt a.M./New York: Campus, 1979).

P. Kmieciak, *Wertstrukturen und Wertwandel in der Bundesrepublik* (Göttingen: Schwartz, 1976).

G. Lehmbruch, 'Liberal Corporatism and Party Government', *Comparative Political Studies*, 10 (1977) pp. 91–126.

M. R. Lepsius, 'Soziale Ungleichheit und Klassenstrukturen in der Bundesrepublik Deutschland', in H./U. Wehler (ed.), *Klassen in der europäischen Sozialgeschichte* (Göttingen: Vandenhoek & Ruprecht, 1979) pp. 166–209.

S. M. Lipset and S. Rokkan, 'Cleavage Structures, Party Systems and Voter Alignments: An Introduction', in S. M. Lipset and S. Rokkan (eds), *Party Systems and Voter Alignments: Cross-National Perspectives* (New York: Free Press, 1967) pp. 1–64.

M. Maurice *et al.*, 'Die Entwicklung der Hierarchie im Industrieunternehmen: Ein Vergleich Frankreich – Bundesrepublik Deutschland', *Soziale Welt*, 30 (1979) pp. 295–327.

W. E. Miller and T. E. Levitin, *Leadership and Change: The New Politics and the American Electorate* (Cambridge, Mass.: Winthrop, 1976).

W. L. Miller, *Electoral Dynamics in Britain since 1918* (London/Basingstoke: Macmillan Press, 1977).

11 A Crisis of the Party System? – An Assessment

HERBERT DÖRING

German political parties have hitherto been remarkably able to absorb protest movements on the Right and Left of the political spectrum. In recent years, however, there have appeared signs of a growing uneasiness with established parties and their ways. Intra-party conflict is increasing, or has at least become more visible than it was allowable in the past; so has intra-party dissent by backbench members of parliament.[1] We have also witnessed a dramatic surge in the number of single-issue movements such as citizens' initiative groups.[2] Public opinion surveys show a steep decline in the sympathy ratings of parties from a peak reached between 1969 and 1971 to a record low after 1974.[3] These findings seem to point to a widespread *Parteiverdrossenheit*, a grumbling disillusionment with party performance. Moreover, an increasing number of people, especially the young, think it right to engage in unconventional political behaviour such as lawful demonstrations, rent strikes, occupying buildings and blocking traffic, rather than just to participate in elections.[4] Over and above this, new fringe groups such as the environmental 'green' groups have sprung up to compete with the parties in the electoral arena.[5]

As all of these symptoms were previously alien to the unmatched stability of the Federal Republic, it should be no cause for astonishment that there is now, among German academics and journalists, talk of an impending crisis.[6] It remains to be seen whether this will be but one more of the many crises in the history of the Federal Republic that never happened. A prediction of imminent crisis has at all events been a constant feature from the very beginning. And with regard to German talent for fearing the worst, foreign observers or Germans returning from long residence abroad have always been amazed to find how a subjective feeling of insecurity contrasts with the stability of political institutions.[7] On the other hand, signs of a new kind of fragmentation in the party system, although somewhat unexpected in the

German context, have been a familiar feature of Western European party politics at times.[8] Thus, the question posits itself: is any prospective crisis in the German party system real or apparent? May it not just be that Western Germany's 'abnormal normality' has come to an end as she has grown more Western European in outlook? Has she just caught up with some of the problems her neighbours have long been plagued with? In order to attempt an assessment, it may be useful to look at some preconditions of the hitherto smoothly working 'catch-all' strategy.

WINNING VOTES – AN 'EFFICIENT SECRET'

In view of recent changes in appearance, if not in character of party politics, it is hardly surprising that even the model of the catch-all party, once a cornerstone of social-science theorising, with Western Germany serving as one of the closest empirical examples, has begun to crumble. Its pretensions remain the avowed aim of German political parties, but political scientists have become aware that there is only a loose fit between what the model of the *Volkspartei* assumes and present reality.[9] Whatever else a catch-all party may be, observers are agreed that its dominant aims are to win a majority in elections and to act as a responsible unit of government.

Vote-maximisation at the expense of any other function a party may have is likely to prevail on one condition: sustained economic growth endowing a governing party with the chance of offering, overproportionately, goods and services to its traditional share of the electoral market; at the same time, in the absence of economic scarcity the governing party is also enabled to distribute resources to all other segments of the population to win broad electoral victories. It is obvious that this 'efficient secret' is more likely to operate if there also exists an institutional arrangement for effective political decision-making by the parliamentary majority. It provides the office-taking winner of elections with the unhampered chance of distributing public goods and services as it thinks fit.

Here, it is somewhat ironical that the party that was first to benefit, the CDU/CSU, initially did its best to prevent a monopoly of political decision-making by the parliamentary majority lest the SPD used the opportunity to bring about far-reaching social and economic changes. Up to 1949 influential sections in the CDU and CSU were hesitant to establish a centralised legislative framework necessary for responsible party government. This was in part due to demands of south German branches of Christian Democracy for federalist decentralisation as well as to certain Catholic teachings. Moreover, widespread talk of an alleged 'absolutism of parliament'[10] was also designed to fend off claims of the Social Democrats for a planned economy, nationalisation of industries and industrial co-determination. It was only due to a compromise in drafting the Basic Law that the federal government was granted sufficient legislative power.

Schumacher, indeed, hoped to win a majority in the first election in order to achieve the chance he had given away in the Parliamentary Council but Adenauer was elected Chancellor, with a majority of one vote. He was quick to realise what advantages rapid economic growth offered to a governing party in order to secure a long-lasting majority. The party offered material benefits to its traditional bases of electoral support, industry, agriculture, and the self-employed, without having to thwart the expectations of the population at large. It may be that by dint of this strategy income distribution in Germany is, even today, slightly more unequal than in some other Western democracies.[11] However, this relatively inconspicuous class bias was complemented by carefully stage-managed *'Wahlgeschenke'* to every-body. All old-age pensions, for example, were linked by annual laws to current salaries, a practice still valid today but increasingly difficult to maintain. The elderly belong to those large groups of the population such as the youth, consumers and taxpayers, which, according to the theory of collective action by Olson, are held unlikely effectively to organise themselves to bring pressure to bear upon government. As even they were presented with material benefits by a generous conservative government, the electoral strategy made a good start.

PREFERRING VOTERS TO PARTY MEMBERS – A DILEMMA FOR THE SPD

In order to understand the difficulties that stood in the way of the SPD of emulating the successful electoral strategy of the CDU, it is helpful to point to a structural dilemma confronting all working-class parties. Most clearly visible in the light of a rational-choice orientation, the argument runs as follows. Once party leaders enter the electoral arena with the desire to win and to translate party programmes into public policies, rather than just giving voice to sectional interests, they face a crucial choice. They are likely, 'to give serious consideration to the opportunities present in an electoral strategy over and against a party strategy'.[12] By a *party* strategy is meant to, 'build and maintain a multi-nuclear organisation to deliver services and create social solidarity incentives for members'.[13] This resembles the 'nega-tive integration' of the Social Democratic Party in the Empire when the party offered its members an ideology and a wide area of services in educational, financial, cultural and recreational fields from adult education through the party press and insurance schemes to sports and music clubs.[14] In a subculturally divided society the party was bound together by members conscious of their sense of isolation in a hostile state. By an *electoral* strategy is meant that the party promises to deliver goods and services to a mass electorate through legislative measures and government policies.

It goes without saying that any party will normally adopt both strategies. However, there is a strong tendency for party leaders to convert the party organisation into:

> machinery to get out the voter rather than to continue to provide information, services, and social solidarity incentives to members. Claims and infrastructure costs can be reduced by appealing to voters rather than members. The former, who can make few direct claims on leaders, are substituted for members who *can* make such claims.[15]

It is worth noting that this general argument, of course, only applies if parties either control government or have the unrestricted power of legislation, or both. The first condition arrived in Germany only long after the formative years of political parties when, shortly before the close of the First World War, a parliamentary system of government hurriedly superseded the authoritarian dualism between government and parliament. With regard to the second, only through bargaining with the monarchical executive had political parties in Imperial Germany been able to enact their own policies, however limited, and see them implemented.

If parties are able to deliver public goods and services to their followers *and* the electorate at large, a central paradox is likely to result. As goods and services can now be obtained through promised public policies, whether one is a party member or not, the question arises as to why people join political parties at all since they are able to obtain those benefits without the cost of committing themselves. Certainly, this logic of Olson's widely quoted theory of collective action does not explain everything, but, surprisingly enough, it explains a great deal.[16] It would lead us to expect that the adoption of an electoral strategy such as defined above would in the long run reduce the number of party members. Indeed, taken at face value there seems to be no lack of evidence supporting this line of argument. There has been, for example, a steep decline in individual direct membership of the British Labour Party as social-welfare legislation increased. In the mid-1960s Epstein believed this pattern to be followed in other nations. However, the continuous rise of membership in all West German parties from the late

1950s onwards runs counter to this expectation, a trend not yet obvious at the time Epstein wrote his comparative analysis.[17] How does this theoretical orientation which is to guide our assessment cope with this apparent contradiction?

The standard answer lies in the concept of selective incentives: in order to induce potential members to join they need to be given additional benefits which can be effectively withheld from non-members. According to a useful typology, these organisational incentives are divided into three kinds: material incentives (monetary returns like business contracts and party patronage for salaried public offices or posts in government-controlled banks, enterprises and the like); solidary incentives (satisfactions derived from identification with the group or membership in party-affiliated clubs and auxiliary groups); purposive incentives (such as the goals of an organisation and its stand on public policies).[18] Organisations often rely on more than one inducement, the mixture of which is difficult to establish; but only if one or all of those incentives are present will the organisation avoid succumbing to atrophy. In Western Germany it is the peculiar nature of the 'party state' that makes it likely that the structure of incentives became predominantly material. As, for example, party patronage has permeated the civil service, the percentage of public officials in the membership of all parties has grown.[19] It can be assumed, then, that material incentives have been largely substituted for the former solidary and purposive ones. This leads us to look at the adoption of an electoral strategy by the SPD leadership after 1959.

'CONTAGION' FROM THE 'CATCH-ALL' STRATEGY

Until Schumacher's death the party leadership and the rank-and-file of the SPD were agreed upon far-reaching changes of economy and society to bring about, as they hoped, socialism with a humanitarian face, opposed to both Stalinism and capitalism. From this endeavour it would appear that purposive incentives to join were particularly marked, over and above the solidary ones traditionally strong in this party. As these policies were repeatedly rejected at the polls, the SPD in 1959 renounced its party line and consented to all the basic tenets of post-war West German politics; not only to anti-Communism which had been prominent within the party since the forced fusion of SPD and KPD in the Soviet zone in 1946, but also to a capitalist economy, mitigated by social welfare measures, as well as to acceptance of military integration into the Atlantic Pact. This 'embrace of the middle' made by the SPD has promoted competing explanations, the two most prominent of which have recently been challenged in an influential article by

Kaste and Raschke.[20] The first thesis holds with Michels that it was the increasing middle-class complexion of Socialist party leaders that resulted in a loss of revolutionary fervour. The trouble with this explanation is that it does not say why a transformation to a catch-all party did not happen when the middle-class status of party leaders first developed – in the decades before and after the First World War. The transformation thesis advanced by Kirchheimer contended that the decline of religious cleavages and ideological preoccupation of the working class accounted for the gradual formation of catch-all parties all over Europe. However, his predictions did not come true for Western Europe at large.[21] Drawing together new research on the history of the SPD, Kaste and Raschke have outlined the special circumstances leading to the change of course in the SPD in 1959.

These reasons were as follows. Sustained economic growth made the SPD leadership aware of the chances of distributing wealth through government policies. It also soon emerged that, while the party preferences of manual workers and self-employed remained stable, those of a well-educated new middle class were open to sophisticated change. This so-called 'new' middle class of salaried employees and public servants, to be distinguished from the 'old' middle class of the self-employed, grew faster than any other segment of the West German population after the war.[22] At the same time the traditional base of electoral support for both SPD and CDU/CSU shrank, i.e. the working class and the 'old' middle class respectively. Therefore the new middle class, akin to the complexion of the SPD leadership, was to become pivotal in gaining an electoral majority. Thirdly, the example of electoral victories by the CDU/CSU, growing from 31.0 per cent of the total vote in 1949 to a peak of 50.2 per cent in 1957, set a 'contagious' pattern for the SPD.

Last but not least, it was a certain type of party leader that favoured the electoral strategy. These were the leaders drawn from the ranks of parliamentarians and office-holders at local and state levels. In contrast to an older group of party leaders returning from emigration after 1945, or to those who had gained their political experience in trade unions, they had been socialised by work in the provincial and local governments of the new republic. What they wanted to achieve in advancing Socialism they thought could come only through legislation and government policies. To obtain an electoral victory they had to win the votes of the new middle class and to do so they had to compromise their policies accordingly. Although Kaste and Raschke write from a rather different theoretical perspective, one of undogmatic neo-marxism, their factual analysis tends to reinforce the view taken in this chapter. Thus, the adoption of the catch-all strategy was in no way preordained by social structural changes or by an end of ideology or some other invisible hand. Rather, it reveals itself as a deliberate choice by one 'career class' of party leaders.

The willingness of the SPD leadership to compromise its policies resulted in an uneasy balance of organisational incentives among SPD 'amateur activists'. While most members had previously been attracted by purposive and solidary inducements, material incentives seem to have taken a lead. This is shown by constant complaints from the SPD rank-and-file about the party now only being a service shop rather than a spiritual home for those caring for the fate of society.[23] It can be assumed that the tendency of party leaders to subordinate any other function a party may have to vote-maximisation is hampered by policy-making desires of party activists since it puts pressure on the leaders' room to manoeuvre in government. On the other hand, it is enhanced by a great deal of citizen detachment from the formulation of public policy, giving leaders leeway to manoeuvre without being hampered by extra-parliamentary movements. This disinterest in politics was, SPD amateur activists notwithstanding, available in abundance – but for reasons that did not augur well for the future of liberal democracy, and hence competitive politics altogether.

THE VIRTUES OF A DEFECTIVE POLITICAL CULTURE

With the memory of Weimar still fresh, when provisions for direct legislation had been abused by right-wing demagogues,[24] the drafters of the Basic Law barred even a modicum of direct democracy that could possibly have modified a rigid representative system. To the absence of direct legislation, somewhat surprisingly, as early as 1949 a majority of the Germans did take exception.[25] It was, however, highly unlikely that their feelings would give rise to discontent since the population did not show much interest in the drafting of the constitution or in politics at all. It is an observation in all textbooks that the immediate post-war period, 'witnessed a widespread withdrawal from public and political matters and an almost exclusive concern with private and familial affairs and above all with material acquisition'.[26] This was understandable enough, since so many people were disenchanted after their initial enthusiasm for Hitler and his henchmen, but also rooted in aversion to conflict, inherited from a more distant past.

What was worse, at the beginning of the 1950s, 'over half of the German population thought an elected parliament an unnecessary institution' and 'nearly as many were unwilling to say that they favoured the existence of more than one political party'; however, acceptance of the political institutions of liberal democracy grew rapidly, and by the beginning of the 1960s, 'two-thirds of the population expressed a commitment to Parliament and three-quarters favoured a competitive party system'.[27] Adenauer's authoritarian and paternalistic style of government, his ambiguous 'Chancellor democracy' appears to have served the purpose of making party government acceptable to a population which was far from having confidence in the institutions of liberal democracy. In view of this ambiguity it is not surprising that German political culture gave rise to concern. And ever since the pioneering five-nation study by Almond and Verba, it has become customary to point to some defective German traits.

Indeed, measured against the concept of the 'civic culture', a type most conducive to liberal democracy, with Britain and the United States serving as examples, there were important flaws to be observed in West Germany. According to this gauge, Germans have no shortage of what is labelled 'subject competence': being politically well informed, they have confidence in those exercising authority. However, this trait combines with a lack of 'citizen competence' in that they are unwilling to become involved in politics and do not think ordinary people should normally do so.[28] This picture appears to be a variation on the old theme of 'the political consequences of the unpolitical German' with an aversion to conflict and a desire for idealistic synthesis, all of which had proved harmful in the past. Combined with an overriding justification of democracy in terms of economic performance, most observers inevitably arrived at the standard question as to whether Bonn was only a 'fair-weather' democracy.[29] In attempting to try and give a reassessment, a closer look at the concept of the 'civic culture' yields an unexpected answer.

It is surprising that Almond and Verba, quite unrelated to their wealth of survey data, clearly state that a citizen's perception that he can be influential, 'may be in part a myth. . . . Yet the very fact that citizens hold to this myth – that they see themselves as influential and obligated to take an active role – creates a potentiality of citizen influence and activity'.[30] Well aware that norms do not match reality, Almond and Verba are nevertheless able to square the circle:

Within the civic culture, then, the individual is not necessarily the rational, active citizen. His . . . relationship with the government is not a purely rational one, for it includes adherence – his and the decision maker's – to what we have called the democratic myth of citizen competence. And this myth has significant consequences. For one thing, it is not pure myth: the belief in the influence potential of the average man has some truth to it and does indicate real behavioural potential. And whether true or not, the myth is believed.[31]

In view of this hard core of the concept of 'civic culture' it might now be argued that German political culture, for all its absence of 'citizen competence', worked as it should in the eyes of the prevailing American democratic theory of the 1960s. A widespread detachment from politics gave political elites an opportunity to make the institutions of liberal democracy work without being hampered by populist or plebiscitarian pressures. For reasons that cannot be justified in terms of liberal democracy, it nevertheless had an effect Almond and Verba found desirable: 'That politics has relatively little importance for citizens is an important part of the mechanism by which the set of inconsistent political orientations keeps political elites in check, without checking them so tightly as to make them ineffective.'[32] Thus, as it was with other seamy sides of German history, the apparent flaws of a political culture may unwittingly have served the purpose of bringing West Germany nearer to liberal democracy.

The concept of the 'civic culture' enjoys some protection from criticism if only because it was fiercely attacked on normative grounds by the then in vogue call for 'participatory democracy' by the New Left.[33] Hence, a short but trenchant critique by Brian Barry, who has a rational-choice leaning, tends to be overlooked. His argument runs as follows: in spite of their wealth of survey data, Almond and Verba fail to establish in which way the two kinds of variables, the 'cultural' and the 'institutional', influence each other. A 'democratic' political culture such as the 'civic culture' of Britain and the USA might be the *effect* of 'democratic' institutions rather than having been conducive to it in the first place. This reversal would, then, lead to the conclusion that 'democracy' produces a 'civic culture'.[34] Developments in Germany after 1945 tend to reinforce this view. Thus, it may be argued that a 'formal' democracy without a congruent political culture brought Germany gradually nearer to a more desirable 'civic culture', if only because it was brought about by the successful and uninterrupted working of the political institutions.

A reassessment by Conradt of changes in German political culture does show that headway was made; on the basis of studies in elite attitudes, he finds: 'There is little of the aversion to conflict and competition that Dahrendorf thinks impeded democratic political development in the past', a pattern matched by the general public.[35] Still, as the concept of the 'civic culture' rests on inconclusive theoretical foundations, it is open to doubt how to strike a balance between the current liberal and illiberal aspects of Western Germany.[36] Germans are often impressed by the calmness and self-reliance with which a protracted crisis is met in Britain, whilst in the Federal Republic there is a tendency to over-react to extremist groups and an amazing proclivity to cry 'wolf' on the part of intellectuals on the Right,

Left, and, most notably, the Middle.[37] On the other hand, among those European nations expressing a confident view in the future of democracy, the Germans rose from sixth place in 1973 to first in 1978 – a surprising change, but far from just betraying arrogance – Germans also put more faith than their fellow-Europeans in the democratic potential of late-comers such as Spain.[38] These results lend additional strength to the presumption that it is the functioning of the institutions which shapes political culture rather than the other way around.

A defective political culture may have had the effect of giving responsible party government a chance and making it gradually acceptable to a majority that had rejected it during the Weimar Republic. But there was another serious obstacle to its achievement during the first two decades of the Federal Republic. At the time the SPD changed its programme in 1959 the majority of middle-class Germans was still haunted by one of the great spectres in modern German history: Adenauer conjured up the traditional 'red menace' of the SPD taking over. The doomsday language used in the conflict between a 'bourgeois bloc' and the Social Democratic Party, with Adenauer insinuating that 'All SPD roads lead to Moscow' and Schumacher accusing him of sacrificing national unity, was not just a rhetoric of conflict derived from the exigencies of a competitive system, as many observers see it today. Rather, it was a remnant of an unholy strategy deeply rooted in German politics. Against this background, the formation of the Great Coalition gains in importance.

CONFLICTING EVALUATIONS OF THE GREAT COALITION

When a unified Germany was first achieved Bismarck tried, with limited success, to put one part of the nation under siege – first the Catholics and then the Social Democrats – in order to rally all the other groups to an authoritarian government. It does not matter here whether this stratagem misfired or not.[39] What matters is that, as a result of labelling the Social Democrats 'enemies of the Reich' and restricting them through law from 1878 to 1890, the fear of the 'red spectre' had lingered on. Not only did it make bourgeois parties hesitant to demand full parliamentary government lest a Socialist majority made use of it,[40] but it also accounts for part of the misreading of Hitler's intentions in 1932/33.[41] Thus, it is not an exaggeration to speak of the 'historic compromise' of the Great Coalition.[42] Rather than just proving the ability of the SPD to govern, it exorcised a spectre that had effectively been used by the bourgeois parties and dogged Germany for almost a century.

In view of earlier suspicions levelled against Social Democrats, it should be obvious why an overwhelming majority of a sample of SPD deputies and party activists interviewed in 1969 approved of the view that the Great Coalition had 'important tendencies toward the equalisation of social differences and the internal pacification of the Federal Republic', while the CDU members of the sample did not; but both were agreed that it was 'bad for democracy'.[43] Indeed, formed without recourse to an election and leaving the role of opposition to the 49 deputies of the FDP against 247 supporting the government, the Great Coalition was hardly in accord with the 'rules' of alternating government. However, major fields of legislation required a two-thirds majority necessary for a change of the constitution, and this was felt to be the reason for a temporary suspension of the Government/Opposition pattern. Both partners were pledged to the passing of a new electoral law of the first-past-the-post kind that would create a two-party system and make further coalitions superfluous – an aim dropped largely for tactical reasons.

Another change was related to the law to promote balanced economic growth which opened up a wide range of possible state intervention into the economy. In the wake of the first post-war recession in 1966/67 it was a widely held and optimistic belief, symbolised by the Economics Minister, Karl Schiller, that judicious state intervention along neo-Keynesian lines would avert future economic crises once the necessary legislative framework was provided. Of course, the day is now long since past when economists, political scientists, journalists and politicians adhered to this view. But in those years it was so strong a belief that even members of the New Left adopted it and argued that the established parties, by their effective use of economic theory and social engineering, would be able to avert crises, form a cartel to protect capitalism, and ultimately become collusive.[44]

Another change to the Basic Law, provisions for an external and internal state of emergency, proved to be the most controversial. The Great Coalition coincided with the world-wide student revolt of the 1960s, waves of unrest unforeseen by behavioural scientists caught up with the 'end of ideology' concept.[45] In the Federal Republic the student movement, forming the extra parliamentary opposition (APO), denounced the passing of emergency laws as paving the way for fascism. While the influential neo-Marxist Frankfurt school gained moral righteousness from its outright rejection of both Hitlerism and Stalinism, one of its more elliptic assumptions was that capitalism itself creates fascism.[46] As this section became more outspoken, there appeared in Germany what might be called an intelligentsia in the general sense used by Hugh Seton-Watson: a substantial section of best-educated persons, whose characteristic feature is its alienation from, and its basic hostility to, the whole social–political regime.[47] By and large, however, this radical critique was part of a universal phenomenon, the attack from the ranks of the New Left on the very foundations of Anglo-American democratic theory of the 'civic culture' type, with its emphasis on citizens' non-involvement.

The strong rejection by SPD activists of the Great Coalition surely makes one 'wonder how well the SPD would have survived a second edition of the Great Coalition'.[48] There is, however, no reason to suppose, as did a German research group, that it was imperative for the SPD to quit the Great Coalition so as to regain flagging support from its traditional *electoral* base.[49] On the contrary, as revealed in a recent study by Helmut Norpoth on coalition preferences of the West German public between 1961 and 1976, SPD and CDU/CSU leaders had little to fear from their 'parties in the electorate'. Rather, *whatever* coalition partner they chose became popular with their voters. With only FDP voters 'punishing' their party for unexpected moves, the CDU/CSU and SPD party leaders enjoyed, 'the role of the representative envisioned and praised by Edmund Burke some 200 years ago'.[50] This staggering discrepancy between the attitudes of voters and party members highlights the crucial tension inherent in party leaders' commitment to serve two different clienteles, the interests of which are often mutually incompatible. For the SPD of 1969, the way out was found in what is now known as the 'euphoria of reforms'.

THE IMPACT OF THE 'LIMITS TO GROWTH'

The promise of domestic reforms by the new social–liberal government was announced under the headline: 'We want to risk more democracy'. There was an overall emphasis on more participation in all sectors of economy, administration and society, from a lowering of the voting age to industrial co-determination. The new moral tone in politics pursued by Chancellor Brandt and President Heinemann took the main themes of the international student revolt of the 1960s seriously. Once again it seemed as if society at large could be changed through party activity, and there was a large influx of young members in the period following 1969.[51] In the light of our analysis, the 'grand design' of domestic reforms, coupled with the *Ostpolitik*, proved to be an ideal strategy. It attracted and integrated the vociferous extra-parliamentary opposition of previous years by purposive incentives. At the same time it secured the traditional basis of electoral support for the SPD, trade unions and the working class, by material rewards. But it also widely distributed material benefits to the elderly, housewives, taxpayers, and the youth.[52]

As far as this broad catalogue of material rewards is concerned, there is hardly a great difference from the rationale of Adenauer's governments. This part of the programme cornered the traditional share of the electoral market while it also wooed the middle class and poured out collective goods to large groups of the population. However, it can be argued that, over and above the 'efficient secret' of an electoral strategy, Brandt's rhetoric of a reformed democratic society beyond class conflict won over the pivotal new middle class of salaried employees and public officials from the CDU/CSU.[53] Indeed, there already had been a change of mood among West German elites before the social–liberal coalition was formed. Surprisingly enough, a survey conducted among the holders of top positions in all sectors showed in 1968 that 51 per cent were in favour of a social–liberal coalition; they also gave a priority to the issues of educational reform, more democracy, and *Ostpolitik*, which is even more remarkable as those elites customarily are said to have a conservative leaning.[54] These findings yield a rendering that is a long way from Dahrendorf's earlier diagnosis of a 'cartel of elites' anxious to avoid social change.

What appeared to be a new liberal democratic strand in German politics came to prominence in the premature election of 1972 following the attempt of the CDU/CSU opposition to bring down the social–liberal government by a constructive vote of no confidence. With the polarisation of the contest over issues, not just politicians, and with an unprecedented level of participation (a record turnout of 91.1 per cent) it could seem as if the 1972 election was a 'critical' one in the sense of Key's usage in that it perhaps redefined the lines of party affiliation for a long time. With the CDU/CSU dependent on the self-employed, the farmers, the old and the religious, and with the issues of *Ostpolitik*, education, abortion and divorce laws being salient, traditional and modern Germany seemed to stand face to face.[55]

For several reasons these expectations did not fully materialise, and the enthusiasm for reforms subsided somewhat in the following years. First of all, the turn of international economic developments, with the oil-price explosion of 1973/74 and lower rates of economic growth, put the financial basis of the heterogeneous package of domestic reform into jeopardy. The recession of 1966/67, rather than leading to doubts about future economic growth, had prompted a reliance on the newly created legislative framework to secure future economic performance. And the social–liberal government proceeded under the assumption that these new instruments of judicious state intervention into the economy would safeguard sufficient funds to maintain an ambitious programme of social welfare. In the period after 1973/74, however, the psychological impact of the 'limits to growth' led to a marked change of mind with an increasing awareness of a pending ecological crisis and a lasting threat to sustained growth. The point to be stressed here is that it was in no small part due to an unprecedented rate of economic growth that a 'catch-all' strategy first developed and worked with unparalleled smoothness in Western Germany in the 1950s and 1960s. As sustained economic growth has become doubtful, a main pillar of the hitherto dominant strategy of political parties appears to be in need of some adjustment.

It ought to be mentioned, too, that the exigencies of the federal system, making legislation dependent on the consent of the opposition in the Bundesrat, watered down a great many reform laws before they could be passed, as did the reluctance of West German entrepreneurs to invest on terms envisaged by the government.[56] Finally, the new middle class took fright at renewed quests for socialism from the ranks of party activists. As a section of those voters abandoned the coalition in elections to state parliaments from 1970 onwards, the SPD leadership contained its socialist intra-party opposition, fended off demands for an imperative mandate and asserted the supremacy of the parliamentary party over party activists.[57] Thus, within the conventions of parliamentary government, an orientation geared towards the vote-casting new middle class again prevailed over attention to the desires of party activists who were previously attracted to join the SPD in the hope of bringing about changes in economy and society.

The endeavour to risk more democracy, on the promise of which the social–liberal coalition came to power, has not completely disappeared, although it has receded. What remained of emphasis on post-acquisitive and participatory values such as quality of life, more say of people in politics and individual self-cultivation found its incarnation in the new concept of the 'new politics', which is now much in vogue. It can be elucidated as follows: If representative national surveys all over Europe put the crucial questions as to whether people rank 'Protecting freedom of speech' and 'Giving people more say in political decisions' higher than 'Maintaining order in the nation' and 'Fighting higher prices', then those who prefer the first alternative are said to be 'post-materialists' adhering to 'new politics' while the others are called 'materialists'.[58] 'Materialists' heavily outnumbered 'post-materialists' in West Germany compared with other European nations in 1972–73.[59] The important thing to note, however, is that the new middle class, whose party preference is likely to decide elections, has now apparently become more liberal and post-acquisitive in outlook than the general materialist orientation of post-war Germans would lead us to expect. Indeed, in 1976 and 1977 it was not only apprentices and students who were in favour of the 'new politics', but also managerial employees and upper civil servants.[60] This observation may lead to a reassessment of some of the foundations upon which the strategy of German parties rests.

PARTICIPATION – A CHALLENGE TO GOVERNANCE?

Given the leaning of a section of academically trained people, occupying responsible positions, to participatory values, three developments are likely to follow. Taken at face value, all of them can be interpreted as foreshadowing a crisis of the party system.

Firstly, intra-party conflict is likely to increase within the SPD and FDP because there was such a large influx from the young and the new middle class into the party during the era of reform after 1969. They not only favour 'post-materialist' values, running counter to the traditional material concerns of trade union party leaders and the working-class electorate at large, but they also advocate unconventional forms of direct participation – for normative reasons unacceptable to an older generation of party leaders exclusively adhering to the conventions of a parliamentary system.[61] Thus, an alliance between young party activists and well-to-do middle-class 'post-materialists' may constitute a lasting line of division and may also lead to an increase of intra-party dissent of backbench deputies. To put it bluntly, school and university teachers, who in West Germany have security of tenure as public servants and benefit from non-contributory pensions, engage in environmental issues while working-class voters are afraid of their jobs. Anxieties are naturally expressed. Thus, German parties, owing to the influence of middle class intellectuals, could lose their ability to act as responsible units of government. While it would be foolish to ignore evidence of a possible trend in this direction, it is worth pointing to the counter-acting forces deriving from the vast kingdom of party patronage and the effects of parliamentary work on the socialisation of those intellectuals entering the Bundestag.[62]

Secondly, a feeling of disillusionment with the established parties is likely to become a lasting feature among both the youth and the new middle class. The argument may be put as follows. The traditional consensus of German party politics rested upon the distribution of material benefits to the electorate at large, whilst policy-making desires of academically trained amateur party activists could be safely neglected. Any prediction of growing unease now stems from the fact that a substantial segment of the new middle class has obviously acquired values which cannot possibly be satisfied by the two basic tenets of the post-war electoral game. It is no surprise that a feeling of not being adequately represented by the present political system increases with the level of education.[63] Indeed, as Conradt puts it on the basis of survey data from the 1950s to the mid-1970s:

> Economic prosperity and rising educational levels have given more people the resources of knowledge, conceptual ability, and time necessary to participate in politics. Data over a period of time on a variety of items – interest in politics, 'talking politics', inclination to join a party, and party identification – show a steady increase in the politisation of the German citizen.[64]

This new evidence necessitates an important qualification to an earlier interpretation. There is said to be a paradox in West German political culture. On the one hand, about two-thirds of the German electorate are still convinced that politicians hardly pay attention to the view of the man in the street and are only interested in getting out his vote; on the other, surprisingly, an even greater part of the same population admits to be 'content' or 'very content' with the political system at large.[65] While it appears to be but a variation on the textbook picture of German detachment from political involvement coupled with an awe of authority, that facile interpretation does not hold true any more for an increasing number among the academically trained new middle class of managerial employees and higher public officials. Their concern with participatory and post-materialist values, laudable with regard to 'citizen competence', nevertheless puts a strain on a strictly representative system with very little outlet for direct democracy.

Thirdly, it is in part, no doubt, a consequence of this new sensitivity to participation in politics that citizens' initiative groups have recently come to prominence. In the first two decades of the republic, such action groups participated in local elections at times. Although they scored impressive results as *Freie Wählervereinigungen* in municipal elections,[66] they were not paid much attention. Now that they have grown in numbers and address themselves mainly to the administration, rather than operate in the local electoral market, they rank high on the agenda of the political scientist.

It is here that we may come back to our theoretical argument outlined at the beginning. In its light, the proliferation of citizens' initiative groups can hardly be cause for astonishment since they neatly fulfil the conditions for effective political organisation as set by Olson's theory of collective action. According to the theory, two factors are thought to be crucial: the size of a potential interest, and the question as to whether a collective or a non-collective good shall be achieved.[67] With regard to these assumptions it is revealing that, in spite of the citizens' initiative groups claiming to have about as many members as political parties, about two-thirds of these heterogeneous groups do not have more than fifty members each; more often than not they are concerned with the achievement of a single goal or the redress of a particular grievance, and their normal life-span lies between twelve months and a few years.[68] Thus, small size and a particular interest appear to be ideal conditions for the well-to-do to face the cost of organising themselves to bring pressure to bear on local administration.

Most of these groups, whether they demand the provision of kindergartens and playgrounds or campaign against building a new highway or a nearby nuclear power station, are only interested in *local* issues. However, we would do well to take account of another type of citizens' initiative group, which, although it runs under the same label, is differently motivated. About a quarter of citizens' initiative groups presents cultural, social, and environmental issues in such a generalised way as to achieve an impact on the whole of society.[69] From the logic of our argument the crucial question now posits itself: What makes people join such an organisation that sets out to obtain collective benefits for the population at large rather than mainly serving any small local group? Perhaps the best possible answer can be found in J. Q. Wilson's concept of the 'amateur democrat' as elucidated in his study of political clubs: he who participates in such a movement sees the political world more in terms of ideas and principles than in terms of gaining political office, is definitely motivated by a cause, is policy-orientated, demands a say in intra-organisational decision-making, and is distinctly middle class in style of life.[70] In other words, what has been labelled 'new politics' is in itself an incentive sufficiently strong to induce people to bear the costs of organising themselves in alternative political groups.

Do these citizens' initiative groups constitute a threat to representative government in the Federal Republic? The New Left, always ready to ascertain some final crisis of capitalism, is, of course, quick to point out that developments such as these herald a fundamental crisis of politics in bourgeois society.[71] On the other hand, Max Kaase, in an empirical examination of the 'crisis of authority' found that in the light of the available evidence there is no sign of the population turning away from the existing political order.[72] However, survey researches show a re-evaluation of direct political participation among important groups of the population. As this shift in attitude cuts across established party lines, the present party system has to take up the challenge arising from demands for more participation.[73]

The important point to note is that a sophisticated version of rational-choice theorising would teach us that parties, due to the very logic of electoral competition between oligopolies, 'do not want to redefine the lines of division in the society, unless they believe they have to'.[74] Hence, there is potential for the German party system to be upset if the established parties do not adapt themselves. It is the young and the new middle class who tend to vote for the new 'Green' party group. Not only was it due to the impact of the 'Green' party that the FDP fell below 5 per cent in the 1980 *Land* elections in Hamburg and Lower Saxony, but in Baden-Württemberg the 'Green' party itself also managed to win parliamentary representation for the first time. It would surely be mistaken to rush to conclusions and to expect the same to happen in the 1980 *Bundestag* election. On the other hand, even if externally the party system evinces stability, a potential disaggregation of interests within the parties has increased.

In conclusion, it may be stated that it was partly due to two factors – an unprecedented rate of economic growth and a defective political culture – that a 'catch-all' strategy worked with unparalleled smoothness in the 1950s and 1960s. Owing to this faulty political culture (seen in comparison with the 'civic culture'), at least one of the factors for the progress towards responsible party government was present at the birth of the Federal Republic. Strangely, this flawed political culture may have served the purpose of facilitating the process of bringing West Germany a good deal nearer to the institutional arrangements if not the spirit of liberal democracy. Any resulting change of the political culture for the better – a gradual development of 'citizen competence' – would entail an unanticipated consequence. Indeed, the very group to which the politics of the German *Volksparteien* were mainly directed, the growing stratum of well-educated white-collar employees and public servants, appears to have developed attitudes which cannot be met by the prevailing strategy of the German catch-all parties, with their ability to seize the opportunities inherent in sustained economic growth and relying on a materialist and detached orientation towards politics. Now, as there are reduced prospects for future economic growth and as an increasing number of well-to-do people demand more say in politics, two pillars of the German *Volkspartei* may have been weakened.

In the final analysis, any evaluation hinges on normative considerations. If we assume that parties ought to be the main agencies of interest mediation, instrumental to a broad range of functions, then the surge of single-issue groups is cause for concern. If, however, we agree that a proliferation of voluntary organisations is desirable for a free society, then it might be argued that those groups act as a welcome counterweight to the materialist and uninspiring supermarket quality of politics that rational-choice theorists envisaged to be the outcome of large and broadly aggregative parties competing in elections and performing governing functions. Thus, any argument of 'crisis' is not only a descriptive account of what happens within the party system, but also includes a strong element of judgment as to what the practice ought to be. Potential for conflict and fragmentation has demonstrably increased within the German party system. Nevertheless, it is the argument here that both a slowing-down of economic growth and the step towards 'citizen competence' have made the Federal Republic more West European in outlook than before. In building a liberal democracy it should not surprise us that Germany now also increasingly shows the symptoms long familiar to her Western European neighbours.

NOTES AND REFERENCES

The author wishes to acknowledge perceptive comments by Kenneth Gladdish and Gordon Smith to an earlier draft of this article.

1. For details, see Joachim Raschke, *Organisierter Konflikt in westeuropäischen Parteien. Eine vergleichende Analyse parteiinterner Oppositionsgruppen* (Opladen, 1977) *passim*. For more recent signs of intra-party dissent by backbench deputies see *Der Spiegel*, 14 July 1980, pp. 19–21, where earlier 'revolts' are also referred to.
2. The leading collection of essays is Bernd Guggenberger and Udo Kempf (eds), *Bürgerinitiativen und repräsentatives System* (Opladen, 1978). See also Jutta A. Helm, 'Citizen Lobbies in West Germany', in Peter H. Merkl (ed.), *Western European Party Systems* (New York, 1980) pp. 576–96.
3. See the diagram in Werner Kaltefleiter, 'A Legitimacy Crisis of the German Party System?', in Peter H. Merkl (ed.), *op. cit.*, p. 602. For recent data, see the Emnid survey conducted for Der Spiegel: ' "Es geht nur um die Stimmen". Spiegel-Umfrage zur politischen Situation im Wahljahr 1980 (V)' Zukunftssorgen und Verdrossenheit', in *Der Spiegel*, 2 June 1980, pp. 48–53.
4. See the data in Samuel H. Barnes and Max Kaase (eds.), *Political Action: Mass Participation in Five Western Democracies* (Beverly Hills and London, 1979) pp. 540 ff.
5. For details see Kurt Oeser, 'Politische Strömungen in der Ökologiebewegung', in *Aus Politik und Zeitgeschichte* (Beilage zur Wochenzeitung 'Das Parlament 49 (1977) pp. 13–19.
6. For instance, see the report on the 1979 Congress of German Sociologists in *Kölner Zeitschrift für Soziologie und Sozialpsychologie*, 31 (1979), pp. 840 f. A broad *tour d'horizon* of the now much *en vogue* 'crisis' theme is given by Hermann Scheer, *Parteien kontra Bürger? Die Zukunft der Parteiendemokratie* (Munich and Zürich, 1979).
7. The point is made by Gordon Smith, *Democracy in Western Germany. Parties and Politics in the Federal Republic* (London, 1979), p. 77. See also Richard Löwenthal, 'Why German Stability is so Insecure', in: *Encounter* (December, 1978) pp. 31–7 and Kurt Sontheimer, *Die verunsicherte Republik*. (Munich, 1979).
8. For details, Raschke, *op. cit.*, *passim*.
9. As elucidated in Peter Haungs, 'Über politische Parteien in westlichen

Demokratien. Bemerkungen zur neueren Literatur', in Haungs (ed.), *Res Publica. Studien zum Verfassungswesen – Dolf Sternberger zum 70. Geburtstag* (Munich, 1977) p. 151 f.

10. Karlheinz Niclauss, *Demokratiegründung in Westdeutschland. Die Entstehung der Bundesrepublik 1945–1949* (Munich, 1974) pp. 73 ff.

11. M. Rainer Lepsius, 'Soziale Ungleichheit und Klassenstrukturen in der Bundesrepublik Deutschland', in Hans-Ulrich Wehler (ed.), *Klassen in der europäischen Sozialgeschichte* (Göttingen, 1979) p. 176 f.

12. E. Spencer Wellhofer and Timothy M. Hennessey, 'Models of Political Party Organisation and Strategy: Some Analytic Approaches to Oligarchy', in Ivor Crewe (ed.), *British Political Sociology Yearbook*, 1 (London, 1974) p. 298.

13. *Ibid.*, p. 310.

14. See Guenther Roth, *The Social Democrats in Imperial Germany* (Totowa, N.J., 1963, reprint, 1979) especially Ch. IX.

15. Wellhofer and Hennessey, *op. cit.*, p. 310.

16. A critical assessment from a sympathetic point of view is Brian Barry, *Sociologists, Economists and Democracy* (London and Toronto, 1970), pp. 23 ff.; for an interesting application of Olson's theory to the development of trade unions in Britain, the United States and Germany, see Norbert Eickhof, *Eine Theorie der Gewerkschaftsentwicklung. Entstehung, Stabilität und Befestigung* (Tübingen, 1973).

17. Quoted in Wellhofer and Hennessey, *op. cit.*, p. 300.

18. James Q. Wilson, *Political Organisations* (New York, 1973) chapter 2. For an application of this typology to American party politics, see Kay Lawson, *The Comparative Study of Political Parties* (New York, 1976) pp. 95 and 113.

19. See Kenneth Dyson, *Party, State and Bureaucracy in Western Germany* (Beverly Hills and London, 1977) p. 43 and the tabulations in Klaus von Beyme, *Das politische System der Bundesrepublik Deutschland. Eine Einführung* (Munich, 1979) p. 72 f.

20. Hermann Kaste and Joachim Raschke, 'Zur Politik der Volkspartei', reprinted in Wolf-Dieter Narr and Dietrich Tränhardt (eds.), *Die Bundesrepublik Deutschland. Entstehung, Entwicklung, Struktur* (Neue Wissenschaftliche Bibliothek) (Meisenheim/Glan, 1979) pp. 168–209, especially pp. 185–9.

21. Steven B. Wolinetz, 'The Transformation of Western European Party Systems Revisited', in *West European Politics* (1979) pp. 4–28. For a differentiated discussion see Gordon Smith, Chapter 4 in this volume.

22. It rose from 20.6 per cent in 1950 to 43.7 per cent in 1976, as shown in Lepsius, *op. cit.*, p. 169. See also the diagrams on these and a number of related data in Ursula Feist, Manfred Güllner and Klaus Liepelt, 'Structural Assimilation Versus Ideological Polarisation: On Changing Profiles of Political Parties in West Germany', in Max Kaase and Klaus von Beyme (eds.), *Elections and Parties, German Political Studies*, vol. 3 (Beverly Hills and London, 1978) pp. 171–89.

23. See, for example, the discussion in the SPD periodical *Die Neue Gesellschaft* (August 1979) especially pp. 678–80. For a detailed analysis, Klaus Günther, *Sozialdemokratie und Demokratie 1946–1966* (Bonn, 1979).

24. As carefully documented in Reinhard Schiffers, *Elemente direkter Demokratie im Weimarer Regierungssystem* (Düsseldorf, 1971).

25. A. J. and R. L. Merritt (eds), *Public Opinion in Occupied Germany. The Omgus*

Survey, 1945–49 (Urbana, 1970), quoted in von Beyme, *op. cit.*, p. 20.

26. David P. Conradt, *The German Polity* (New York and London, 1978) p. 55.
27. Gerhard Loewenberg, 'The Development of the German Party System', in K. H. Cerny (ed.), *Germany at the Polls: The Bundestag Election of 1976* (Washington, 1978) p. 24.
28. Gabriel A. Almond and Sidney Verba, *The Civic Culture: Political Attitudes and Democracy in Five Nations* (Princeton, 1963) pp. 225 ff., 250 ff., 428 f.
29. Conradt, *op. cit.*, p. 51.
30. Almond and Verba, *op. cit.*, p. 481.
31. *Ibid.*, p. 487.
32. *Ibid.*, p. 483.
33. For this attack, see the collection of essays in Charles A. McCoy and John Playford (eds), *Apolitical Politics: A Critique of Behaviouralism* (New York, 1967); also Henry S. Kariel (ed.), *Frontiers of Democratic Theory*, (New York, 1970). For a reply, see Peter Y. Medding, ' "Elitist" Democracy: An Unsuccessful Critique of a Misunderstood Theory', in *Journal of Politics*, 31 (1969) pp. 641–54 and Giovanni Sartori, 'Anti-Elitism Revisited', in: *Government and Opposition* (1978) pp. 58–80.
34. Barry, *op. cit.*, pp. 48–52.
35. Conradt, *op. cit.*, p. 53 and *passim* draws on his article 'Changing German Political Culture', in Gabriel A. Almond and Sidney Verba (eds), *The Civic Culture Revisited* (Princeton, 1980).
36. With regard to anti-terrorist legislation, see the balanced statement by Wolfgang Krieger, 'Worrying about West German Democracy', in *Political Quarterly*, 50 (1979), pp. 192–204.
37. A point made by Wolfgang J. Mommsen, ' "Wir sind wieder wer." Wandlungen im politischen Selbstverständnis der Deutschen', in Jürgen Habermas (ed.), *Stichworte zur "Geistigen Situation der Zeit"* (Frankfurt, 1979) p. 208.
38. See the sources in Beyme, *op. cit.*, p. 39.
39. For the debate among British and German historians over the effects of *Sammlungspolitik* against the Social Democrats in Imperial Germany, see Richard J. Evans, 'Wilhelm II's Germany and the Historians', in Evans (ed.), *Society and Politics in Wilhelmine Germany* (London, 1978) pp. 11–39 and Volker R. Berghahn, 'Politik und Gesellschaft im Wilhelminischen Deutschland', in *Neue Politische Literatur*, 1979, pp. 164–95.
40. For a detailed analysis, see Dieter Grosser, *Vom monarchischen Konstitutionalismus zur parlamentarischen Demokratie. Die Verfassungspolitik der deutschen Parteien im letzten Jahrzehnt des Kaiserreichs* (The Hague, 1970) pp. 60 ff. and 163 ff.
41. For evidence, see Hans Fenske, *Wahlrecht und Parteiensystem. Ein Beitrag zur deutschen Parteiengeschichte* (Frankfurt, 1972) pp. 342 ff.
42. Peter Pulzer, 'Responsible Party Government and Stable Coalition: The Case of the German Federal Republic', in *Political Studies*, 26 (1978) p. 185.
43. Frederick C. Engelmann, 'Perceptions of the Great Coalition in West Germany, 1966–1969', in *Canadian Journal of Political Science*, 5 (1972) p. 37 f.
44. Ekkehart Krippendorff, 'Das Ende des Parteienstaates?', in *Der Monat*, 14 (1962) pp. 64 ff.
45. For instance, see S. M. Lipset and S. Rokkan, 'Preface', in Otto Stammer (ed.),

Party Systems, Party Organisations, and the Politics of the New Masses (Berlin, 1968) mimeo.
46. Friedrich H. Tenbruck, 'Deutsche Soziologie im internationalen Kontext', in Günther Lüschen (ed.), *Deutsche Soziologie seit 1945. Entwicklungsrichtung und Praxisbezug*, Sonderheft 21/1979 of the *Kölner Zeitschrift für Soziologie und Sozialpsychologie*, p. 74.
47. Hugh Seton-Watson, 'Thoughts on Intellectuals and Intelligentsias' (Paper at the Seminar 'Intellectuals and Social Change in Europe', University of London, School of Slavonic and East European Studies).
48. Engelmann, *op. cit.*, p. 54.
49. Bodo Zeuner, 'Das Parteiensystem in der Grossen Koalition', in Dietrich Staritz (ed.), *Das Parteiensystem der Bundesrepublik. Geschichte – Entstehung – Entwicklung* (Opladen, 1976) p. 193.
50. Helmut Norpoth, 'Choosing A Coalition Partner: Mass Preferences and Elite Decisions in West Germany', in *Comparative Political Studies*, 12 (1980) pp. 424–40; quote on p. 437.
51. See Feist *et al.*, *op. cit.*, p. 182 f.
52. For details, see Manfred G. Schmidt, 'Die "Politik der inneren Reformen" in der Bundesrepublik Deutschland 1969–1976', in *Politische Vierteljahresschrift*, 19 (1978) pp. 201–53.
53. See the arguments of M. Rainer Lepsius, 'Wahlverhalten, Parteien und politische Spannungen', in *Politische Vierteljahresschrift*, 14 (1973) pp. 295–313, especially pp. 308 ff.
54. Rudolf Wildenmann, 'Germany 1930/1970: The Empirical Findings', in Wildenmann (ed.), *Sozialwissenschaftliches Jahrbuch für Politik*, 2 (1971) p. 57 f. See also Christian Fenner, 'Das Parteiensystem seit 1969 – Normalisierung und Polarisierung', in Staritz (ed.), *op. cit.*, p. 203 f.
55. Pulzer, *op. cit.*, p. 195 f. Manfred Küchler, 'What has Electoral Sociology in West Germany Achieved? A Critical Review', in Kaase and von Beyme (eds.), *op. cit.*, p. 27 points to the heart of the matter: 'With the clear election victory of the Social–Liberal Coalition a constellation came into being which was completely new in German history. This made it necessary to answer the question of whether 1972 was a normal election with a short-term interference factor or rather a 'critical election', i.e. the starting-point for a long-term reorientation of relatively broad strata of the electorate.'
56. For details, see Schmidt, *op. cit.*, pp. 215–21.
57. Kaste and Raschke, *op. cit.*, p. 197.
58. Ronald Inglehart, *The Silent Revolution: Changing Values and Political Styles Among Western Publics* (Princeton, 1978) p. 27 ff.
59. *Ibid.*, p. 38.
60. See Table 10.4 in Chapter 10, by Pappi and Terwey, in this volume.
61. On the basis of survey data, this supposition is made by Max Kaase and Hans Klingemann, 'Sozialstruktur, Wertorientierung und Parteiensysteme: Zum Problem der Interessenvermittlung in westlichen Demokratien', in Joachim Matthes (ed.), *Sozialer Wandel in Westeuropa. Verhandlungen des 19. Deutschen Soziologentages 1979* (Frankfurt and New York, 1979) pp. 535 and 568. Their prediction is aptly illustrated by recent conflicts in North Rhine-Westphalia, see *Der Spiegel*, 4 February 1980, pp. 43–5.
62. See the revealing results of a study which interviewed a panel of newly elected

members of the Bundestag over time, Bernhard Badura and Jurgen Reese, *Jungparlamentarier in Bonn – ihre Sozialisation im Deutschen Bundestag* (Stuttgart, 1976).

63. See survey data quoted by Gerhard Schmidtchen, 'Ist Legitimitat messbar? , in *Zeitschrift für Parlamentsfragen*, 8 (1977) p. 238 f.

64. Conradt, *op. cit.*, p. 56. See also M. and S. Greiffenhagen, *Ein schwieriges Vaterland: Zur politischen Kultur Deutschlands*, (Munich, 1978).

65. Recent data in the Emnid survey of 1980, published in *Der Spiegel*, 2 June 1980, p. 51.

66. See Heino Kaack, *Geschichte und Struktur des deutschen Parteiensystem* (Opladen, 1971) p. 498 ff.

67. For this argument, see also Wolfgang Jager, 'Bürgerinitiativen -Verbände – Parteien. Thesen zu einer funktionalen Analyse', in Guggenberger and Kempf (eds.), *op. cit.*, p. 218 f.

68. For estimates of the number of members, see Udo Kempf, 'Burger- initiativen – Der empirische Befund', in *ibid.*, p. 359. For the normal duration, see *ibid.*, p. 366. Compare also Helm, *op. cit.*, p. 577 f.

69. See the breakdown in Kempf, *op. cit.*, p. 361.

70. James Q. Wilson, *The Amateur Democrat: Club Politics in Three Cities* (Chicago, 1962) pp. 3, 13, 19 and *passim*.

71. For instance, see Michael Th. Greven, 'Parteiensystem, Wertwandel und neue Marginalitat', in Matthes (ed.), *op. cit.*, p. 581 f.

72. Max Kaase, 'The Crisis of Authority in Western Liberal Democracies: Myth and Reality', in Richard Rose (ed.), *Challenge to Governance* (London, 1979).

73. Kaase and Klingemann, *op. cit.*, pp. 556 and 566 f.

74. Alan Ware, 'Competition, Oligopoly and Electoral Markets', in Ware, *The Logic of Party Democracy* (London, 1979) pp. 32–52 and 46 f.

Index